IN MY E

Immortality and Its Critics

Robert Geis

University Press of America,® Inc.
Lanham · Boulder · New York · Toronto · Plymouth, UK

Copyright © 2010 by
University Press of America,® Inc.
4501 Forbes Boulevard
Suite 200
Lanham, Maryland 20706
UPA Acquisitions Department (301) 459-3366

Estover Road
Plymouth PL6 7PY
United Kingdom

Library of Congress Control Number: 2010930497
ISBN: 978-0-7618-5265-0 (paperback : alk. paper)
eISBN: 978-0-7618-5266-7

To the memory of
Frances Caryll Houslander

TABLE OF CONTENTS

PREFACE   vii

I. MORE THAN CONSCIOUSNESS

QUANTUM THEORY AND REALITIES OF DISTINCTION   3

METHODOLOGY   13

CONSCIOUSNESS   21

OTHER   35

COLOR AND OBJECTIFICATION   45

THE EXTRALINGUISTIC OBJECT   55

II. CONSCIOUSNESS IMMORTAL

DISINTEGRATION AND PARTIBILITY   65

DEATH AND PURPOSE   75

INDIVISIBLE SENSATION AND "ZOMBIE" THEORY   77

COHERENCE, PERCEPT, *QUALIA*   83

OTHER DIFFICULTIES FOR NEUROPHILOSOPHY   93

CONCEPTUALIZATION, MEMORY, IMMATERIALITY   113

ANECDOTAL OR EVIDENTIAL?   135

SENTIENT IMMORTALITY   151

ANOTHER WORLD   163

NOTES   173

INDEX   217

ABOUT THE AUTHOR   227

PREFACE

For most of the past century, and previous, many of the books that treated of immortality began with the implicit premise that there is a world in which individuals live, from which they differ and are other. These books went on to relate relatively uncomplicated arguments for the immortalist claim, then stories about how individuals speak to the dead, have apparitions, or have precognition of the time of their death, etc. Popular editions today— we all know them— those that are also quick reads and easily paged through, proceed no differently.

The arguments in these works, e.g., as late as Dr. Jeffrey Long's estimable 2010 book, *Evidence of the After Life. The Science of Near-Death Experiences*,[1] are simple compared to the academic literature of the past three decades or so. These "popular" presentations do not address what we will here. As the past thirty years or so have passed, the academic literature has built on previous studies becoming in fact ever more complicated and difficult to read, or to which one can give credence. This is because of how many studies now on our subject proceed. Unlike the general readership works to which we just referred, these proceed as if there is no world separate from the individual. Or they assume (or is it only postulate?) that if something can be proven of a small portion of the brain in terms of some model, then all of consciousness can eventually be understood in the same way.

It is not so much that these studies make the statement overtly as it is that the process and grounds for the process of their argument tacitly assume that there is no real or metaphysical distinction between the individual and the world. Or, short of that, that consciousness makes its world. Protracted study and analysis is required to uncover this, making the study that follows here neither a simple task nor a quick read.

We can look a bit more closely at the process of exposition in these writers, what we, in shorthand shall call here "the neuroreductionists." If studies and theories in their conclusions go directly contrary to our experience of the world, one imagines that those arguing them would in some way adjust. After all, if consciousness—my consciousness—is the world, with whom are these writers communicating? Their studies argue that the real fact of experience, or all we can know about it, is that only one's consciousness constitutes the world. This means only I exist. If only I exist, and these writers are communicating such theories, their writings contradict what is implied in their very activity of writing, and therefore what they must be tacitly assuming. Their position contradicts or renders strange any reason why they would be writing. Writing, after all, is a means of communicating. If only I exist, to whom or for whom could these writers claiming only consciousness exists be writing? To avoid self-contradiction, they must assume I do not exist. To avoid them suffering such an embarrassment of contradiction, such a weakness and faultiness of reasoning, should we assume instead those for whom they are writing their books etc., like you and me, are simply imaginary and unreal entities, products of and dependent on their imagination?

A bit of detail as to what has taken place is in order here. Precision of presentation requires we explain what has occurred in the terms, words, and language of the processes and forms of arguments in these academic and scientific studies from neuroreductionism that have brought us to this point. What the everyday individual has most probably assumed, sc., that the world is different than he is, and that his passing away does not include that of the universe, is not how much of the academic study of mind and consciousness has proceeded since the 1970s. The language in which it has proceeded has made the study of the subject especially obfuscated, limiting access to it for those who want an argument to be simple, clear, and to the point.

In the past few decades modelings of sensation and quantitative electrochemistry in neuroscience philosophy have tracked the well-known advances in software applications improvements. This has seen a movement in those decades to equate philosophy of mind, the venue for discussions of immortal personhood, with algorithmic calculations of cortical electrochemical events. In turn, a marked shift to identification of the individual and world has occurred where the two are nearly indistinguishable. They are, in the extremes of various current arguments, actually identical. Only consciousness exists—my consciousness. What I call the world is actually, and only, my consciousness.

We address this development here and note why the indistinguishability of individual and world—the identification of the two—makes the question of immortality moot. We then set out to establish the real and actual, distinction between the two. They are not the same. They exist independently of each other. While consciousness is *of* a world, it is not *the* world. Its existence is not all that there is. A world can exist without consciousness. Only then can we turn to the question of immortality.

Towards this end we have divided the work into two parts, the first (entitled "More Than Consciousness") treating of the question of an actual world outside of me. The second ("Consciousness Immortal"), confident that the first part has succeeded in establishing the reasonability of its claim, proceeds to the more imponderable question of immortal consciousness and why it has a plausibility that cultures over the millennia have accorded it.

No essay that seeks to establish what can only appear as recondite and insensible as immortal existence, the obfuscations of the current literature notwithstanding, can be a leisurely read. Truth is not easily achieved, as Aristotle writes, especially when it comes to our subject.[2] When it is reached, it usually has come about only through the most intense reflection and arduous deliberation. If we rely only on the senses for knowledge, the casket presents us with what can only be the end to everything. Human intellection, however, does not end at sense-prehension. It only begins there.

The underbrush through which we will need to traverse here will appear dense and obstreperous. Some realities indeed do not lend themselves to felicity or ease of expression. Consciousness is one of them. Because, however, the stakes are so high as to the outcome of what one can perpend and think through in the question "Is death simple nothingness?" the effort and trouble it takes to understand the positions and possible solutions available as an answer seem a small price to expend indeed.

This essay, then, is for the reader, frequently called the specialist, current with the vagaries in current philosophies of mind, and not unaware how off compass the directions of some of those are. For example, because the rejection of the world as an actual fact takes on so many guises in our debate on consciousness, we have had to repeatedly respond to the objections to a "real world" in the forms they have taken in neuroreductionism. We have had to spend much time on the "otherness" of a real world, of a world that actually exists. Only with the objections to the world as an actual existent other than me addressed can a present day inquiry into immortality have any value for those who want to see the arguments of neurophilosophy and reductionism addressed.

Some commentators advancing their positions ask us to imagine different models and the like that can, for them, increase insight into this reality called "consciousness." The further those models take us from what appears to us as what consciousness is, of what a non-inferential awareness of the world comes to us as, the more suspect, however, should become those models. Some writers tell us to think of "possibilities" that can add to an understanding of what we are examining. However, some possibilities, if the realities of our experience have natures, essences, cannot apply to those things because of the natures these realities have. Their natures, essences, are given with *this* world. Their essences are as creatures of *this* world. "Possible world" debates, then, have no application to what we are discussing here: the nature of the human individual in this existence in this world. The recommendation to engage in imagining "possibilities" is of no service then.

I know of no systematic work that addresses these most recent permutations in theories of consciousness that, the reader of this work will find, have no semblance to what the everyday individual takes consciousness and his subjectivity to be. A prior work, *Personal Existence After Death*,[3] only touched on these issues. That is the reason for this work fifteen years later. In addressing reductionism, materialism, and neurophilosophy as the current undertaking does, it reinforces the legitimacy of discourse and questions about "immortality" and one's destiny which denial of a world outside *my* consciousness has made almost a caricature.

Often, if one begins an inquiry with an assumption what is implied in the assumption is the outcome on which one eventually lands. We have tried to avoid that weakness in reasoning. It is an avoidance which alone can start us on a resolution to anything where truth is demanded, and whose price for missing in the question of immortality is inarguably too high to pay.

ἐν βυθῷ γάρ ἐ ἀλήθεια

(Diels-Kranz, *Die Fragmente der Vorsakratiker*, B 117)

I. MORE THAN CONSCIOUSNESS

QUANTUM THEORY AND REALITIES OF DISTINCTION

Bodily death is perhaps not as dreaded a notion as extinction of one's consciousness. We seem to think that the death of the body may not necessitate the end of awareness, of contact with a world that, though different than perhaps this one, is not its alternative, sc, unconditional emptiness and complete absence. Something seems to tell us that body and self do not each carry the destiny of the other with it, that the two are not the same.

One looks upon the ashes to which the person one knew has been reduced, upon the crystals to which the body once strong and vibrant has now become, and thinks, "this is not the person I knew; this is not what he was." That is why bodily death does not appear to carry with it the fear that accompanies extinction, whole and entire, of one's awareness. To say "this is not the person I knew" implies within it that therefore "this body is not the person."

Said otherwise, we seem to think that we are not just a body, that body is not the entirety that the individual conscious subject is. The sentiment takes expression in the phrase, "This can't be all there is," when one thinks of one's own life and what death seems to mean to it. "This is all there is?" is a question that emerges to the individual confronted with the fact that at some point there is possibly nothing else left for the individual to experience, to undergo, to know. "It makes no sense" is an alternative expression that declares it an absurdity that life was simply the blink of a light, a momentary incandescence, that could not endure between two endless nights.

In what follows we want to look at whether death is the extinction in every entirety of consciousness, of awareness of any sort. There is something about awareness that seems to tell us that the body is not its *sine qua non*, that the body is not what determines it. Conscious life, living, is not simply the body with awareness. Life is not just the body such when the flesh of the living being putrefies all is eternally, endlessly gone. The body and consciousness appear to differ. We wish to examine here whether they do, to what extent they do (if they do), and, if they do, if what is true of one need not be true of the other.

One would think a study of immortality would be sufficient if it set out to discuss whether the body survived bodily dissolution. While that may be complicated enough, it is no longer adequate, given the discussions of neurophilosophy over the past few decades. Unchecked in many instances over the past decade especially, neurophilosophy has been able to make a respectable platform for a view that renders dubious the existence of sensations as experiences of a living subject other than what it experiences. In its stead, it has argued for a view of sensations as neurochemical phenomena of a cortical substrate sufficiently complex, an assertion which finds the postulate of a subject in those phenomena redundant, if not outright superfluous. Percepts are not events other than those neurochemical phenomena. They are precisely those phenomena, and it is only because society continues to speak in terms of conscious events as other than neurochemical molecules and formulae that we are still misled, according to neurophilosophy, as to the exact nature of consciousness. Consciousness is a neurochemical process *tout court*. Actually, "consciousness" itself is simply an outmoded word for what is actually occurring in the brain. There is no consciousness, actually: there is only the cortex and its extensions through the sensory apparatus of the physical body.

To avoid being accused, therefore, of having taking anything for granted in our study we have sought to establish what one would seem to think is unquestionable, but which modern science has, through a reductionist approach to the subject of awareness, tried to argue has no basis in actual neurophysiology. This will become clear in our examination of whether besides consciousness there is an actually existent world other than it. While the answer may seem obvious, on an issue so important as one's eternal destiny the obvious may just not be sufficient for looking at how we come to examine the question of eternal life. We will see in this work's chapter entitled "Difficulties For Neurophilosophy" the Botvinick-Cohen suggestion that all of experience may be accounted for totally by brain events. That is, that what we call "experience" is the product of the brain, which never reaches what our non-inferential, "commonsense" posture holds we do, sc., the actual object, the actual world "out there." "Consciousness" is strictly brain events in contact with nothing demonstrably other than it.

What has taken place, i.e., in the recently completed last century of the philosophic study of consciousness, especially since the Turing machine success, is a gradual withdrawal from the acceptance of the world "out there" as a source of our knowledge. In its place has arrived an assertion that either the object in the world is an electrical event achieved by many cortical gradations and actually nothing with which we are really directly in contact or, a position that actually traces back to Hume, the world we believe is "out there" we cannot prove. All we know is consciousness such that it might in fact be that when we speak of the world we are speaking of our own conscious states, and not the world. In that case, if all I know is my conscious states, there is nothing that lets me have access to other conscious beings. In the extreme, there might be no conscious beings or objects at all except me. I might be the world: my consciousness might be all that there is.

In a world where there is no "self" to which events relate, every event becomes isolated from each other. There is no continuity. You have only pieces, extensions of consciousness, neither of which has any link to any other. Absence of a self means, equivalently, absence of a subject inasmuch as a subject is just as improvable as is a self. This has led to a denial of the "subjective" element in experience. We will see that these are the *qualia* which are irreducible to any quantitative or reductionist expression and which involve its neurophilosphic opponents in denying their own experiences for the sake of a philosophic position that is totally alien to everyday experience. Neurophilosophy in its purest form will leave one with neural events in an atomistic world where snippets of awareness constitute "world." In the end, one cannot even use the words "I" or "ego." These are merely linguistic manners of expression, and not what true science actually calculates in its studies of what we call "experience."

Subjectivism in the end leads to the end of a subject, and thus an end to an individual that is immortal. In its present-day form argument against a self and a subject unfolds almost a cosmos without any individuality. Awareness is without the individual who is aware. What we are left with is simply consciousness in a fragmented state of unrelated awarenesses.

If there is no self, no "I," one cannot scientifically say "mine" when speaking of events or what is experienced. These are merely linguistic turns. In its purest form subjectivism will lead one to simply speak about "what is experienced" without allowing any attribution of the experience to a "me." Yet to even state these words have no basis in actual fact the subjectivist (the one denying a world other than consciousness) has to acknowledge who it is that is making the claim. It is an omission that subjectivists have not recognized and for which they cannot account. To simply state "words are said" without saying who said them the subjectivist is in danger of leaving his whole world of discourse in chaos. Such are the results to which extremes, such as reductionism and neurophilosphy will be shown to have, lead.

If only consciousness exists, i.e., if only mine does and thus constitutes all reality, its extinction would rule out any heaven or hell since, on the grounds that only my consciousness exists, nothing else could exist. Hence, heaven and hell would not. Immortality, then, would not be an issue at all for study since immortality implies something other than this existence—a heaven or a hell. Each is a state other than this one.

This implication, which the Botvinick-Cohen outlook has hardened into "scientific stature," is totally consonant with, if not a derivative of, subjectivism. In its extreme form, to which we just alluded, it is a skepticism of anything existing except me, as one finds in Hume's *Treatise*.[1] I cannot prove an external world exists, or that I am a perduring entity through change.

A hard look at immortality needs to address these assertions if we are to have a realm that exists which we know is other than *my* consciousness. We must address the proof or existence of a world that is not consciousness, that is not my consciousness, given the thought trends of today and the claims to which some of its outlooks, as we shall see, have led. To the extent that we have succeeded in avoiding taking things such as the "external world," a world other than my consciousness. for granted, to the extent that we have established something other than consciousness as a real existent, we will have been engaged in correct reasoning.

Was man born to die? After all, every individual that has been born is either dead, or will die. Would that make life's purpose death? Is it that life exists for death to come about? If birth brings about life that always ends in death, does not one have to say birth brings about death? Hence the question just posed, whose repetition is apt here given the profound impact of death to every living person: Was man born to die?

Reflection upon the issue of death invites two queries almost immediately: why do so few consider death in their everyday thinking, and why is it that we do not have an immediate awareness of, a direct recognition of, a life beyond death—if there is such? On a question of such seeming import it stands as reasonable that one should know, without much plodding or difficult thought, whether bodily death means (or implies) total extinction. Why is it that we do not have such a recognition, if in fact bodily death does not mean the end of personal existence? This addresses the status of immortality more than as an ontological condition. It takes it up as a personal condition, a condition about *me*. This question, it seems more than obvious, is that to which nothing is more important to the person than its closure.

Shall I, a conscious living being, exist once the body decomposes? Not only I, however, but whatever has had consciousness? Is consciousness, once brought into being, indestructible for the individual being that has received it? In this regard our essay here goes materially and importantly beyond just the question of immortal existence as it pertains to the human being. Now we address the issue in terms of the reality that consciousness is. Is it, in its reality, immortal? Animals are conscious. Are they immortal?

So our essay begin with consciousness, and what it is and means. Individual conscious agency, how it takes its place in existence and its world, and how this signifies a possible dimension to it that explanations seeking to reduce everything and every event to matter deny, comes in for discussion.

Consciousness has a correlate, however, the "other." Not everything that exists has consciousness. It is this correlate of consciousness by which we here mean the term "other," in addition to the conscious existents in one's world. We will take the "other" precisely as "other," without regard to whether it is conscious or not, and seek to understand its relationship to consciousness.

Examining that "other" precisely in its structure of "otherness" brings us to an existence that is not dependent on consciousness in any way for its existence. Is this "other" of a being what makes it clearer that perhaps consciousness and it are different enough that what applies to one does not to the other? Can we show that the differences found enable us to set one apart from the "other" that is without consciousness as that which has no possibility of immortal life?

In the process of our exposition, we frequently find ourselves using the regress (vicious circle) argument against opponents whose arguments would stop immortality in is tracks were their arguments binding. That we expose their regress weaknesses shows they are not, in much the same way circular argumentation of reductionists, as we showed in our book *Personal Existence After Death*, made it clear their arguments were without suasion.

Importantly, we look at the quantum physics[2] debate of "bitless" reality (is it?) and argue that irreducible components go to make up our creation. This allows us to argue for the distinction between materiality and immateriality, and all the conclusions that argumentation permits.

A grave self-refutational error at the heart of modern sub-atomic physics arises in our examination of what it claims for the structure of reality. The error, in point of fact, renders moot much of its outlook on "physical matter." Its tools for its claim come from a portion of the cosmos which represents, by its own admission, only a minute portion of the cosmos. The minuteness of this portion, however, is our only access to a universe far greater than this comparatively minute speck (vibrational increment) allotted to us by quantum physics. If our access to the universe is only within this narrowest of bands that quantum physics has argued, and it is from such a narrowest of vibrational bands that his materials to deal with and hypothesize about the universe come, how can any physicist postulate findings of the nature of the universe that he can consider authoritative? In simplest language there is so much more that has not been taken in and, apparently, cannot be given the minute access to the universe which our senses allow—by the very assertions of quantum physics itself.

Can the modern theory of consciousness, seemingly originated from various models of quantum physics, have authority given the core tenet of those models? Quantum physics tells us we have access to only one half of one percent of the universe: this is the only band to which we have access given the nature, structure, of our sense capacities. The tools, though, that tell us we have almost no access to the universe are tools that miss ninety-nine point five percent of the universe. This holds by quantum physics' own assertion that our sense prevent access to almost the entire electromagnetic spectrum. We have access to only that one-half of one percent portion. But that is whence the tools which give us access to our portion of the universe come and by which tools we asserted, in the first place, that we have access to only one half of one percent of the universe. If we have access to only such a small amount of the universe, how do we know anything that we say about the universe binds? If our tools for examining reality come from only one half of one percent of the electromagnetic band, how can we say that the tools are in any way dexterous enough to yield the entire truth of the universe? It appears that the quantum model gives no possibility that from the rest of the universe could come tools of different capacity that might override the claims that quantum mechanics has made—claims based on the tools which originate from the minuscule portion to which it claims we have access.

The argument, as a rebuttal to our quandary with quantum physics, that the laws throughout the universe must obtain in the same fashion does not help the physicist here. By his own assertion the rest of the universe is unlike the band to which we have access. It is of a different frequency. That would allow the inference that the laws in the remaining bands would be "unlike" also.

Quantum physics, as this self-refutational postulate we just pointed out would show, does not provide us the rigor we need for addressing the subject of endless life. We argue in our essay that the destructibility of the things of our universe coming about through their separability into ever smaller portions constitutes the most reliable way of looking at how destruction happens, and how in its absence (non-partibility) one may argue for indestructibility. Said in the plainest possible way, the self-refutational flaw we have just identified seems to show quite clearly that quantum physics is without the grounds on which to offer us indisputability into the nature of matter and the mind. On the other hand, the evidence of destruction through separation into parts is before us in abundance everyday. In fact we feel directly our own destruction (partially), e.g., when an arm or leg is severed. To suggest that the truth of matter, of the ultimate constituents of our universe, lies at the sub-atomic level offered by instruments that do not reach ninety-nine point five percent of the rest of reality seems a wayward rejection of the rules of evidence—especially given our incontestable knowledge that our destruction takes place at the gross level. Things are "real" at this level far removed from the sub-atomic, and it is this "real" aspect of life that a study of immortality must explain.

If this is our position (and it is), we must explain how what experience tells us is not a mistake or false compared to what quantum physics argues. Skepticism about the constituency of the cosmos, what goes to make it up, and what arrangements in space and place that make-up fills, has made the study of immortality of especial difficulty in the past half century. The argument about partibility and decomposition (that one leads to the other) become suspect if we do not have a basis for stating that all things in the end are divisible into smaller components and this divisibility constitutes their corruptibility. Are the items of the world actually physical inert bulks, or must we state that their major constituent is space (as quantum theory sets forth). Their corruptibility into parts becomes problematic then inasmuch as the objects of our experience may in their actuality simply be spatial fields through which float and orbit bits that are in no way congealed one to the other at all. There is no accretion of bit to bit at all. We are really confronted with an existence that is primarily spatial, and if so what value does the argument about partibility and decomposition have?

As the world's components are declared ever smaller, our certainty that the world is as it appears becomes ever less. The student of this subject of immortality, fresh to his first inquiry into it, would not begin to understand how physics and various theories of causation and "observation" argue against the world as it appears to our five senses. Reading studies from a century ago which could not have anticipated the new contentions in physics today cannot help the student of today looking at this problem. One needs, in the study of immortality, to actually take up the challenge of science and see where science fits in the study of immortal life. Are the old arguments supportive of immortality useless? Or do they have application today once we see what science today has actually accomplished, and not claimed to have accomplished?

Magnification powers make everything different than the unaided eye sees. It is the same eye that sees, but now through a different medium—the medium of enlargement. The medium has changed what the eye sees. We know from particular experiments (where predicted outcomes of subatomic behavior were verified) that the medium is not giving us a "false" reality, only a different one. That is, what we see without the medium, though different than what we see with the aid of a magnifying medium, is not "unreal." Because the two things we see, one without a magnifying medium and one with, differ does not mean that what we are seeing in either case is not what the thing we are seeing really is. It "really" is the thing we see through the medium that we are looking. The question then, "Which is the reality of the object that we see—is it accessible only through an electron microscope, or does the unaided eye see what the thing really is?"—is moot.

The object as it is unaided by any magnification process is the object as it is "in Nature." It is how the object is meant to appear when encountered by the animals or beings to whom Nature has provided eyes (or sensation). Intelligence has given man the ability to see different objects with different acuity through the power of intellection it has given him. With it man has come to make new tools for investigating things that the unaided eye does not. Yet, we know that birds have far better sight than us. Is what they see, then, a reality different than what we see? Or is it that we both see the same object, but it appears differently because our sense powers or tools of sight may differ?

We see the same object, but differently. It is not different in itself, It appears differently to each sense power or tool of magnification. Our sense powers do not make the object be what it is. It is independently of sense perception what it is. Observation does not make the object be what it is. Were that so, the automobile racing towards the man crossing the road should be able to be different if the observer had power over the reality of what was approaching him. We somehow get the sense if he does not move quickly enough out of the way, however, the automobile will kill him. Were it mostly space, as quantum physics wants to tell us, that should not happen at all.

It is this sort of reality, the fact that I might die if I think of reality different than my senses present it in the case of the onrushing automobile, that makes us argue that the world of quantum physics is not the actual world, the world as it really is. It is the world as seen differently, the world as seen with tools that transmit to our sense powers data differently than in the manner or to the power to which the sense organ is accustomed. And yet the material for those tools themselves, as we have pointed out, come from such a small increment of reality that we must surely question whether those tools quantum physics is using to describe "reality" describe reality or only a small portion of it, sc., the portion on which that their tools are focused. What "reality," that is, is quantum physics yielding to the inquisitive mind? If we leave aside the question of the type of tools that quantum physics is using, whether they give us "true reality" or not, ad look at the results of the magnification process to which those tools give us access, we can point out nevertheless that magnifying the sense particle does not mean that its reality has changed. If, through the magnification tool of quantum physics, it appears to be saturated with space and not the solid I perceive, it is because my senses and the object before me are proportioned differently than what the magnification affords to a sense power that is not proportioned to the sense object the way the magnification would have it be proportioned.

Without the sense power in the first place we could never have contact with any reality in question. Thus, simply because a tool of magnification can change the proportion of the object's dimensions differently than to what the sense power is normally accustomed, i.e., to what it grasps without the tool of magnification, does not mean the sense power is not in contact with the object's reality as it is. The resistance of the object is real, whether or not there is a tool for looking at the object differently. The magnifying power of the microscope does not eliminate the impenetrability, the "solidity," with which that the object, e.g., the onrushing car, confronts me.

That impenetrability, that solidity, is as real as the fact that the object has space between its electrons which powered to a certain exponential make it appear as almost total space. Total space does not give me resistance as a solid does. If the object does not permit me passage, it is not because it is really space and my inability to pass through it is an illusion. The object is not "really spatial" at all. It is "really spatial" only when viewed on a level different than what unaided sense organs transmit, those very same unaided sense organs which tell me when an auto is rushing towards me that it is "really" rushing towards me. I use the word "really in that case because I have no doubt that that is the actual reality confronting me. The car rushing towards me may appear when broken down into sub-atomic parts as primarily empty space through the magnifying powers of various ocular media. But the sense organs are telling me what will really happen if I don't move out of the way.

It is for this reason that one is not far off in viewing what the unaided sense powers transmit to us as being that which actually constitutes reality—however else other tools of science may view it. And on that level of sense transmission, the level of sense power unaided by instruments that change what the sense apprehends, we know that objects are in fact divisible into smaller components into which eventually destruction and perishing actually occur. If a being's reality is measured by the effects it can produce, reality for human consciousness comes to it not through instruments (electron microscopes, etc.) that alter how the human sense perceive things, but by those very effects produced on the conscious agent by the thing in question. And that thing, as in our example of the car, is a reality that comes to be and passes away by the accretion of and separation of parts. What quantum physics gives us, then, is not reality. It gives us an aspect of the world that evades sense powers, but an aspect that no more qualifies it as being what reality actually is anymore than the absence of an effect tells us what reality is not.

The most important conclusion for the distinction between partibility and non-partibility of anything that exits is, arguably, that we have evidence from this distinction of a consciousness that once come into being does not perish. Consciousness is indestructible. What the senses transmit as bodily decomposition and perishing does not go far enough in telling us what the reality decomposing before us is. Different sentient beings, as we noted in the case of the sense of sight in birds and man, have different powers of sense. It may be that our belief the corpse in front of us is the sign of consciousness powerless and moribund comes on account of a sense apparatus that cannot penetrate to that which the mind, in opposition to plain sense presentation, reasons. For it the evidence warrants we assert immortal existence of the body the senses show as simply dead. Immortal existence, the mind reasons, because of partless existence that all consciousness evinces. The senses transmit a reality to us; it is just that the reality so transmitted is not the entire truth of that reality.

If consciousness has this indestructibility, is it limited to one species of conscious being? Or is it that consciousness itself has an indestructibility about it essentially? Can we suggest that animal species other than the human have this indestructibility? Neither philosophy nor science has the capability to address this in the way it can with human personhood.

However, to the believer Scripture is a road to truth not accessible at times by reason. Does Scripture allow for the belief that other embodied conscious beings beside man retain their consciousness intact, that bodily dissolution is also not the destruction of their consciousness?

A metaphysical outlook that sees being as a perfection will not accede to a theory that suggests consciousness "below" the human level is annihilated upon bodily decomposition. If what the Divine has brought into existence as *Genesis* (1:31) declares is "good,"[3] we think Aquinas, whom we will have reason to discuss further, is well served with his belief that only annihilation brings into absolute non-being what has come into being. For the Divine, he implies, to have permitted a universe into existence for so long without bringing it into non-existence, or creature to have existed for any amount of time without destroying it, does not allow for a view (which he holds) of being as that which is diffusive of itself into infinity.[4]

METHODOLOGY

In the examination of a subject for which there is apparently no physical datum, sc., human immortality, the question of how one approaches it is paramount. Methodology[1] becomes overriding as a concern, only because the consequences for having chosen the wrong one are so profound—if one holds that immortal existence is the most pressing issue of one's own personhood.

Methodology must be compliant not only with what is to be examined but also with what does the examination, with what tools are used to undertake it. We expand on in our exposition in what follows that on which we briefly touched in the previous chapter, sc., the assertion that our senses register only electromagnetic impulses within 0.005% of the frequency band that provides for all stimuli. We have access, i.e., to only one half of one percent of the world, and the universe. We already argued that quantum physics cannot present to us what constitutes reality, however sophisticated its tool are. Not only because of the question what value can tools derived from materials, components within such a narrow band of reality possess; but also because reality is measured by what effect something has on something else. We saw that though quantum physics may describe an automobile in terms far, far different than what our perception presents, the reality of the car is not reducible to what quantum physics argues. The effect the car has on us is far different than the sub-atomic parts to which quantum physics reduces it. Those parts are not what kill us if the auto runs over us. The car's reality is something other, as is the reality of all extended objects in our experience. Their reality derives from the arrangement of their parts into which they corrupt or out of which they come to be. What quantum physics wants to present as the reality of the object, therefore, it cannot.

Our question now is: Given a limit to our sense capability, as quantum theory has hypothesized, how is it that we can say what we say about our eternal destiny has sure and closed validity? Do not the senses afford access to only a fraction of reality? To what extent can our comments have surety, have certainty that cannot be undone, e.g., by access to further fields of experience that any of the remaining 99.95% of the vibrational band quantum physics asserts exists may afford?

This outlook of the current science, quantum physics and its correlates, merits examination frequently throughout our essay. If for no other reason than its self-refutational core has rarely received critique. Had it to the degree it should have, one asks what significance would it play in the epistemology of immortality? Very little, it should appear, if self-refutational structures of thought are seen to be the weaknesses they clearly are. On the self-refutational flaw in quantum physics, that reality is not as we perceive it, and quantum physics has the tools to prove it, tools whose materials issue from just a sliver of reality, however, so much has been built. It has made approaches to the question of immortality in terms of addressing matter and the immaterial through composition and dissolution by parts seem almost irrelevant, if not also quaint. They are neither.

With this critique of quantum physics, detailing its self-refutational claims, we can further proceed. Questions of truth have always involved the credence that one can apply to the avenues of knowing. If in the case of man those avenues are so narrow, as science today explains, what methodology did we use to gain this understanding of how narrow the capability of what we are using to address this problem is? We used scientific equipment whose wholeness and solidity was available to our sense powers, so we imagine. Yet the methodology in question, quantum theory, states that what we are measuring and saying is solid and definitive is simply a complexus of empty space within which orbit irreducible charged particles. Between the particle and the outer "limits" of the object in question is all empty space. The same, however, holds for the tools we have used to come to that finding, that conclusion. They are made from an empty space composed by irreducible orbiting bits.

Accordingly, if the tools we use themselves were put together and assembled in this most limited vibrational frequency, the only access to which quantum physics allows, how is it that we can say those tools actually tell us what constitutes the real dimensions, the real status, of what it is we say we know when we say we know an object? If the tools are fashioned from material which we selected from this smallest area of vibrational frequency, sc., the world of our everyday—a miniscule portion of the frequencies constituting the entire cosmos— how do we know that what they present to us has any mark of certainty since that from which they come, the 0.005% frequency vibrational band, is itself so confined and limited a part of the universe? The instruments we use, such as electron microscopy, particle beam efflorescence, and the like use particles and components that come from an area that represents only a miniscule segment of all the galaxy. How sure can we be of the dependability of electron microscopy or particle beam smashing in yielding access to what represents all of the cosmos, given the so limited piece of the cosmos from which their components come?

Does one want to say that we can extrapolate from these to the rest of the universe's matter and say that is how all of the matter in the universe would act? Can one say from one-half of one percent sampling of the universe that laws for the remaining 99.5% can be said to be similar to those of the one-half of one percent?

Surely the conclusions about truth that are wrapped in the equipment of quantum physics give us pause, give us difficulty, when the scope and expanse of what we have used to come to those "conclusions" is so limited, so inconsequential, it would seem, when set against the largeness of the remainder of the galaxy to which our sense powers, according to quantum physics, provide no access. The new physics tells us the closer we examine physical matter, the more we find that "matter" does not exist as we thought. Electron microscopy zooms us past protons, neutrons, etc., past orbiting particles into energy fields. How do we come to accept this when the tools that brought us to this conclusion come from the material that goes to make up only one half of one percent of our cosmos?

One's findings are only as good as the tools one uses. This is a principle of experience that does not appear limited to results one has encountered in this smallest portion of the vibrational band that we have been discussing. For the principle has not come about by using the tools of quantum physics. It has come about by active intercourse with the world, however quantum physics wants to describe that world or specify what amount of the universe we can experience. The principle, i.e., does not appear dependent on what quantum physics has to say about what it is that we experience. Applied to the findings of quantum mechanics, what probity do the claims of the new science have if the tools it employs, by its own admission, carry with them only the smallest portion of the universe?

This is the problem of methodology that confronts us as we begin our inquiry. Which maxims can we declare legitimate, and which not, if the field of evidence for our findings, on which we are basing those maxims, does not represent any significant portion of the galaxy? Oddly, quantum physics has separated us from a universe about which, yet, it wishes to make claims that it postulates are all we can know.

If this point of the failure of the latest methodology in science is clear, if the failing of our experiments, because of the limits to the tools we use, is clear, where do we begin a study of establishing, if we can, endless life? What is the methodology we can use? Can we use tools that tell us how narrow our access to the universe is, while those tools themselves came from that area which is such a miniscule portion of all that exists, and which minute portion is that alone to which we have access? Clearly we cannot depend on tools whose origins are so confined that we do not know if access to what the rest of the universe contains would overturn the result to which those tools led us.

What this means, it appears, is that we cannot rely on those tools to tell us our fate at death because of the frailty we have located in them. Tools constructed from materials derived from a wider vibrational frequency field might in fact show a world totally different than the world of 0.005% vibrationality. Add to this, the difficulty that vibrations require two points within which the vibrations occur, we must ask which two points in our quantum vibrational world we are to pick so that we have picked the correct vibrational frequency with which to understand the rest of the universe. It seems obvious that there is no criterion by which we can know which two points they would be. One's findings, as we already noted, are only as good as the tools one uses. In this regard, quantum science's findings for any study of immortality do not appear to provide what such a study needs.

We had already intimated this criticism in our example of how the onrushing car cannot be quantum mechanics "spatial" reality to the exclusion of its solidity. The fear that the individual who sees the onrushing car experiences evinces for us an understanding of reality that quantum mechanics simply does not capture. In this observation, we did not lay down a methodology for the critique of quantum physics like we have just done above. Yet, we showed that an endeavor which dismisses or contravenes what the experiences afforded by our sense apparatus transmits is not a methodology the search for truth can abide. Our very behavior towards the onrushing car, sc,, jumping out of the way as fast as we can to avoid injury or death, shows this. In that respect we have indicated one branch of a methodology the tree of knowledge must put forth—the testing of claims that may not square with sense data against how one behaves. If behavior acts contrary to what particular claims set forth is the truth about reality, it might be that the claims do not meet the criteria all methodologies directed at truth must have. This clearly seems to hold in the case of quantum physics. At best it tells us something about reality. We cannot depend on it to tell us what is reality.

A guiding maxim for any methodology in a field of knowledge is that results must be, and can only be, proportionate to (1) the transparency of the subject being studied, and (2) to the ability of the inquirer. Further, (3) the inquirer must know whether he is starting with the right tools, (4) on the right path, and with (5) the right questions. He also must know, if he has taken the right path, that (6) the right path means each step taken is successively coaxed by a further step which adds further to the incontestability of the conclusion one needs in order to claim truth in an inquiry.

One process towards incontestability of approach is that one proceed without prejudice, let the field that is being studied open up as it is with as little interference from the investigator as possible. One wants it to stay as untrammeled and unsullied as possible, so that it presents itself as aboriginally as knowledge allows. Disclosedness is the effort. This means interfering with nothing in the disclosure, otherwise there is the possibility of something being concealed, not letting be seen, which is directly contradictory to letting something be "as it appears."

If this is so, we want to begin with a methodology that remains faithful to the world in which we live, that lets what we are investigating open itself up to us as it is. The quantum tools surely cannot advance this given their undependability that results from their status as instruments culled from only an infinitesimal slice of the universe. Their findings, as we saw, are immediately suspect given the nature of the instruments used to reach those findings.

Methodology must seek never to result in what is suspect. Denying that one needs to let things disclose themselves as they are requires one disclose why that precise principle is not the proper way to proceed. Letting things "be" to the extent one can appears the most salutary way to truth.

Phenomenology, as a method seeking the pure essence of whatever it is that appears (presents itself), would appear to have a preference to the "pure" observer inasmuch as the goal of all phenomenology is to proceed without prejudice and preconception. The method is self-correcting if there is prejudice found because one would imagine that one would not find the prejudice that was found if one were prejudiced in the first place. The point is important as a reason to employ phenomenology, as well as a defense of the approach. Phenomenology's self-correcting process makes it a viable vehicle to the "pure" inquiry necessary to the study of the question of immortal existence.

The claim that there can be no "pure" or unprejudiced approach would hopefully, we might add, come from an individual who himself was without prejudice, i.e., who could make his claim from a "pure" standpoint. Failing it, his own objection to any possibility of a "pure" approach, a "pure" account, of any situation or reality would seem to have no consequence since he claimed already that no "pure" approach was possible in the first place—including, therefore, his own. We encounter once more a self-refutational position. On these grounds, it appears that we can use phenomenology as our method to examine consciousness in our undertaking inasmuch as it seeks to proceed without prejudice and is self-correcting, as we just noted, if it finds prejudice.

The phenomenological method is one that uses pure description, as we shall see, for its basis of examination. Proceeding though "pure description," one comes to the underlying structures and laws governing the appearance of what one examines. Is this an adequate approach to the study of the human person in the world? Phenomenology rules out presuppositions in its descriptive approach. That is what it means, in one sense, by its "purity."

"Pure description," unlike the tools of science which we just saw, seeks to let things come before us unsullied, as it were, by tools for which, as we now see in our criticism of quantum mechanics, we cannot vouch. It suggest that we enter inquiry not with the attempt to alter how things appear, (which tools such as a microscope do) but look at things in their "natures," and not as interfered with by mechanical devices that man has fashioned. Indeed, to what extent such instruments "alter" the appearance of the object as it appears in Nature makes the mechanico-scientific approach suspect in that we have not reached the object as it appears in its originality, in its primordial setting, but as "tampered with" by the "scientific" investigator. That does not appear to be the way the student of existence should proceed.

Consciousness, as an object of descriptive undertaking, comes to us in sharp relief and determinability if we reach it without presupposition, prejudice, and tampering. How can what is purely descriptive, after all, involve prejudice? If it is actually "pure" it cannot. This is how we will seek to present consciousness in our essay. In so doing, in presenting it "purely," we can arguably claim we have established consciousness, in fact, as a reality of "aboutness."

This is important as we move to see whether the world has an existence independent of consciousness. As we discuss consciousness in its pure "structure," it will be important that we discuss at length that which is independent of it, sc., the "other." We cannot leave the existence of the "other" as a matter of simple "unimpeachable" common sense. We have to go into great detail regarding the establishment of the actuality of its existence given the importance the demonstration of that plays in a discussion of immortality. Without an "other," consciousness is simply one subject sc., I. And if all exists is the "I," its dissolution at death obviously is the total dissolution of all that is—as well as the elimination of any after-life. Accordingly, our methodology is to proceed towards those experiences, here they are "resistance," the perception of "color," "language," and the obvious immediacy of directionality (of which "curiosity" or "wonder" [by another name] is a derivative reality in some respects), and argue these experiences point to a world actually independent and "other" than the "I."

The method of syllogism, as a further amplification in methodology used here, seeks to take an entity's nature, and from that, or towards it, make observations that are included in the very nature of the entity but which analysis and explanation have to break out. If consciousness has a nature, the syllogistic method, as we have described it here, gives us increased certainty that what we are examining is not an entity that is simply a binary or trinary processor of electrical pulses in the brain. Consciousness emerges as something that is not reducible to a processor of "open" and" closed" sequences within neuronal histology.

It is here where the method question becomes paramount. How do we know that using binary structures, trinary paradigms, is not the way to examine what we "folkwise" call "consciousness"?[2] How do we know that consciousness is not more exactly and correctly understood as some algebraic "zombie"[3] that acts as a super algorithmic processor?

This is the tenor of the current thinking called neurophilosophy. Neuroscience, neurophilosophy, calls emotions and feelings language and words that neural specifications and physiological studies in our study have antiquated. Why are not these terms superannuated byproducts by now of a less sophisticated, less scientific, literati? We continue to make distinctions between a neural event and an emotion, and have done so over the millennia. Neurophilosophy tells us that this is due to absence of understanding in what actually, which is to say what neurally, occurs in each sentient entity.

Once the sun orbited the earth. Once there was a consciousness that was distinct from bodily operations. Now, the new understanding calls us to accept that what exists is only a world of the brain's doing by which whatever we believe and think comes about. There is no external reality. There is no self. What the world is is a matrix of interactions and actions networking through a complex of multibillion microscopic neuronal moments putting together a world that we think is something independent and separate from us—but is not. Only in our era, according to neurophilosophy, have we come to understand this.

A methodology is known to be inapt if it lacks a certain "feel." If there is something about a methodology that goes so contrary to what our immediate appraisal and attitude regarding something is, we can either question the acuity of that immediacy in taking attitudes and appraisals, or simply disregard them and say that each new development in science is what we must accept and to which we must adhere.

The only difficulty with that is that we do not know what criterion to use to tell us whether what we immediately think is the case is an acceptable criterion or not. Absent the criterion, we have to ask ourselves on what basis we would accept a view of the world and ourselves that goes so contrary to what we immediately, non-inferentially, accept as true and evidentiary. That is, on what basis would we accept a view of the world whose methodology reduces all experience and consciousness to algebraic formulae or material platforms and residue? One has to ask that especially if there are exceptions that continually creep into the neuro-reductionist or materialist approach that indicate problems with that approach.

Skepticism towards neuroepistemology abets the methodology we have chosen here to approach the subject of life after death, personal existence beyond bodily dissolution. If the world is itself not all that is within our sense capacity to grasp and prehend, we need to question any system or approach that reduces all existence to the material and the totally corruptible. A system that dogmatizes such an assertion does so at the cost and risk of disregarding what evidence tells us no serious inquiry should disregard.

That is the avenue we have taken here as we start with a phenomenology of consciousness, reason by that to the existence of an "other," and look at the interaction that occurs within the conscious field, and why then eliminative materialism and reductionism, and their subclasses, cannot give us a final answer on the question of immortal personhood. Knowledge does not stop at sense-prehension. To say it does is itself to have gone beyond sense-prehension. Because knowledge goes beyond the senses, we are able to address the question of immortality in a way meritorious of the appellation "science."

What gets us closer to the answer, and thus further from the state of question, is the approach of looking at why reductionism and other similar approaches do not end our inquiry. Why do they leave it with more queries than an approach that shows their inadequacies in favor of data that bring us closer to believing that immortality might in fact not be a chimera after all? And in doing this show it a possibility for which it is wiser to prepare than not.

CONSCIOUSNESS

We have argued that electron microscopy and other like approaches to reality actually distort the reality of what is being examined. If the concrete items of experience are "in reality" primarily space, then the approach that holds that is saying when an individual is hit by a car, what has killed him is primarily space or spatial. What differentiates this from why certain spaces cannot destroy someone seems a problem for any doctrine that holds the basic constituent of any thing is space. Space of itself is without occupation, so that how in one instance something primarily spatial (the onrushing automobile) can kill, while in another case it cannot leaves one questioning what criterion must be used to identify what is reality and what is not. We have argued that reality is known in large by its effects, such that a car approaching me is known not to be "really" primarily space at all, but an object of mass that can end my life if it hits me with enough force. Quantum science cannot give such a criterion for how I ascertain what is real. For this reason we have had to dismiss it as any procedure that can aid us in understanding reality as the individual human encounters it. A different scale is needed because quantum science presents only an aspect of reality, one under the altering media of lenses and electromagnetic manipulations. It does not present us with what reality is. That comes to us through the senses, and these transmit a totally different world than in quantum science. The senses present us with a world of resistance, weight, impenetrability, not simply of extension and interchanging areas of pressure and motion. While this such world is what they convey, that to which all this is conveyed shares in none of these features of the reality of mass and bulk we experience everyday. This reality is further removed from electron microscopy than they are and possesses a feature that none of them do. It cannot be broken down into a constituency less than it.

Reflection on the first time we erred in our assessment of a situation before us, that is, made a mistake in perceiving what was in front of us, such that what we thought to be before us was in fact not, gives us cause to identify a gap between what we sometimes know as opposed to what we think we know, but do not. There is a difference in what we think versus what is in fact the case. The long history of this problem as a philosophic issue came to a crisis in Descartes who decided that the many errors that dependence on the senses caused required that we acknowledge that only one datum gave me indisputable truth, sc., the knowledge that I exist. No matter how I sought to doubt this datum, I needed to exist in order to doubt it. Greater certainty, if not absolute certainty, was nowhere else to be located.

Descartes famously went through the case of the *genium malignum*, *"summe potentem et callidum"* the Evil Genius who may be deceiving me into thinking that I am in contact with a world.[1] The thought experiment gives me reason to dismiss direct awareness of the world, unmediated indubitability of contact with objects themselves. If I can make an error in sense-perception, what is there to stop me from allowing the possibility that I am not in actual communion with the world but only with at best a representation of it? To go further, if I try to point to any evidence that I suggest gets me out of this difficulty, what is there to show that this evidence itself is not manufactured by this Deceiver? I may not be in contact with any world whatsoever, only with thoughts and mental representations of a *malin genie*.

It seems, however, far easier to accept the direct participation of the world in my thoughts than the convoluted scheme Descartes suggested. Far easier to say that I in fact have direct acquaintance with objects, and that this is good reason to allow this to be the starting point of all my deliberations. Keep explanations to a minimum, as Occam argued, which certainly a doctrine of direct acquaintance with the world does as opposed to postulating some wicked demon out to construct my entire world and all the machinations it must devise to keep me in that belief.

Error, we can say to Descartes, comes from the mind introducing into an object what is not there, from combining with the subject a predicate that is not actually in existential synthesis with the subject. We will make mistakes in perception, for sure. But this is not grounds to dismiss any direct prehension of the world. We do not need the method of rigorous doubt to get us back to our moorings of living in the world among objects with which we are in direct contact. We need only to be sure that errors are avoided, which means to leave be the object as existence synthesizes it before the mind, and with which the mind becomes immaterially identified as the immaterial synthesis that all knowledge is.[2] The senses, contrary to Descartes' admonition, are not where error occurs. It is in the judgment, that all knowledge is, where error resides.

What we do know, indubitably though, is that in error there is a difference between what is actually the case and what we say is. This allows us to ask whether there is a difference between what does the prehending, and what is prehended? That is, is there a difference between the world that comes to awareness and the nature of awareness itself? Are the two in any way similar? Or is there a difference between them that cannot be joined, a difference that metaphysically separates the two and makes them totally unlike the other?

Embodied consciousness—corporeally situated sentient prehension—in its state of actual awareness is the direction of a bodily sentient being away from itself. The direction is towards everything that is other than it. "Direction" is a spatial metaphor. In its meaning here we understand immediately two points, one from which an event commences and a second on account of which the event has commenced in the first place and in which it terminates or is realized. The event's points in question are the individual that is conscious and the second is that of which he is conscious. Directing himself towards that second brings to his existence that which was not previously present. It brings an entity that is not the result of his doing, not the result of his making. That entity emerges in awareness without any mediation, or steps in thought, as that which is not the being which has directed itself, turned its "attention," to it.

"Direction" is a cognitional movement towards an entity that is not it, by which that entity takes on a new being, that of "being known," that of which some "other"—the consciousness directed towards it—is "aware." By this directionality of consciousness this entity, of which consciousness has become aware, takes on that new being in virtue of that which has moved towards it. "Awareness," to use Husserl's language, "is being minded in a descriptively determinate fashion."[3]

Critical in the account here is the term" minded." "Body" and "mind" are two existents neither of which the other in any way is. Nothing about either can be said about the other except that each "exists." Beyond that everything is different. Neither can do what the other does. Neither originates from the other. And, we will argue here, neither ends where the other does.

The movement of consciousness as "direction" to an "other" has been otherwise known as "intentionality":[4] The Latin language heritage manifest in the word makes clear that "intentionality" from "in-tendere" means (as the Latin root "tendere" evinces) a "tending towards," a "tilting towards." Immediately in this term an "other" towards which this "tilting," "tending," is occurring emerges without opacity, without any confusion. The very structure of the act contains within it a "duality," a "two-ness." Without the "other" there is no consciousness taking place, there is no "awareness" that has come about.

Consciousness in its act is essentially "towards something other" through which that other becomes that of which the movement towards it can now be called "awareness." "Every mental phenomenon includes an object within itself." "Object" simply means whatever is encountered in consciousness. As such, consciousness is "immanently objective" in that it is, of its very essence, related to some object.[5] Every mental event is with an object. It always refers beyond itself, in sharp contradiction to the merely physical. No physical object intrinsically refers to anything beyond itself, while each conscious act is that whereby we are always able to be other-referring.

In the act of consciousness, that "other" is never again by itself. Its being is forever changed by being that of which something other than it is now "aware," or "of." There is no hearing without that which is heard; no believing, unless something is believed; no hoping unless there is something hoped for; no loving unless something is loved.

Consciousness is that by which we are related to an object, "which may not be actual but which is presented as an object."[6] In this way we see immediately a difference from the physical world where objects interacting are indeed real, are indeed "there," "outside of me." But in this relation of awareness to its world, the relation towards what is "other than" is not constrained necessarily by an "object," in the way the "object" is so in the world of force and movement against each other. The object of the act of consciousness is always at least immanent to the act, to the consciousness, whether or not there is an object that is "outside" of it (an object not dependent on consciousness for its existence, an object that exists whether or not consciousness does). That object, not dependent on the act of consciousness for its actual existence, is immanent to the act once it is "present" to consciousness. It is both "inside" consciousness, and "outside" it. It is "immanent" to it only by first being extrinsic to it, by being metaphysically its "other."

Consciousness, as the essential structure of that which is always "object-directed," "object-related," differs absolutely in itself from any object in the world that needs no such relation at all to be what it is. The billiard ball can be the billiard ball without any directionality towards anything outside it. Consciousness, however, cannot be consciousness unless there is this "otherness" about it which we understand as its correlate. Consciousness is essentially "correlative being," and it is in this correlativeness, in fact, that its essence lies.

In the act of intentionality has come about a structure wherein beings of the world take on a relationship towards each other as object and subject, as that towards which the "intentional" (cognitional) movement occurs and that whose movement constitutes consciousness in act. In this structure there is that of which the totality of objects, as well as each and every object, is correlative, sc., consciousness, which in turn in act is that alone by which any object takes on its status as "object." Consciousness becomes the subject to which all objects "appear," become "sensed," "known," once they have come within its domain.

In this construct of "subject-object" arises a world other than simply things, but now a world of "things for," "things by," and "things to which." At once vanishes a world of isolated and unrelated entities, but instead a world where perspective, attitude, and estimation give the object a status other than it had without there being consciousness in its world.

Billiard balls, one against the other, react and interact, but not in the way the movement of consciousness and object, subject and known, does. In the one the action-reaction is purely mechanical, through physical forces one plied against or intersecting with, the other. Consciousness and its object, however, are not a similitude of forces in presence to each other. More than the mechanical—no, something totally other than the mechanical—is operant here.

Already we are coming to the route by which we will begin to answer the question whether there is a difference in some way between beings that are "aware" of the world as opposed to those without awareness. Our billiard ball example evinces a way of interaction and reaction that is other than the way consciousness and object relate. Something about them is not reducible to the obviously unintended movements of the balls. Something in the being of consciousness indicates an approach to its world that the billiard balls do not possess.

For the being that is conscious, in this world comes realization of otherness and ability to calculate otherness through means and media not available to our billiard balls. There is possession of abilities not within the domain of our billiard balls that enables movements and motions not available to the balls. Stopping without the interference of a counterforce causing the stop is one such power.

This shows for consciousness an independence from forces around it inasmuch as it can act contrary to those forces without physical contact from them. It can begin on its own, stop on its own, "focus" this way or that on its own and take on the being of what it encounters in a way that strictly material objects cannot. Presence to it occurs in way other than simply contact, place, or attraction. Consciousness is changed in a way that physical force or extension does not and cannot accomplish in material existents that lack it. The object of which the conscious being for the first time is aware now becomes ingredient to that conscious being in a way not within the capacity of an entity not possessed of powers of awareness.

Consciousness, awareness, furnishes an existent a status that the entity without awareness does not possess. We see in it an independence, a freedom, a power of origination that the unconscious being (our billiard ball) does not have. At some precise juncture the philosopher must ask himself what it is about the conscious being that provides for this capacity. What gives the conscious being the power to "start on its own," and what is lacking in the unconscious being that this power of "on its own" is absent in it?

If the world of objects, e.g., is something occupied by entities constantly perishing, constantly decomposing, constantly passing into non-being, does this mean that what does this prehensions of such a world, that is, that wherein this awareness of all that is passing away takes place, is it also subject to the same strictures of decay and passing out of existence? Or is there, to which we have been alluding and which we shall argue, a difference between the two? A gap, as it were, that shows the two worlds, sc., the objects of our awareness and the world of consciousness, in total metaphysical opposition, opposition in their very being, to each other? Is the one, i.e., unlike the other, imperishable, incapable of dissolution, incapable of passing away?

Awareness of color indicates a difference from what physicists quantify as its different places on a chromascale. Red may be a certain quantified wavelength, but my perception of red has no correspondence at all to the quantification. My perception is not a quantity, it is not a length. What the scientists tells me "red" is is not what I experience. So also with all the colors, and also with sound. The rate of vibration in the instrument is not the "sound" I experience. The mathematical formula that identifies pitch is not my experience of tone. A general principle surfaces that is critical: whatever sensation I have is not like the event in the body, my physical matter, whence the stimulus linked to the sensation originally derived.

Furthermore, consciousness as "intentional" existence is not "intentional" towards "formulae of mathematics." When we "see," we do not see a sensation,[7] nor a mathematical formula. There is no evidence that we see by means of a mathematical formula. Similarly, for hearing: we do not "hear" a mathematical formula, nor a sensation. The hearing itself is the sensation.

The object is given, towards which consciousness has been open as "direction-towards," and with which directionality arises the sensation. In sensation, the object occurs to sense faculties of a living body; not a mathematical equation. In memory, sense faculties do not "possess," no longer bear, the sense datum, sense content; nor in imagination. Intentionality and object relate non-bodily in memory, but in no less a reality than occurs in the instance of embodied awareness. The manner is in accordance with structural capabilities intrinsic to the powers of the consciousness in question.

If consciousness is not a quantity, does it thereby escape one obvious precondition of dissolution, sc., being divisible, broken up into smaller parts, quantities? How consciousness as an actuality comes about in everyday contact with the world asks us if the way it does also means that there is a further difference between the world that comes to my awareness and the awareness by which that world does so occur.

More importantly, does this level of consciousness of which we speak apply only to human, or does it apply to consciousness in all sentient beings on the planet? In other words, if we are coming to evidence that consciousness has about it a feature that is totally other than that of which it is the consciousness, are we coming to a state of being that is not only different from the material world in human beings, but in all sentient beings?

Consciousness' indivisibility protrudes as obsidian evidence to the materialist. It is not like a pie that can be cut, a piece of wood that can be sawed. You cannot take one's consciousness and by division come up with two. The claim, in this regard, that so-called multiple personality disorder poses a material objection to the indivisibility assertion actually is without merit. We see patterns of behavior fragmented, the one from the other, in such a situation and clearly have no grounds for arguing the fragmentation means two conscious streams occupy one space or body. Split-personalities, a subset of this multiple personality argument, themselves each requires the streams of consciousness that characterize and differentiate the awareness of one person from the other. But there is no way of showing that the stream of consciousness bifurcation claimed in split or multiple personality cannot simply be resolved back into one consciousness behaving in two different ways. For this reason, the claim of indivisibility as a feature of consciousness has to remain one that the thinker needs to take seriously, especially given the ramifications of such indivisibility.

If there are these differences in the being of consciousness versus that of the physical world, consciousness steps out as evidence to suggest a form of existence not limited to material destructibility. We have a platform other than that of "mind" for arguing that life other than human may possess that indestructibility. "Mind," taken to mean the ratiocinative and conceptualization process[8] in the human by which various abstractions are possible which do not appear to be in other sentient life, is not the only possible datum to suggest to us that existence is not totally and completely material. Besides this faculty of "mind" is the faculty of consciousness. Consciousness is wider than mind in that it is not limited to ratiocinative processes but goes beyond them to things themselves that become part of the subject's world. They become an aspect of that subject in ways that strictly material beings cannot. Consciousness comes to the world in more than just concepts as we understand human mentation to. It is not necessary for us to show whether sentient existence other than man has concepts, mind. Our point here is that consciousness itself suffices as evidence of an existence that is trans-material.

Consciousness and body appear to be at polar opposites, if not at opposites that reveal contradictory properties. Body is in space and can be located, consciousness is nowhere positionable in the sentient being. Consciousness appears to be in space only insofar as it is situated in the body that experiences the world. Try to specify it by any coordinates and it escapes being in any way pinpointed. Half the color red in consciousness remains "consciousness of red," though we can remove a limb from an extended object, a tree, and we end up with a limbless tree. You cannot divide a "sound" in two, and yet you can cut a piece of wood in half. More importantly, while I can know the same house you live in, can have familiarity and experience with it, I cannot have *your* experience of the note your ear has picked up and is now registered in your consciousness as a "tone." Nor of the "stars" that come into your consciousness after you have suffered a blow to the head. Both are private, incommunicable.

If I look in your brain for where the musical note in your consciousness is, for what could I possibly be looking since an electrical event does not resemble the sound in my consciousness? I look for the consciousness "red," I cannot find it. The touch of velvet one experiences, the smell of freshly cut grass—where in consciousness does one find these?

If awareness is to have no limits, it would stand to reason that it must in some way be unlike everything of which awareness comes to be. If, on the other hand, it has limits to providing contact with the world, one could argue that that could derive from it itself being in some way like the things of the world. Only if it is not like anything with which it could possible be in contact, which could possibly present itself to consciousness, can consciousness have no limits on what can come into its sphere. In that no one has yet come to see just what limits on awareness do exist, has never been able to specify what in the material world could not be present to it, one can argue that what is material, as well as spatial or extended, is totally unlike it.

Were consciousness and the body identical, conceiving of one without the other would be impossible. It would be contradictory, in the same way conceiving of a square circle is impossible because of the contradiction entailed. Yet, nothing about "mind" stops me from conceiving it as other than body, in the same way nothing about "refreshment" requires that I think only of "water." I am involved in no contradiction if I think of refreshment other than water, while there is nothing about water that tells me to think of something else that refreshes is contradictory. Nothing about "Babe Ruth" stops me from thinking of some other major league ball player as hitting sixty home runs in a one hundred and fifty-four game baseball season; but if I think of Babe Ruth, to think of him as not one such player is to involve me in a contradiction. It is inconceivable to think of him as not having accomplished this total in home run hitting because in this world he did. It is the events in this world, as measure of the truth of statements made in this world, that precisely make it inconceivable.

To want to extend the term "Ruth" to every possible world, and thus avoid the charge that one is always involved in a contradiction if one denies Ruth and sixty home runs are mutually implicative, does nothing to reduce the power of the argument that "body" and "consciousness" are not identical. There simply is no world, possible or actual, where my thought of body is impossible without the thought of consciousness. I can, in point of fact, however, think of a two-by-four piece of wood without thinking of consciousness, or of it as being conscious, as it possessing directionality to something other than itself no matter which universe or possible world I visit. For in the very nature of the entity in question,—wood— consciousness cannot be in its composition.

Conceivability, we should note, as a measure of an entity's metaphysical status has, for the realist, questionable probity. Thinking of something as possible or impossible does not add to our understanding of the actual existence of what comes to be or exists. The principle of non-contradiction became a measure in some way of the possibility or impossibility of something's existence in Aristotle. Permutations of that principle's application in philosophic arguments have run the gamut from application in skeptical methodologies to tests of realist assertions. Hume seems to have given it a prominence of only which he was capable, which we have treated at length elsewhere.[9] Suffice it to say here that there appears no actual criterion to justify an entity's ability to exist or not simply based on the conceivability of it.

There is nothing that tells us the principle of conceivability itself has the applications claimed for it simply by reason of the fact that nothing assures us that what the human mind finds inconceivable translates into actual impossibility of occurrence. Creation, the bringing to be out of nothing, surely is an inconceivable occurrence, if not an outright contradiction. To make something be from nothing is to use nothing in bringing the existent to be, as well as bring it out of nothing. If, however, to use nothing in a thing's coming to be means it came to be without anything, i.e., that nothing was used in making it come to be, in its coming into existence, and we also claim that it came from nothing, we have the instance of an entity's popping into existence without any agency or means. Creation is declared inconceivable, and yet creation as a doctrine of the universe's emergence has respectability throughout the millennia and in a multitude of religions. Acceptance of the doctrine is a recognition that something about the human mind is not so encompassing that it becomes the arbiter of whether or not existence is possible, or whether simply because the mind declares something inconceivable, it is. How many instances of inconceivability, therefore, do we dismiss as criteria for an entity's existence, or different entities, for that matter, if the pivotal instance, creation (*creatio ex nihilo*), does not have the persuasiveness that claimants to the inconceivability criterion want?

Such are the questions, just to begin with, in which this criterion of inconceivability can involve us, much to what one may not have expected. It is what immediately confronts us, that towards which the senses are directed as the conduits for awareness, consciousness, of "presence to me," that appears more serviceable as the basis for introspection and reflection on what actually constitutes experience, than on what conceivably may or may not.

It is in fact this immediate given, that consciousness is "about," is "of," that takes it out of the Evil Demon's grasp of solipsism and gives the conscious entity its sense of being thrown into an environment, a world. It is not one of consciousness' making. Were it, this sense of "about," of "of," that consciousness, that the conscious being, takes to its very existence, would be impossible. These terms convey an otherness, a "that which is not of one's making, but is beyond it." The being "about" a world confines consciousness to that which is before it, and is that which grounds, validates, the conscious being's claims about its experiences. Confines in the sense that it is the measure of whether consciousness', the conscious being's, declarations are true or false, factual or imaginative.[10] While it does not have the infallibility that inner perception must yield, that our inner mental life bares plainly to us (can the conscious agent doubt its interior perception is other than it is?), consciousness as the other-directed act by which the world is engaged achieves the object as it is when the object before it is allowed to appear as it is *tout court*.[11]

So ingredient to consciousness is this feature of "about," "of," that it is a law, a universal, of consciousness itself. There can never be a consciousness in act that is not "of," something. Consciousness without an object, without that towards which it is directed, is lawless, is an epistemological impossibility.[12]

Corollary to this is the notion of "givenness" (*Gegebenheit*), that all experience is experience "to someone." In all consciousness there is, irreducibly, a "to whom." In every act of consciousness there is an intentional correlate— consciousness' intentional correlate. The manner of the experience, that according to which the object is experienced, comes under the aegis of the powers of awareness in the conscious agent, powers for which sense capacity is the limiting factor, followed by the power of imagination (image making), and then the higher cognitive capacities.

The experience also can come under different modes, e.g., that of temporality (as in remembering), which is different from the actual experience itself. Remembering (bringing the past to the present, but as past) a blow to one's body is not to be hit again, nor is remembering an error committing it again.

Consciousness, that is, is not a determinant of sense powers. It is the other way around. The sense powers determine consciousness to the extent that the content[13] given to the consciousness in question is so according to the sense powers of the conscious agent.[14] Thus, whatever is sentient is a conscious being, an entity with awareness which, of its very nature, is other-directed, and which does not remain forever circling around and within itself, as it were. It is, as a sentient-conscious construct, ever the tendency towards engagement with an other as a "content," or, more than that, a "meaning."

Content as other than consciousness is the true meaning of object,[15] for object by its very meaning is other than subject, which is the entirety of consciousness' ground. This existence as other than me is not an immediate correlate of conscious existence. It comes about only as I, as conscious being, come to prehend certain distinctions among objects which differentiate their mode of existence one from the other. Whatever exists is an existential synthesis of predicates with its subject. By existential synthesis we mean existence synthesizes all attributes of a subject with that subject, and by that synthesis the subject becomes the existent that it is in time and space. That existential synthesis occurs in consciousness either as internal to its world or external to it. This takes place immaterially (intentionally, not bodily or physically). Features of the synthesis for the external object when made part of consciousness speak to it of an object not only other than it, but also other than its existence.[16]

In all consciousness there is a subject, and an object for that subject. It is this "object" that for humankind can, we know, become "meaning," not just "content," as we are restricted to express the "object" in the animal world, the object for animal awareness. Unlike the actual act of consciousness, the actual, here-and-now individual conscious act, "meaning," as Husserl has pointed out,[17] has no such restriction. It is repeatedly instantiated in other acts of the same awareness, is not just an awareness event that happens only once. "Content" is the "other" that both animal and human consciousness share, to which their awareness is "directed"; "meaning" is content under a different guise. It is content that becomes the basis for language.

"Meaning," to further define it, is accessible to many, if not all, in a way that the object is not. It is not restricted to "this particular space and time," "this particular instant." "Meaning" is known as having been grasped because meaning is that on which the human conscious agent acts, it is that which directs the agent this way, or that. Presented with a content, the human conscious agent will either remain unmoved, or will engage in motions which otherwise would not have occurred. "Meaning" is at a level of awareness where what has entered into (human) consciousness can be manipulated and prehended as compatible or incompatible, compossible or incomposable, with other "meanings."

This further separates it from our term "content," which we said is applicable to the form the object takes in both animal and human consciousness. We do not know if what activates the animal consciousness ever comes under the abstractions inherent in the terms "composable," and the like. We can simplify the distinction by noting that "meaning" has to do with words and language, and "content" strictly with the object as present to consciousness.

These response activators, the sense faculties of humankind, which move the subject, differ sharply from simple forces of Nature. The human agent, in our cases of it moving "on account of this or that meaning," has a relation towards that which in this case is moving it which is absent in the instances of simple raw forces of Nature working on, in, against, or for each other. "Meaning" is a motivator on a level other than that of a howling wind, a driving rain. While it can induce the same motion as the wind or the rain, how it does it is essentially different. Meaning, i.e., does not operate out of Nature. As we look into the structures of consciousness, awareness, we see "meaning" is not a tool of Nature.

"Content," as we have described it here, is more of an "immediacy" with Nature as "other," that "meaning" surpasses. Meaning is an occurrence between a human conscious agent and his awareness that is not limited to the individual content in his presence. "Content" is confined to the here-and-now. "Meaning" takes the conscious agent to other objects with the same "content" that need not be present to it in its here-and-now. "Meaning" also gives the human consciousness a "look" behind the content to possible structures and relations that can give the "content" greater intelligibility, give the human agent a larger awareness of what his consciousness has prehended.

"Meaning" also occurs in human agency and awareness as a time reality. No "meaning" occurs to the human agent without the co-presence of time as an intrinsic accompaniment. "Meaning" in the human being's consciousness, i.e., is through the medium of time, a medium totally transparent to the conscious being. This time in no way obfuscates or "bends" the "meaning" of which he has become aware. Time as co-present with the meaning at hand conveys to the human consciousness that the content or object prehended is not something that occurs only in the instant but is an ongoing reality before and after it is an "object" or "content" to the human consciousness. The transparency of time means that "meaning" is not in consciousness through a veil, but is direct to its gaze.

We do not have insight into animal awareness in a way that we can analogize from our own individual awareness to that of other fellow-human beings. Since content appears to me also as "meaning," I conclude for fellow human beings this is also the case. For the human, consciousness always carries meaning-correlates: every object to it is a meaning. With the animal existent, our inability to "see" from or "into" an animal's perspective limits what I can term regarding the "object" for the animal's awareness. If, however, we allow inference from behavior to enter into our analysis of how the object presents itself to the animal consciousness, to the individual animal aware of what is before it, we need to examine whether there is a pattern in that behavior which mirrors the human pattern in its encounter with what we call for it "meaning."

Analogizing this way is not a new occurrence for the philosopher. Clearly we analogize from our own awareness of parts on our body separated from one another to that of distance between objects, to the space that contains them. Similarly, we analogize from our own experience of causal efficacy, as in our instructions to the arm to move, to the same efficacy that reason has presented us in our search for the manner in which things come to be. We argue for certainty that there is a power between the objects we perceive in the same way we know of a power that goes from the mind to the arm in its instruction to the arm to move. We experience that power in that action, and in the same way we ascribe, via analogical principles, such power to objects that we know cannot come to be of themselves.

This delineation of "object," "meaning," and content" in our study here offers a step beyond what currently has been the accepted view, sc., to discount animal consciousness and the animal's possible prehension of "meaning" in accounts of subjectivity and world. "Meaning" for Husserl was a world of idealized structures, essences. Descartes, and Malebranche we can also add, saw nothing in the animal being that could ever possibly move it to a similarity to human experience. Animals were automata. If "meaning" because it is replicable endlessly, is able to be instantiated numberlessly, is something therefore "transcendent," and is by that outside of the animal awareness, animal awareness is incapable of the "objectification" of "meaning."

However, if, in fact, prehension of "meaning" is a cause of activity, movement, such that without the prehension the movement or activity would not occur, how we look at animal awareness as, like we do human awareness, different in kind than that of which it is aware, sc., inert, physical bulk, becomes an issue in the question of sentient immortality. Its resolution may bring us to a different, and perhaps more accurate, understanding of animal awareness and the possibility of bodily survival.

We have, however, limits in our analogizing. While at first we analogized from other individuals who appeared to us as we do to ourselves, sc., the same or similar in shape, behavior, needs, and the like, to the actual interactions with them that confirmed what we had analogized, sc., that these individuals are also "selves,"[18] are also possessed of the cognitive capabilities that I have, with animals we cannot so analogize. We cannot see whether animal consciousness shares this access to "meaning" which we have been ascribing to the human consciousness. We communicate with the animal world through symbols, signs, gestures. None of them, however, is abstract, is non-physical, in the way that "meaning" is. Meaning as a language expression in a word or sound to us does not appear to have the same resonance in the animal consciousness. It seems to have an "otherness" to the animal that makes it either uninterested in what is before it or incapable also of what is before it.

Animals, i.e., appear incapable of ascending to the level of "meaning" in their commerce with the world. Yet, this does not mean they are without the capacity of transcending material existence in the way man is. We just saw that all consciousness presents itself as other than material reality. We will be elaborating this in much more detail in the following pages. Our emphasis here is that animal consciousness and human are similar enough to suggest that at their core both will share the properties that the other does. We have been able to conclude to this because we have looked at the structures of "consciousness," "intentionality," "directionality," "towards," and "awareness," and found in these a similarity between man and animal that seems to end only when we come to the essence of "meaning." Animals, we cannot assert, have access to "meaning."

That, however, is in no wise a reason to suggest that the difference between animal and man in their "structure" of the consciousness native to each means that one cannot have immortality, and the other can. We will argue, as we already have begun to, that consciousness as other than that which is material, makes it uniquely possible to remain indissoluble despite the disintegration any material factor with it encounters. The separation of the bodily parts does not signal necessarily that consciousness once there has been dismembered as a result. If it is by partibility alone that something can end in existence, the fact that consciousness is without parts, is not "partible," argues that, being partless, it may also not be susceptible to an end once it has come into being.

In both the sentient human and the sentient animal there is a means of encounter with the world that, unlike in the case of strictly physical matter, only intentionality describes. There is, it appears, from the outset of their sentient existence a transcendence to it, an "exteriority," as Levinas calls it.[19] It will find further expression in Merleau-Ponty's view that in fact one cannot think of either without the other. The world cannot be an object unless there is a subject, and there is no subject unless there is an "other." So constituted, consciousness and world emerge inextricably as a self-enclosed totality each enriching the other and whose existence is impossible without the other.[20]

OTHER

We have, in the previous chapter, given a phenomenological account of consciousness—of how it appears to the "pure" observer. Now we must establish that consciousness, that "directionality towards," does not make its own world such that all that exists is consciousness. The hint has already come from our "pure" account of how consciousness is a "directionality towards." Further pure description of the occurrence of consciousness will bring us towards establishing its "other," not as something that is of its own making, but what is simply not consciousness in any way.

The manner, as we have just finished discussing, in which the object comes before consciousness, in accord with our requirement "purely appears," sc., as content or as meaning, indicates the level of consciousness with which we are dealing. The level of consciousness, however, we have argued, and will discuss further on, does not indicate whether the consciousness in question is immortal. Our methodology is to begin with realities as they "appear" and, should that appearance beckon further for elucidation, we will take up each step that the appearance provides. We will hold that all consciousness is immortal.

Content versus meaning, the distinction that held our attention in the past few pages, is simply the way in which consciousness makes its acquaintance with the "other." As "meaning," the other before consciousness is seen in the greater of its potencies and possibilities than would be the case in its being simply a content. Content is what every "other" before consciousness must have in order for it to be what it is in its otherness from everything else before consciousness.

If consciousness is, as it "purely appears," essentially other-directed, it seems that there must be something in addition to consciousness in the world. Else wise, consciousness, as "directionality-towards," would be directed to itself. In such a setting, would not then everything exist for it all at once since consciousness itself exists all at once? In being directed to itself, were it everything at which it was directed, anything at which it was directed would have to already exist. Consciousness would be the sum totality of all at which it was directed. In other words, the sum total of all at which it was directed would be directed at the sum total of all at which it was directed. The impossibility of the consequences from such a situation makes for the recognition of an actual "other" to consciousness.

The point about "other" is inviolate, essential, and of the most pressing importance. This "other" feature of consciousness is given with consciousness at once, as soon as consciousness takes place. It is of immediate evidence, something that cannot be simplified, reduced, or proceed back further. It is its own evidence.

Consciousness cannot take place unless there is something of which it takes place. Without something other than it, there is no consciousness. Intrinsic to the very actuality of consciousness is that which it is not, that which is "other" than it. We already saw above that that of which conscious is cannot be wholly itself if it is essentially other-directed. It can be aware of itself in its knowing the other.[1] But its essence is not directedness-to-itself. Its essence is other-directedness, which other is grasped by me in every conscious act.

There must be something in addition to consciousness in the world: consciousness is not the entirety of existence. In this chapter we shall be working towards excluding as persuasive philosophic positions that want to raise as questionable any objective, independent, status one wants to give to this "other." We argued in our opening pages the need for this approach in a study of immortality especially given, as we shall see later, the claims of the Botvinick-Cohen model, Unless one can have epistemic conviction, a high degree of certitude derived from evidence, that one's consciousness is not all that there is, that one is not simply a consciousness in a world that is not independent of that consciousness, the possibility of an existence beyond this life becomes absurd. If I as a sole consciousness am all that there is, my end becomes the end of all that is. If I am all that there is there is no "other" that can exists independent of me. My death, then, is the death of everything if there is nothing objectively existent except my consciousness.

A look at what "otherness" means begins to take us out of this solipsistic condition. We have, however, difficult terrain to traverse if we are not to have been accused of taking things for granted, e.g., being accused of assuming that there is a world other than consciousness. It is by no means clear that one can rest with such an approach of "appearing to take for granted" given the continual argumentation over the centuries about the impossibility of demonstrating that there is a world other than me. What is striking to the historian of the problem is how Hume's argument against a world external to me differs so sharply in form from today's neurophilosophic objections. More striking, how these two different argumentations go against what a non-inferential, immediate take of existence gives to consciousness—which is, there is a world other than it.

Otherness, which consciousness, immediately as consciousness, encounters defines consciousness as that which makes consciousness be the directionality that it is. As "directionality," it is "activity towards." It is an act of something that is other than that at which it is directed. Consciousness is therefore an individual. This follows from the fact that in showing there is something other than consciousness, we have established at least two items in existence. Where there is plurality there is individuality.

As individual, it is possessed of an identity by which it is the individual it is and nothing else. Because it is a directionality, we know that it is not a passive element in existence[2] but has about itself an agency that gives it the ability "at," "impetus towards." That at which it is other-directed cannot be that which activates, directs, consciousness as an agent power. It is not that which "turns," (in the manner of a light switch as it were), the conscious being "on," and by that activates its consciousness. Efficient causality can never be at a distance. Consciousness, then, as directionality is an agency, a directionality-towards, of its own. By its nature. It is an individual agent. It is not brought to be by the other.

Consciousness is transparent to itself. It is aware of itself as being aware, and this transparency is not found in that towards which it is directed. Consciousness does not experience a "hardness" against itself, an inertia through which, of its own, it cannot pass.

Consciousness, as embodied sentience, feeling, and knowing (and precisely as embodied), shares particular characteristics of those physical objects it encounters in its field as physical objects. Contrarily, the physical objects of its encounters lack all transparency, all permeability. They are opaque to themselves as inert bulks lacking any outside immanentation, any realization of being anything but what it is as the physical object. No physical object lacking conscious power can take into itself anything that it is not and remain what it is. Consciousness, however, in not being anything towards which it is other-directed, can encounter everything towards which it is directed. Intentionality is a way of always reaching more in a virtually endless number of ways and manners.

We already saw that the attempt to suggest the world is a total illusion foisted upon one by an Evil Demon breaks a fundamental rule of thought, sc., Occam's razor. The simpler explanation is the better, so long as the complexity in question fails the simplicity the question admits. Were this maxim derived from an experience not yet disproven to be the work of an Evil Demon, what probity does it have? Yet if we accept the theory that a *malin génie* is deceiving us, that all experience is actually his deception, we are violating Occam's razor, sc., the simpler explanation, solution, is the better.

How do we get to say that the world I am confident is not part of my making, is not any of my doing, actually exists as that towards which consciousness is the power and act of intentionality? By establishing that, we take the first step towards the question of immortality as a mode of consciousness.

If one wants to claim that consciousness is a product of the conscious agent's own doing, that the agent is he who makes his world, brings to be the conscious states he has because he brings to be the objects of which he is becoming conscious or having his awarenesses, we encounter a problem of how these objects are differentiated by this consciousness. If consciousness has all these objects in its inventory and becomes aware of them only after "rolling out" each object, or "state of affairs," how does one account for what we know as "the unexpected." If I want to maintain that all conscious activity originates from the objects and content *I* produce, how did we ever come to be aware of "the unexpected"? If consciousness precontains all its objects, how can it ever have the experience of the unexpected? That would already be precontained in it. Already contained, it cannot be unexpected.

Of more mortal concern is why would consciousness ever bring forth a state of affairs where tragedy and sorrow are encountered? Yet, this is what we must maintain it does if we want to offer that consciousness "makes" its own world, brings to be all the awarenesses that fill its life.

If that difficulty becomes insuperable, and one is willing to acknowledge that consciousness does not "produce" the objects of its world, does this mean that we have shown that "the world" is in fact something into which each consciousness enters, and which in fact precedes (in the sense of being "independent of") its existence and awareness? It is important that we be able to establish this because we are seeking to show that the "world" of which consciousness in its awareness is conscious is not consciousness, but something "other." Consciousness is not that of which it is aware when it is aware of the world. Consciousness is other than the world that comes into its field.

If the world of which we hold consciousness is aware does not precede it ontologically, but is co-temporaneous with some activity of consciousness, or with the activity by which consciousness takes on its world, we have the problem of what we shall call "ontological simultaneity." I and the world are simultaneous in our being if the world is really simply consciousness aware of itself. Nothing has preceded either.

If there is no "other," if only my consciousness exists, the question of immortality is an absurdity. If only my consciousness exists, when I say there are those whom I have met who are now dead, what can it possibly mean they are now dead if these individuals are simply a product of my consciousness? If my consciousness alone constitutes the world, if there is no such reality that is not myself, the death of those I claim in my experience is strictly something consciousness—me—has created. What possible meaning, then, could the question of surviving this "death" which I creatively construct for those in this world that I alone constitute have? Approached this way, questioned in these terms, it becomes clear why we must establish that existence is not simply my consciousness, but that there is the "other."

What other possible difficulties surface in asserting only my consciousness is the "world"? Stories or accounts of things as before my existence become puzzling to a consciousness that we above have argued the reality of the unexpected shows cannot be responsible for what comes into its field. Not only can I not explain how "the unexpected" is part of my doing, but how can I explain accounts as being long before I came to be as indicating events for which no one in my conscious field will allow that I was responsible? I cannot claim responsibility for the Mona Lisa (I cannot say I painted it, or came up with the idea of it), because no one will allow that I did. Everyone will look at me as if I were a madman. I cannot claim responsibility for the dropping of an atomic bomb over

Hiroshima. It is something that happened for which no one will allow my claim as the pilot who flew the Enola Gay.

Yet if all these events are really simply consciousness, are simply me (which is what saying the world is consciousness is) how can anyone challenge my claim to the Mona Lisa or to being the pilot of the Enola Gay? All those objecting to my claim are, in this setting, simply, actually, the doings of my own creative imagination, of my world that consciousness, in our hypothesis here, is. If the whole world is simply my consciousness, why would there arise in that consciousness objections by persons I created telling me that things I had claimed I did I actually never did? That these objections do arise in any claim I may make about events I could not have possibly mastered, or in which I could never have been involved, argue that the world and consciousness are not identical. The world is not simply my consciousness, and nothing else.

Even more dramatic, and more personal, if I originate all the objects in my world, if the objects in fact are nothing but *me*, do I claim a child to be mine which everyone knows cannot be mine? Next, do I create those individuals who will not permit that I fathered a child, and this is how it is that I cannot claim paternity? Is it the same with the Mona Lisa and the bomb over Hiroshima? If my consciousness is the world, if it constitutes the entirety of all, do I create those individuals, those objects, who will flat out deny I have fathered a child, I painted the Mona Lisa? Would I create those individuals who are denying those claims of mine? Why would I?

But that is what I would be doing if the world is simply *my* consciousness and there was no such entity as the "other." Such a world has no independence of my thinking it or fashioning it. This is what we mean by consciousness as "ontologically simultaneous" with its world. Consciousness is its world without any "other" because it is simultaneously the world.

If the inability to explain the "unexpected," as we have just discussed, is not enough to make us pause and think that maybe this world is not one that I created, we can point to the sorrows that we note the world contains. What consciousness would advance its own cancerous condition? What consciousness would create as its mother one who dies a horrific death from ovarian cancer? What consciousness would fashion a baby in a crib to die from a terrorist's knife? If what I call a world is not other than consciousness, is where consciousness and "world" are no different," one is confronted with a situation of a consciousness causing suffering and untold harms that are simply itself. For the world of which we are speaking in this case is none other than one consciousness and nothing else.

The reality of language seems to present a difficulty to one who holds that there is no actual world other than a consciousness, that no world, object, exists—consciousness, *my* consciousness, is the totality of anything experiencable. Nothing except my consciousness is real. With language I come to know "words" that I did not know before. If such words are of my own making, why are they made in the first place? What function do words serve, and how is consciousness their originator? Words imply communication. Yet if I am the originator of, and entirety of the world, what purpose does "communication" serve? After all, in such a situation where consciousness—my consciousness— is the world, where there is no "other," it would simply be communicating with itself.

If consciousness conjures up language for communication to avoid "loneliness," why not in this world—where only my consciousness is world, as we have been hypothesizing—conjure up alternatives that can take me from that loneliness? If consciousness is the world, it has "created," those people from whom it feels isolated in its "loneliness," consciousness can simply eliminate them from its thought. They would no longer exist from which to feel isolated. Or, even more, never bring these individuals into consciousness in the first place. This is a power it has because on our hypothesis here, it is its world. What is the need for language when there are other methods that one can use to address this emotion? If communication is meant as an "aid" in my living, why not simply eliminate what is perceived as a hindrance to the living that this one sole consciousness desires instead of coming up with the phenomenon of language? If consciousness is the world, eliminating any hindrance in that world is within its power.

There is also the reality of words we do not understand. They are not familiar to us in the way we ourselves speak. These are words of a "foreign" language. Yet, what purpose is it for consciousness to construct such a method of communication if words in the first place are meant to enable communication, to facilitate existence, and avoid emotions (such as the loneliness we hypothesized above) that are bothersome to us? That there is a language I cannot comprehend would suggest to me that the world and consciousness are not the same, that in addition to consciousness there is an "other."

Language, of course, is not the means by which we constitute our world (fill it with objects) or come to knowledge. If we say we come to our world only linguistically, that is through language, and not directly, we end up in an infinite regress. If language is the way I come to awareness, by what language do I come to an awareness that language is the way I come to awareness and so on?

Knowledge is not only by way of concept, and concepts are not linguistic in derivation. Concepts are not products of a community or society's language from which we learn, come to know, or constitute our world. Intrinsic to the very conscious agent we have been discussing, the one that is in fact in contact with a "world" that is not he, is the ability to prehend "meaning" in the "other," some of which meaning takes the form of concepts.

That concepts are not linguistic, a matter of language, in origin is important in that we want to hold that concept formation evinces an ability that is beyond the bounds of a language that society forms, that the world brings. Concepts are the workings of a mind whose tools society does not provide, but which of its own has the ability that society as a unit does not afford. In the same way society does not give us "mind," it does not, the point is, give us concepts. It may give us language, but that is not the same as providing conceptual ability. That originates elsewhere. It originates in a capacity that is not society's to bestow. If concepts come from one's capacity for mentation, and language from elsewhere, we have established an existent other than consciousness.

So also with "meaning." Our ability to come to awareness of "meaning" is not a societally endowed capacity. "Meaning," the ability to see relations between and among concepts, which requires that the concepts are prehended in the first place, is not a linguistic or grammatical phenomenon. While society, as we said, may provide language, that is, may provide the vocal sounds or inked forms that one associates with the concepts one has, it does not provide "meaning" to the mind. "Meaning" the mind arrives at through what consciousness—the awareness of the world before me—presents to that capacity of awareness that can see structure, relationships, possibility, modal rigors of thought, beyond what the world presents to consciousness.

"Knowledge by acquaintance," a term it is perhaps Bertrand Russell who made most famous,[3] is certainly non-conceptual. I do not first have a concept of a "cow" when I see a figure that looks like it for the first time. What I am acquainted with is an animal that chews cud in a field, gives milk, and flips its ears while chewing its cud. The first acquaintance with such an animal does not give me the concept "cow." It is only after a number of instances with such animals that I come to a concept of them.

I cannot have a concept of something that I have seen only once. I can know it as an object that I have seen only once, but I cannot have a concept of it, have a grasp of its "whatness," or "quiddity," because I cannot only from one seeing tell you "what" it is that I saw. This is especially the case if I only saw the object for the first time. Nor can I tell you "what" I saw if I never see the object again, but in fact only see it once. At best I can only describe it. I thus have an "acquaintance" with the object, but not a conceptual prehension of it. Yet I have knowledge of it. Thus, not all knowledge is by way of concepts or, therefore, a community

If language is the product of a community in that the concepts I use are supposed to be from the community in which I have lived, the community which is part of my *Umwelt*, it is being held that I cannot have a concept of an object or of anything in my world without the community. I can only have an "acquaintance" with it because knowledge is either conceptual or by direct acquaintance. Language does appear to be evidence for an "other" in my world, that I (my consciousness) am not the entirety of the world after all.

Language, however, does not make the concept. The concept is the mind's reaction to what it encounters in the world on a number of instances. Language appears to follow upon concept when there is a communicative setting. To say that society has originated my concepts is to suggest without society I could never conceptualize. Society has originated language, but only after individuals agreed upon a sound or word they used for a concept they all have and found they had only after comparing their knowledge with the others in that society. They found themselves able to form classifications, class names, because the objects in their experience provided for the classifications.

The world in which I am, then, does not originate from a linguistic apparatus. Consciousness' world is pre-linguistic. But with language comes evidence that the world is not just one consciousness, mine. Language indicates that there must be something besides a solitary individual consciousness. What is the purpose of language if language is a communicative medium and there is only one entity that exits? Language is expressed through concepts and verbs, concepts being about objects or actions, motions that take expression in verbs.

Concept gives more than acquaintance. It signals that other objects of my acquaintance, if they are all red, e.g., have something "in common." This I can know without society.

We already saw that not all knowledge is by way of concepts. Something before me that I have never seen before need not find expression in a word to say that I "know what I saw." I have knowledge, but it is not conceptual.

The concept forms when the object's similarity (or action's) to other objects (or actions) emerges in my consciousness; and when I come to realize the objects (or actions) can have certain properties and not others. For this I do not need society. It appears that my concept is not linguistic unless I decide to name the object, apply a word (either by voice or writing) to it. It is too elementary to discuss whether it is society that brings about the need for language. The point about language and concept here has been to note that concepts require language, words, only when we are in a society. We do not, i.e., need to have words in order to know something, to have a concept of it. If we want to communicate what we know, then we need a means to do so. And this is language. This is not to say knowledge of the world does not grow with knowledge in society, only that knowledge of the world does not need society.

Thus, language (words shared in common) is ultimately conceptually derived, not societally originated. Language appears to be necessary if we are to transmit what is in our consciousness to another conscious agent equally capable of that transmission. To whom are we speaking in language if not to someone other than ourselves? What need is there of language if we are only to communicate with ourselves? If the individual is alone in the world, if there is nothing except the individual that exists, to have language means the individual has fashioned an apparatus with which to communicate to himself while, in fact, the concepts he has, we have argued, suffice for his knowledge of the world. He is not in need of language, words at all. The fact of language points to a world other than the individual, then. Language tells me there is something other than me that exists.

Our original suspicion, our original inclination, that consciousness is defined in part by the term "other" is well-founded, then. There is a reality that is not consciousness which completes consciousness' mode of other-directionality, other-directedness. It gives consciousness its totality. It accounts for consciousness' wholeness, its not being a dirempted entity in "search" of always its complement to complete it. With the "other" established as an existent reality that is not consciousness, consciousness emerges as a being that has found its primordial structure in the world.

Identifying more characteristics that specify this "other" that rounds out the being of consciousness is important. While explanation should be adequate, Occam's razor does not permit it to be parsimonious to the extent that its worth has fallen short of what actually accounts for being an explanation.

That which we have called "other" is "publicly accessible." There is nothing about it that makes it the exclusive domain of one individual. There is nothing about this "other" that says it is proprietary to only one consciousness, and no other. While we have yet to establish that there are other conscious agents, we do know that nothing about that which defines the "otherness" to consciousness is privileged to just one consciousness.

COLOR AND OBJECTIFICATION

Concepts arise independently of a linguistic framework or provenance, and language is based on concepts that society does not produce, but which are the workings of the individual mind. This we have established. Added to the fact that consciousness cannot be a "directedness" towards itself, but must be at something "other," al this points to fixed grounding for the assertion of existence as comprised not only of consciousness, but of that which is not consciousness.

It also appears that not all that is said about this "other" can adequately speak of "consciousness." We alluded to this in our prior chapter in the example we cited about color.

Our eyes can perceive only so-called luminous matter—that which reflects light within a certain frequency range. Our physical world is just one of numberless wavelengths, frequencies, or dimensions. We can only see objects when there is light reflecting from them. In a room with no light source, one in pitch black, we see nothing.

This holds, in fact, in the larger, universal, scale. Ninety-five percent of the mass in the universe is called "dark matter." It does not reflect light in a way that is humanly visible. The electromagnetic spectrum is just 0.005 percent of the matter/mass (dark energy/matter [95%], ordinary nonluminous matter [4.5%], ordinary luminous matter [0.5%], electromagnetic spectrum [0,005%]) said to exist in the universe. The human eye, however, can only register ("see") a fraction of that 0.005 percent, that fraction being known as "visible light." (It does not "see" gamma rays, x-rays, microwaves [and sub-bands], or radio waves]. We have access to these, but not without aids to the senses, as we saw. In other words, the eye detects only an infinitesimal percent of the universe. In this percent color is a dominant feature.

Color is spoken of as wavelengths (in units called "nanometer[s] {nm}" [a billionth of a meter], 700nm beginning the infrared spectrum, 400nm the ultraviolet, with bees apparently being able to detect wavelengths of 300nm, but no known species able to detect above 700nm).[1] Color is also referred to as being sourced in a seeming ocean of electromagnetic radiation occurring from a discordant and conflicting pattern of wavelengths reduced to a narrow band coterminous with the middle range of the sun's radiation spectrum.

Others may speak of color in terms of "frequencies," some as a "flux of ions in little bits of jelly in my brain."[2] These are all ways the scientist describes it. The same scientist tells us "color" itself is the product of light (electromagnetic radiation which itself is totally without any color) emitted, refracted, diffused from a physical object impinging on the eye's photoreceptors, and similar receptors. Traveling up the optic nerve is the neurosignal these receptors send (mediate) which effectuates a particular brain occurrence that is the percept "color."

Yet, color in my experience is nothing "quantitative"; it is in no wise a system of numbers (as we have above just described). Were it, color blindness would be inexplicable. The wavelength is the same in each case for the one who can "see" the color as well as for the one who is "color blind." Yet in the one there is the experience of color, but in the other there is not.

Quantitatively, color is the light energy distribution of a particular wavelength. If one knew this distribution he would (in theory) know (be able to calculate) the color being experienced, provided of course he also had the measurements of other ocular variables (among which being the cones,[3] retina, opponent response functions, retina size, foveal capability, etc.) This "knowledge," however, this ability to "number" the phenomenon, is not the experience of the color. Our experience of color is not numerical.

It is in fact incommunicable, inasmuch as one who is blind has no capacity to understand what I could possibly mean in an attempted description of it to him. One can explain or know it only ostensively, that is, as something that one needs to point to and say, "There it is, that is what I mean by 'color.'" We know color only in virtue of an acquaintance with it, which acquaintance, however, cannot be described. Indeed, the acquaintance itself is colorless. It is that with which I am acquainted that is not.

"Color" is an experience someone who is sightless will never have, it being specific to sight. And yet I can tell him about the length and depth and width of the surface which may occasion this phenomenon. Thus, the blind man may very well have an appreciation of my arithmetic statements regarding the "size" and "shape" of what is colored, but about this reality that I call "color" nothing can convey what the experience is.

This point is material inasmuch as it shows us that even knowledge of the wavelengths, etc. (all the mathematical quantities), that comprise a color do not give us "knowledge" of the color. One can know all the facts about "color," as Frank Jackson has pointed out, but that in no wise is the same as actually encountering "color."[4] Textbook knowledge of color will not save anyone from walking right past its occurrence and not recognizing it. If upon walking past the color someone tells you "there's the color red, I thought you knew what it was," you will have definitely learned something new. But how can this be the case if you argue that you knew all about the phenomenon already because you had studied everything quantitative, mathematical, numerical, there was to know about it except actually having the experience? So, if all the physical data were present to you and you did not know what color was until it was pointed out to you, then this experience of color cannot be a physical datum. This is especially pointed by the fact that registering the neuroelectric charge that corresponds with what the neuroscientist wants to call the "color event" still does not give the experience that the awareness of color shows itself to be. Otherwise, whenever the charge was effectuated, the result wherever the neuroelectric charge is effectuated should be "color." The plain fact, however, is that this is not the case. Otherwise propagating that charge in the cortical matter of a blind person should give that person this experience called "color." It does not, however.

That the awareness of color is so universal throughout the species makes it difficult to understand why its neuroelectric replication should be so difficult. If knowing the electromagnetic quantity is, as the neuromaterialists hold, the same as knowing the "spectrum occupancy," (i.e., the "color"), taking the specific neuroelectric quantity (say for "red") through cortical matter should bring about consciousness of "red." Mimicking the cortical structure through various silicon chip patterns and the like should be an adequate substitute for a model of the human experience of color. Reduce the "color" experience to an algorithm which, upon activation, causes the position of valence and bonding to mimic what occurs in the neuroelectric charge called "color." "Color" as the human subject knows it, despite the mimicking, does not occur. What we have in this algorithmic event is simply a spark, a flash of current. If all these quantitative, physical quantity, attempts at color result in no percept that we can identify as "color," it appears that the identification of color with an absolutely physical quantity, physical datum, fails at an adequate description or account of what the percept entails.

"Color," that is, is not reducible to covalent bonding and ionic charges and counter charges. Electrical polarity does not issue in the origin of the percept called "color." One would imagine, if it did, replicating that polarity and bonding and valency in the lab would give us the ability to see color coming to be right before our eyes. Replicate the histology of the neuronal cell. Place all its structures in the arrangement it has in the living cortex, and spread the neuronal material over a plate, or any surface one wants. At some point the scientist should see this percept called "color" coming to be right before his eyes. If all he sees is simply disaggregated, uncoordinated, sparks, flashes of electrical events, he will be seeing exactly what we know to occur in all cortical events of consciousness. But we won't be privy to the consciousness occurring in these events. Just as the scientists will not be privy to the percept color in our suggested experiment above.

If the disaggregated, uncoordinated, flashes of electrical charges do not give us the percept of color, is it because there is no unifying power that strikes the charges in such a way that the percept "color" is realized? If color is not the disaggregated flashes of electrical charges, is there a unifying force that gives us what comes to be the percept color?

If the unitive force comes by way of antipolar charges, those charges in the cortex must be continuous. But there is no polar charge that is a continuity in any electrical field. They cme by way of ions and the like, but these are all separate and distinct in their flow. If the force is a unifying constant that holds all the flashing of electrical bits together, it cannot be electrical. No electrical bonding of itself survives the instant. This, if quantum physics has shown anything, is the subatomic phenomenon of electrons appearing and disappearing; they do no actually "move" to different orbits. While some have held this interferes with the maxim that matter can be neither created nor destroyed by ordinary means, for our purposes the fact that electrons have no existence keeping them the same throughout, e.g., four nanoseconds, five minutes, two hours, thirty years, would argue against an electrical force that unifies the electrical sparks and flashes that the materialist wants to hold account for the percept. A unifying force is necessary if consciousness takes place in a way that these electrical events neither portray nor (given their instantaneous existence) can provide. It appears that it cannot be material or physical in origin.

Not everything in the world, that is, is "physical." So also with, on a more complicated level, the textbook knowledge of what it is like to be pregnant. There is nothing a comprehension of all the medical data regarding this event can convey that the actual state of being pregnant will. One would be left with the absurd inference that a male physician, if he knew everything in the world there was to know about pregnancy, would therefore know what a woman knows about pregnancy when she is pregnant. He would know what it is to be pregnant. The same reasoning applies to the claim that complete knowledge of the physical, the quantitative, aspects of color (its electromagnetic properties and formulae) gives us an account of it that is true, accurate, and complete. This is what materialism wants to hold, but cannot, once reasoning tells us, as here, that mathematics is no substitute for experience.

Color is always of something. It is never in isolation. That with which it is always found, sc., shape, can be traced with the sense of touch. Shape seems amenable to bifurcation, division. Color never divides. It is unanalysable, further, which is why it cannot be described. Instead, it is that which characterizes, and thus that with which one describes.

Above we spoke of covalence and electron activity in the phenomenon of color. A bit more detail here adds to the argument against the percept "color" as something strictly materialist or physical. Color, as simple optics experiments over the decades have shown us, is a phenomenon issuing from the conduct of the electrons in its field.[5] Their rate of transition from one level to another is a vibrational reality which, in concert with the particles (wherever they might be, e.g., the sky) that diffract it, and the speed at which it moves through the various media (high density to low, or vice-versa), account for the presence it assumes in nature.

But more than this, different crystal structures in the transparent objects through which it passes, say rubies and emeralds, also play a part in how the color of these jewels "comes to life." The temperature of atoms (their rate of activity) and the ions with which it interacts also give this reality called "color" properties which appear in perception in different intensities and the like, depending on that temperature. "Color," that is, does not reside in "things," but rather results from a rate at which things radiate light (photons) from their surface and strike the neural receptors that register the stimulation "neuroelectrically."

And this rate, as we just saw, has a number of variables all of whose differences among themselves account for the color that one actually "sees." E.g., one surface may absorb wavelengths of light that go into the composition of a certain color, while a surface ever so different might, instead of absorbing, reflect it. All of a sudden, in just this very example, we have the phenomenon of different rates of propagation of electrons. Then, there is the angle of reflection, too.

More than all of these variables, is the question of the actual physical entity with its optical receptors that absorb these transmissions from the objects we have just discussed. Said in simpler terms, different living organisms, different animals, it is a well-known fact, perceive different "colors" off the same surface, or through the same transparent medium. If we take just the act of human sight, and the relation of the sense-organ, the eye, to the data transmitted: at what level is there any similarity between the data in the external transmission and what the retina "takes in"? The density of the receptor arrangement in the retina is not of the density of the electrons transmitted from the object. The eye itself has various organic components, such as blood and humor, which in no wise can be said to mimic the data the object transmits to the "seeing" eye. And the actually socketed eye, as is well-known, is in constant motion, but the color experienced is never blurred.[6]

Also, the chromatic/achromatic (color/black and white) ability is situated in the number of cones [(for color), of which there are varying spectral capabilities {short-,middle-, and longwave}, depending on the neural signal it generates when stimulated by the photon wavelength)] and rods (black and white) in the eye. Yet, the owl has no cones: it only sees in black and white. The chicken, on the other hand, never "sees" this way. The acuity of the color capability also depends on the number of quanta of light (phota) stimulating the cones and rods that can be absorbed. The extent of that capability determines how colorful the animal's world will be.

The distribution of rods and cones in the eye, the way components of the retina (like the macula, the ganglion cells, their rate of input/output transmission up the optic nerve) are situated before the data activating its response receptors—all these are intricately involved in making of what is strictly quantitative (the electromagnetic wavelengths) into the non-quantitative experience we have. The firing rate of neuronal components in ocular activity is also of great importance in the experience of color. What provides for the contrast between shades and actual color vibrancy (called lateral inhibition) comes under this aegis of firing and is material to how the individual can "see" his way through the world that comes into his range of vision. Similarly, with analogous mechanisms in other animals.

Thus, in the case of man, what is moving through the transparent medium to the eye will register definitely different "color" experiences to the receptor that processes the data. The retina is an active, almost "producing," as it were, through successively ever higher visual centers, component in the experience of color that the human has, just as similar ocular organisms in other animals are. In this sense, the ocular organ becomes, so to speak, an extension of the brain (hence, the term "eye-brain") that is constantly processing and interpreting the spectral composition of radiation wavelength that it encounters every moment of every day.

How do we say if color is *in*, is a property of, the physical object[7] that resists us, that we come up against, in our daily routines (a position held by James Cornman.)[8] Or is it an arrangement of wavelengths in the atmosphere, not found *in* the object, but hitting off the physical object that bounces back to the photoreceptors of the eye, after which through neural transmissions a "color" comes into perception? I.e., is the experience of color an instance of phota of certain wavelengths, say 575nm, that reflect off a physical surface to phota specific receptors in the eye, which excite a neural signal up the optic pathway to give me "yellow"? Or does registering the wavelengths stimulation into a coherent percept require something other than neuroelectric activity excited by phota stimulation? And must this capacity be due to the object whose color is perceived?

Aristotle held color is *in* the object as the *cause* of what the eye sees, and comes into human awareness via the sensible form that actuates the medium through which the form becomes one with the sense organ in question. Aristotle's notion differs sharply from the atomistic theory of current neurology, as well as that of Democritus. The form of color in the object is not an aggregation of atoms that activate the sense tissue. Color for Aristotle is a ratio (λόγου)[9] that activates the transparent, the medium through which, by way of light, color is sensed.[10] If it is by light that color is perceived, light itself cannot be a body because air is a body and were light a body we would have two bodies occupying the same place, which is impossible.[11] This is why the atomistic theory of light propagation, whether in the inchoate form in Democritus, or in today's science, has a challenge to it that the Aristotelian argument continues to hold. How do we give color any quantitative dimension if that by which its awareness comes about, sc., light, itself must be without dimension?

Sensible form for Aristotle is immaterial, and the sense organ's reception of the form requires an immaterial capacity. For the eye to take on color, it must be colorless. To perceive color the eye must have the potency for the color, and in perception immaterially becomes the color through the sensible form. If it is the eye by which we see, and to see all colors it itself cannot be colored but must be without color, the only way the eye furnishes us the awareness of color is by a principle of potency in its constitution which allows it to become that color.

In this regard then color is not some higher order mode of adverbial seeing. "I see greenly" is not what I mean when I say "I see green." An awareness of color is not a disposition to behave in a certain way of speech or language, either. It is hard to see how "I am aware of color" means only that I am speaking "colorly," for that seems to mean my mode for speaking is outside of any basis except language. That brings us back again to the infinite regress impossibility that we noted previously. Add to this that there are "shades" of color that I claim to experience. Does this mean there are shades of speaking "colorly?"

Couching experience of color adverbially, it has been argued, is the more appropriate way of presenting the experience, of speaking abut it, because such a manner helps with hallucinations and double-images. If I am seeing a blue object in a hallucination, rather than have the embarrassment of being corrected and told it was a hallucination, if all speech of color experience is done adverbially, that is, here I say "I see bluely," then there is not the problem of the object's ontological status. I can be seeing "bluely" without the blue object at all. It takes care of the hallucination, and at the same time is not an incorrect statement with regard to the actual perception of a blue object. In both cases, I see bluely.[12]

Problematic, however, with this is that we already say that we do not see "color" alone. Color is always of something. Hence, if the color blue in this case is of a blue ball, I have to account for the roundness present to me in the perception, as well as the blue. To say that I am sensing a round object in a hallucination, I have to say I am sensing "roundly." So in this case, am I sensing "roundly" or "bluely?" Which has priority in my mode of expression?

Importantly, even if the adverbial mode falls short of adequacy in accounting for the percept "color," the fact that we can have different percepts simultaneously—adverbially or not—surely argues for the belief that the individual having the percepts must be other than the percepts. Whether color is "in" the object, or a result of electromagnetic reverberations that hit the eye, we cannot state that consciousness is the cause of the color we experience.

Turning back to this adverbial mode accounting for "seeing," an individual at once who sees "bluely," experiences "toothachely," and feels "warmly," has to be other than these experiences, otherwise we have a warmly toothachely bluely way of perceiving. While sounding bizarre may be a basis for suspecting that it is not reflective of actual perception, the toothachely bluely way of perceiving all at the same time will be contradictory of itself in that while a tooth is rectangular, the ball is round. This contradictoriness itself is basis enough for dismissing the identity of the percept with the perceiver.

The "adverbial" cover for sense-theory, sc., that I see "bluely," I feel "roundly," raises the further issue of how any state of affairs can be "bluely," or "roundly." Even more so, how any state of awareness could be "blue" or "round." Further, how could anyone verify this "blue" presentation if there is no object itself that is blue? It is to deny, it seems, an intentional object to awareness. I.e., to make it difficult, if not impossible, to ascertain when it is that we are having a hallucination (which, as we saw, is why the adverbial manner of speaking came to be a hypothesis about color vision in the first place) and not in fact an experience of an object that it incontestably real. For if it is not incontestably real, how do we come to differentiate, as in fact we do, between a hallucination, or an after-image experience, from what is neither, but what is identified as an actual object in our field that presents itself to awareness as different in color than an object not giving us that awareness?

On the other hand, however, how successful are we in identifying where color resides? We have argued earlier the importance of showing that there must be an "other" in our universe if the question of immortality is to have any seriousness for us. This is why we have gone so extensively into the issue of the perception of color. In our just completed discussion on the adverbial way of speaking we seem to have shown that denying a distinction between the subject of perception and the object perceived leaves us in ludicrous difficulties. Do we gain any further position on the claim that the awareness of color points to a world other than a subject in our discussion of the "location" of color?

When we opine that color is "in" the object, exactly what is it that we mean? We certainly do not mean a wavelength of a certain formula that the object reflects and sends to our eyes. We are saying that object possesses a color, that color is ingredient to its very structure. "The object is red" means that its possesses an actuality. That actuality is such that the eye sees it in a certain way, and that actuality is not dependent on the eye for its being. It is not "red" because it has acted on the eye a certain way. It is "red," whether or not there is someone who exists to "see" it.

This is a way of speaking that no scientist permits today. In current theory, no micro-structure of any expanse in any object that we take is homogeneous. Any look under a microscope will show that. Yet, we claim that all color is equal to the expanse in which it is "found." That is how we experience it, which is why we say color is "in" the object. How can it be "in" the object, however, if it is not equal throughout the expanse of surface of which we claim color for the object? Unequal throughout the expanse of the surface in question means some part of the surface is without color. If, then, we are to have a direct acquaintance with color, it appears that we cannot, under current physical theory, state that it is the object that provides the direct awareness. Color does not appear as occurrent with the "micro-structure" of the object: it is not found with the object as a property of the object precisely because the object, while presenting itself to us as fully colored, in reality, because of the unequalness of expanse, is not colored. It is we who ":make" it colored by filling in the expanses where it is not "colored." It seems suddenly that our appeal to "color" as evidence for the objectiveness of the "other," of the "world," may be in peril.

Yet, the notion of sight wherein it is the activity of wavelengths in interaction with ocular instrumentalities has its own problems. For this notion, to say I saw "red" means wavelengths interacted with the eye that I possess and effectuated a nerve pathway excitation to the cortex. While this gets rid of the "expanse" theory of color, it simply replaces it with another problem. It assumes an atomistic theory of sensation wherein all sensation is by virtue of electron vibrations in various configurations. The problem here is that these are all quantitative in their exercise.

No sensation, however, is quantitative under any instances. Measuring a neuroelectrical charge does not measure a sensation. Thus, no sensation, no percept, meets the test of a number. And stimulating a neural pathway does not tell us how an arrangement of electrons takes on the reality it does (sc., the percept 'color,' a reality that in no way resembles the electron activity or the brain disturbance) when the cortex absorbs the neural message, which message is totally electrochemical. At best, and we shall look at this later, one can only say that sensation may start with excitations from sensory atomistic data but in no way can sensory atomistic excitations equate with perception.

We do know, at this juncture, that color is not "in" the object per se, nor is it the result of some agency in the conscious being. In the latter, his causing it would mean it was already present to him, in which case he would already be experiencing it. And in the former, the microscope shows gaps in the physical constituency of an object, but we do not experience color as perforated, as spotty (spots against a background)..

In cases where there appears no way out of a dilemma (we have the percept color, but neither horn accounts for it), we can only, it appears, give a "best explanation" case. That is the one where, as in the empirical sciences, predictability and stability, just as we experience the world, accounts for what it is that we are experiencing.

How, our problem is, do we account for a world where color is believed to be "in" the object (while the expanse theory shows it cannot be), and yet we know it cannot be the product of our own consciousness? Since color cannot come out of nowhere, what is the "somewhere" of its origination? The "best explanation," "best efforts," hypothesis would have us present the schema of a causal mechanism where both the agent and patient in interaction bring about the experience.

The solution? Color is caused. It is not caused by me (otherwise I would already be having the experience). Therefore, it is caused by "the other." Color, therefore, need not be "in" the object to give me evidence of some reality other than myself. "Color" is not the product of consciousness (were it, color would always be present to consciousness). At the same time, it is not in an object the way commonsense suggests. It is "in" the object as what causes the excitation, either by Aristotelian form or Democritean atoms, of ocular instrumentalities. These either take on the actuality of the color in the same way the signet ring leave an impression on wax (Aristotle's argument) or, through cortical excitation by which the percept takes place in consciousness. In neither case do we have an electrical flash that constitutes the percept. Something else goes to make up this percept, and it is this that has eluded the materialist model.

THE EXTRALINGUISTIC OBJECT

What we have established so far, then, is that evidence of an "other." Adding to this evidence is the phenomenon of resistance. This looms large for the notion of "a world independent of me" inasmuch as I cannot be resistant to myself. Yet I experience resistance. Since it cannot issue from me, I must look "elsewhere" for how this resistance, this solidity that I encounter, comes about. That "elsewhere" is the world independent of me.

This brings us to a "causal" theory of perception, and moves us further away from the possibility that all that there might be is a solipsistic ego, a consciousness, and nothing else in the world. My awareness is caused. Take the simple example of a basin of water feeling differently to the two hands of a person placed in it. The temperature is the same throughout the water, but not to the "feeling" hands. No matter the condition of the hands in question, the point is the sensation in the two differs. It is not the hands that cause the difference because without the water they would not have the stimulus. That suggests a cause of the disturbance not in me, but independent of me.

The argument, e.g., of Ayer,[1] that there is a time delay in some sensation from the object to the perceiver means we do not experience the object itself, leaves us with the uninviting prospect that we are not experiencing anything. The object no longer exists (say, the sound we hear) and so what is it that we are "hearing?" We are hearing something that occurred a nanosecond go, but what actually made the sound is no longer making the sound. That is like "at what point is the house to which I am walking" actually "the house to which I am walking."? Surely, I do not see the house simultaneously with the waves of light it emits to my eyes that bring it to my awareness. Does that mean the house does not exist? Or that it exists only at the point that it comes into view? If there is always a delay in "perception at a distance," is it that distance is that upon which the object in question depends for its ontological status?

When something touches me, I am in simultaneous contact with it. I don't doubt the existence there, but in the case of distance, using Ayer, I would have to. Distance becomes the criterion for the entity's existence, but on that basis the entity does not come into existence except when it, or something about it (the light waves it reflects by which I see it) has traversed a certain distance. But that would seem it would already have to exist in order for it to traverse a distance. Or it just "pops" into existence like a Humean impression, ready to go out of existence as soon as the awareness ceases. But, on that basis, why the need for the "light waves" theory of causality?

Which brings us to the question, if something just "pops" into awareness (equals "pops" into existence), whence did that which "pops" into awareness (existence) come? If it came from the consciousness into whose awareness it has just "popped," that consciousness would have to have had that item that comes into awareness already. Otherwise, whence could it have come? If it had the item already, what triggered the percept, the awareness, at the time that it did, that it "popped" into existence at the time that it did and not at another time? It seems an overwhelming amount of consciousness' experiences would have to be addressed this way because of this problem of "at a distance" causation of sensations. The "suddenness" of our sensations in many, many events seems to argue that this "trigger" cannot be consciousness at all, cannot be some mechanism in the conscious agent. It is, the realist would argue, the object itself in the world that is the "trigger."

Ayer's argument is important to address because again we encounter a proposition, a point of view, that wants to keep us away from an "object," keep us out of touch with the object. The argument that the world is a product of consciousness in some way, of which Ayer's is a variant, keeps us away from establishing that beside consciousness there is another existent, one independent of it. And, as we have argued in the preface, if only consciousness exits, that is, if it is only my consciousness that exists, the question of immortality is an absurd one. For if all that exists is my consciousness, and nothing else, when my consciousness perishes there can be no existence into which it enters upon death because nothing else but it exists. Therefore, at its perishing *ex hypothesi* everything perishes and there can be no immortality.

This is why establishing the reality of an existence where there is more than just me, the subject, is of critical importance in a study of immortality. It cannot be gainsaid. The skeptical view that no self exists (because a "self" is not provable), that no world exists save consciousness (because nothing beside consciousness can be proven to have existence) has been an underlying corrosive to the immortality position for a number of centuries, especially since Hume. Addressing that subjectivism, that skepticism, from the many different angles we have here gives us a basis for arguing that in fact consciousness is not all that exists, that my consciousness does not constitute the totality of existence, such that upon my perishing everything would therefore perish. Establishing an existence other than simply my consciousness opens up the possibility that we may argue for immortal existence, which skepticism and subjectivism every so subtly have been used to prevent as an argument that has merit.

We can, accordingly, continue this process of arguing for a world besides my consciousness. If it is recognized that observation or experience always occurs under certain conditions, then we can acknowledge that those conditions may be germane to how and what it is that we experience. The conditions of observation themselves are never a matter of observation. It is by and through them that what we observe we do in fact observe.

Hence, if I see a stick in the water and it appears bent, but it is not, is that a basis for doubting that I can reach the object "as it is," i.e., directly? Or that in fact there is an object which presents itself to me at all? If I move from where I am viewing the object, perhaps the light casts differently. Perhaps there is an angle that eliminates what I had just perceived. Also, the condition of the sense organs involved, and how trained my ocular apparatus is, are all situations under which the observation, the perception, of that "bent stick" takes place. If I give up reliance on sight alone and move towards the sense of touch, suddenly I detect that this stick is not bent at all.

To what sense, then, do I give priority or credibility? Am I on incondite grounds if I argue that repetition of this experience over time has indicated to me that it is not always the case that reliance on one sense will transmit the object to me "as it is" but other senses must come into play to balance out the data that are presented to me about the object?

Is it the case that senses cannot be trusted, as Descartes argued, because one sense may be fallible in what I take to be its transmission? Is the work of one sense alone the basis for dismissing all sensation as a means of knowledge? What about the other four? If they, in fact, in their combination give me a much more tangible mental grip (so to speak) on the object before me, do I still follow Descartes' methodic doubt as the path to knowledge?

Descartes was never able to present how it is that doubt is the path to knowledge in the first place, or epistemic certainty. Without the ability to show that it can bring us to the knowledge we all seek, on what grounds do we follow his Augean process? It is by no means clear, then, that we can dismiss the conditions of perception in our question of whether we can have a direct acquaintance with the object that we seem in everyday parlance to want to claim—that object which tells me that there is more to existence than my consciousness.

When, however, we talk about conditions of observation, we must be very careful to avoid claims of "what the normal observer" would sense. "Standard conditions" for sensing seem to have no basis in the real world where so many variables in the environment come into play in the activity of sensory experience. It is almost as if we are saying the object has to be disposed in a certain way in order for us to have the correct sensory input from it. But to know what the correct disposition is we seem to need to know already what the actual object is like under the correct circumstances. It is, however, precisely those correct circumstances that we first need to know.

An inquiry and examination of the conditions of our perception seems to suggest that a number of avenues (touch and sight together, or taste and touch together) may correct together that about which one alone has caused us to be mistaken. Dismissing sense acquaintance as a means to knowledge, as a means to a world other than, independent of, consciousness, when only one of its conduits has been used raises the question as to what would allow one to do that initially. After finding that the senses can provide a correction of one to the other (touching the stick shows me that the eye's seeing a "bent" stick is a mistake), it appears that dismissing all the senses based on the action of one sense is either a precipitous move, or one that is based on a prejudice of one sense in favor of the other. That would be, however, a prejudice for one sort of datum over another. That, though, is not a route to truth.

We are getting closer, then, to stating that we can accept as reasonable and evidential that a world other than my ego exists. That is to say we are therefore getting closer to stating we have evidential grounds for discussing whether immortality has an objective basis.

This "other," this "world," that I encounter, then, is not of a being that consciousness is. Otherwise, it would be consciousness. Yet much of what I encounter in the world is without any awareness, is not possessed of a consciousness. It is rocks, leaves, water, sand, automobiles, benches, pens, desks, paper. None of these items presents me with a capability of a "directionality towards" on their part which issues "somewhere from within them." They are lifeless, static, inert, empty of any content that could compare with me as an agent who has consciousness.

We have spoken of "intentionality" as the identifying mode of consciousness. It is clearly an absurdity to attribute any such "intentionality" to the objects we have just named. If "intentionality" is not susceptible to a believable materialist or reductionist account, then by that very fact not everything we encounter is explicable by a theory, hypothesis, or worldview which says that only what is material, physical, exists.

This is precisely the problem that the reductionist has with the account of color. He will say that it is language that makes the description of color to a blind man impossible, not the fact that color is not instantiable in his consciousness. "Understanding color" in such a claim is, as we saw in the last chapter, to equate a physical, quantitative, description with a complete description. "Knowledge" of a color" equates with a numerical account of a wavelength in the color spectrum. This, in turn, equates to a "percept." The individual who has knowledge of color by direct acquaintance, sc., one who can see, supposedly has the same understanding, then, as the blind man. The blind man's grasp, or anyone's for that matter, of the numerical quantities involved in color, after all, for the reductionist, is all that is needed to grasp "color." This, of course, is an absurdity. Color is not a quantitative event. Its measurement is, but not the experience.

An argument against acquaintance with the object itself, against the claim that I have a "direct acquaintance" with a world other than me, is the attempt to offer that consciousness is not actually of an object, is not a direct interaction with an object. It is strictly of a linguistic turn. This is another variant of subjectivism which, we have stated, makes the question of immortality moot. Absent something other than me, as we have noted, immortality has no meaning since upon my extinction nothing else exists if only I, my consciousness, is what constitutes the world. Each argument against the object's reality which has arisen we need, then, to continue to address if we are to make our case about immortality at all.

The "linguistic turn" argument states that consciousness that I hear a sound is not the same as consciousness of the sound, such that I cannot say consciousness of a sound is identical to a linguistic expression equating the consciousness with the sound. Language as a product of consciousness does not provide me with the object that becomes a content of consciousness.

To say that speech of an object (an entity independent of my consciousness of it) is merely a disposition to speak (whether the disposition is governed by "rules" or agreed upon pre-conditions) in such a fashion, and has no grounds in what I am observing or experiencing independent of so speaking, gets us into a vicious cycle. My disposition to speak this way is supposedly speaking of an object, but speaking of an object is a disposition. This, though, brings me right back to where I started and my needing to acknowledge again that speaking this way is a disposition only, which I am claiming is at the same time, speaking of an object.

We break the cycle only by acknowledging that the "other" is not constituted by a disposition. It stands there outside of any relation to the subject, sc., consciousness. Further, just as intrinsic to it we find certain properties, such as it must be spatial, it must be extended, we find upon our own awareness of ourselves as conscious agents that "intentionality," being about an object, being directed away from the self to something other, is intrinsic to our very being. It would appear that the difference between being "directed towards," and "that at which something is directed" could not be more different. So different that they could never be one and the same thing. Were they, then that at which something was being directed could at the same instance be that which was actually doing the directing towards. It would be receiving that which it was giving. In that case, however, it would already have what it was receiving before receiving it. This was our argument, in terms only a bit different, on why the world could not be consciousness. As directionality consciousness as the world would mean that which was "directed" at was doing that directing. That which was directed at was what was dong the very directing at. It was both active and passive in the same act.

And one would want to argue that the intentionality must be intrinsic to the being in question. To deny any intrinsic intentionality whatsoever, i.e., to say that this "intentionality" claimed of consciousness, sc., the fact that something by its very nature is "about" something else, would seem to get us in a circle where the one denying the intentionality is himself setting forth a denial "about" something, a denial of which in turn would be a denial "about" and so forth. At each step a denial takes place, about which the denier must be aware, otherwise how would he come to make the denial in the first place? While the regress does not prove the affirmative, it makes the denial (in this case, that of intentionality as intrinsic to a perceiving subject) incoherent. The denial, to be coherent, would have to be that about which the subject is making a denial.

In this respect, the argument that the concepts we have are a result of some linguistic behavior likewise fails. Berkeley and Hume, in the heyday of nominalism, offered the theory that the concept was a product of convention, the linguistic behavior or society. We use "universal" terms not because universals exist, but because habit and custom dispose us this way.

When to use the convention, however, requires the very cognitive activity the nominalist wants to deny. We must know when the convention applies, and this requires identifying a sameness in circumstances otherwise different. This is precisely what a "universal" is, however. Inasmuch as it is not singular, it emerges as something "other" than the objects of the world which all exist singly, as singular existents. As singular they are incommunicable to any other existent and cannot be said about other existents. E.g., I cannot be predicated about Julius Caesar without the person making the predication realizing a direct error, a complete misstatement. Nor is my existence communicable to any other existent. It cannot be "shared."

Universals, however, concepts in the mind, can be said of things otherwise different but same in one respect. Three-sided figures differ in shape and angularity, but the word "triangle" obtains in each instance. It is too elementary to state that I do not have an awareness of something that holds in addition to the figures of which I have this understanding of "triangle." Language has not disposed me to speak this way. Something about the activity of awareness gives me the ability to disregard all differences in things and perceive throughout those differences a sameness by which they can be and are known, and subsequently classified. It is the concept, a manner of existence that things ground for me, and not a linguistic prejudice.[2]

Showing that the claim of convention as accounting for the use of class names actually is to admit the existence of universals, which the argument for convention was meant to disprove, is to show that there is an aspect about awareness that is not confined to material existence. Convention as a societal origination of linguistic class nomenclature is part of the outlook that claims we never get to the object "out there." In the case of class names as a linguistic turn of society, what we reach is not the actual content of things themselves. We are simply manifesting a disposition of economy, a predilection towards shorthand. "Class names" (universals) are a means of making the language simpler. In this view, concepts and language are what society tells us they are. Concepts are strictly means of expression in language.

We can reject the notion that all experience is, in the end, linguistic legerdemain, perhaps even linguistic kaleidiescopy. Rorty expresses this thesis best when he opined that, as proof, if we used neurological terms, rather than the terms we do for "pain," "intense," "sharp," and the like our experience would have a different way about it. How we "experience" depends on the concepts we choose for the description of the experience involved.[3]

The concepts we form, however, are not the workings of a society. We can press that argument here further than we did in the prior chapter. The position that language is a societal phenomenon is supposed to prove that we never do get to the object "out there" after all. The view that I cannot have experience without concepts is the view that all awareness is societally conditioned, that I come to "speech" only in a community and that without it I cannot make sense of what it is that confronts me. Language is how I deal with experience, how I make it intelligible to me, and this intelligibility is conveyed by the words and symbols society over the aeons has fashioned and reinforces in its members over their own trial and error with its usage. It is not things, objects "other" than us with which we are in direct contact. Rather, it is the words we use with which we are in direct contact. They are media to whatever the objects themselves may or may not be. Language becomes the "other" for consciousness in this instance, and not the things themselves.

Here, again, however, we have the problem of regress. If awareness is only through language, if it is language that is the cognitive "space" for my interpretation and interaction with the world, is it a linguistic event that gives me this insight? That is, did I come to this awareness only through "language"? If so, how can I know that I am in fact correct since I cannot step outside of language to verify my claim? I need language to verify my claim, however, because I have said that it is only through language that I can say I have contact with this world about which I am making any claim. The argument cannot have demonstrated validity unless I am able to step outside of language, which the argument does not allow me to do, however. It, therefore, must be dismissed as ineffectual. What is has stated it will do for me it, by its own premises, cannot.

Accordingly, in all consciousness, whether human or in species different, language is not an essential particular to what consciousness in itself is. Consciousness exists extralinguistically, is not concept bound (otherwise we could never have "knowledge" of anything after just one acquaintance), and is not rendered determinate by convention, disposition, or practices of communities in the past or present. It can take on different approaches to the world depending on the species in which it is embodied.

By arguing, as we have here, against the linguistic straits in which consciousness is supposed by some to traverse for its commerce and activity, we at the same time allow ourselves to look at animal consciousness as a possible mode of immortality. In showing that consciousness is not language bound we are able to argue for a state of existence in which animal and human being share, and by which state they have more than a similarity in being material embodiments of consciousness. Now they are possible participants in a state of being that is not embodiment bound as it is in this world of which we and the animals are conscious. Consciousness can now take on implications for us which many have been wont in the past, with few exceptions, to ascribe only to the rational being that Aristotle also qualified as bipedal.[4] To order that all in a way that steps out in a sequence that is intelligible and truth endeavoring we can now turn.

II. CONSCIOUSNESS IMMORTAL

DISINTEGRATION AND PARTIBILITY

We have established in the prior chapters, the first part of our study, what we said we must establish in order to bring up the question of immortality. To show that it was not moot, we needed to set forth the existence of the world as a reality more credible, more substantiated, than its denial. This we did by showing the vicious regress, the circular argumentation, and the *petitio principii* arguments in which those denying a world other than *me* engaged. We chose the arguments from the reality of color (which do not depend on the quantum assertion of vibrational banding, though in the arguments we have allowed that assertion *ex hypothesi*)). Then we focused on the actuality of the "concept," concept formation, as an accomplishment of the individual human mind, and not his social environs. It is independent of language, and actually makes it possible. Language, however, is a phenomenon that only a social fabric can adequately explain. Thus, we have society outside of just consciousness.

We also argued as to what constitutes reality. Magnification, we argued against quantum science, reaches reality only if reality comes in ways smaller than what our unaided senses give us. Quantum physics gives "reality" only under one aspect—that of being magnified by media or instruments that give the senses, especially of sight, a different "look" at what is before them. The "other," whose actuality we have come to test and conclude in the prior pages as independent of consciousness, is not a reality only under an electron microscope. Its reality engages all the effects it can power, not simply microscopic elements which of themselves do not in any way give us the reality before us. On the supposition that reality was only in the elements of an entity before us, the car would not be the extended machine it is that brings us back and forth and can run over us. Instead, it would be an aggregation of atoms unable to account, of themselves, for how it is that the car does what it does.

We may now move in our second part, with look backs from time to time on what we have already established, and move to the reason for undertaking this study in the first place—to show that immortality is a condition of conscious life.

If we have given reason and probity to the claims that more than conscious-ness exists, that that about which it occurs is independent of it, we can proceed to looking at a feature that seems to characterize both: corruptibility. What brings it about? If composition by parts is ingredient to everything that exists, is any existent immune to decomposition?

This is the question of "simplicity," the query whether there is any existent such that any reduction, deduction, from, diminution of, it would mean it no longer is, is no longer an existent. Again, we cannot skirt over what seems to be simply obvious. We stated in the preface this is what books in the popular press on immortality do. In writing on immortality, it mentions nothing that is argued in the current philosophy of mind and the literature in which it funds expression. For the thinker on immortality it is imperative, however, to argue for and justify every statement he makes about material existence and to the detail, however seemingly obvious some points may seem, necessary. Accordingly, we will have to look at not just the object that is independent of consciousness, but that in which both it and consciousness exist. This is space, place, and how they relate to decomposition, and how they may not. Because space is that in which corrup-tion occurs, its reality as a fact of existence has taken up discussion here. In the same way we argued for the "otherness" of the world, even though it may have seemed obvious, the sakes are too high to simply have passed it along as "com-monsensical." The discussion on space and place here, then, are under the same caution of discussion. We have not addressed the arguments in neurophilosophy sufficiently, as we have said here we must, if we do not discuss them.

Loss of a limb does not necessarily mean the non-existence of the individ-ual who has lost it, though clearly this is an instance of reduction. In all objects that are spatial, as the individual who has lost the limb, their possession of, composition by, parts would stand to reason. They will be complex, composed through parts, as evinced in the fact their spatiality dictates their occupation of different parts of space.

Is there any entity such that any total loss of, diminution to, some aspect of it would not necessarily mean it no longer exists? Only for that which has no parts could this not occur. If it has no parts, it can only lose all that it is at once. Absent parts, it appears destruction cannot occur to that which is without them. Termination of existence, if it did occur, would have to occur in a way that is without parts—partless. We know of no such occurrence in material bodies where they simply vanish without a severance of the parts to them first.

Corruption occurs by the severance of bondings among atomic constituents in the material entity that corrupts. Once stated to be caused by the break-up of the "matter" in a material constituent, quantum mechanics has moved us to question whether there are any absolutely indivisible bits that in the end go to compose each "material" existent.[1] Are these existents in point of fact simply vibrational realities at certain frequencies without any ultimate bits, that cannot be further divided? Does the argument that divisibility of a constituent, as in the experience of all that is around us, is the cause of its dissolution no longer hold?

If it is the break-up of "matter" that causes the decomposition of a being, is it that without the possibility of such a break-up decomposition could not occur? The argument reduces to the distinction between "material" and "immaterial." Is the distinction valid can be answered in the affirmative only if there is a realty known as "matter" of which all entities that perish are made, and the breakup of which causes their perishing. Are there not, i.e., irreducible components, as was held by thinkers since the time of Democritus,[2] that ultimately go to make up the physical realities of the world?

Or is it the case that it is not that physical reality is an illusion, it is just that in adhering to a doctrine of matter we are mistaken about its actual being? Matter is simply vibrational fields. Impenetrability is simply the power of one vibrational arrangement being superior to another Therefore, talk of diremption of parts as the cause of destruction is misguided. In the end, according to this point of view, what we call destruction is strictly the rebalancing of vibrational forces. Nothing massed here has been lost. Only identity of what was one vibrational field has been lost since a new balance of forces in that field has come about. This is what is really destruction. There are no absolutely minimalist "parts" that go to make up what we consider to be a "material composite." Therefore, perishing is not by way of the separation of these parts. It is simply vibrational realignment.

There is in this question a certain irony inasmuch as a completely physical description of the universe would eliminate any being called "consciousness," (asserting, to the contrary, that nothing but matter exists). Yet, a doctrine of reality as strictly a system of "wave functions" would eliminate any talk of matter at all, while not necessarily eliminate a place for "consciousness."

The vibrational theory of matter, proffered by quantum physics, will not do for a look at the constituency of the reality we confront everyday. Accepting that beyond our sense perception are atoms ingredient to the constituency of everything resent to our senses,, as even quantum mechanics holds, reason moves to the conclusion that there must be a terminus to each bonding of these atoms. Otherwise, they would run on to one another. Force fields would simply be without definition, without that by which they were separated. Separation occurs at points—that is, indivisibles. Without such indivisibles—units which could not be further broken down—separation could never take place. Always another step before the separation, difference from another entity, would be required.

The fact that things are separate means that any similarity among them has come to an end. This, though, would be impossible were always another step necessary to eliminate the similarity. The step where the first difference the one from the other is achieved marks them off from each other and must be irreducible and indivisible for the difference, the dissimilarity, to take place among them. Difference requires an ultimate starting unit, the first of which unit makes for the difference of the entity in question from anything else.

These are the irreducible bits, the indivisible component, of reality, that quantum physics has seemingly discarded in favor of frequencies that are without irreducible realities in their composition. For it, we apparently have simply waves in which is nothing that is ultimately impervious, nothing ultimately an absolute resistance to penetration. We have shown, however, that differences require endpoints between the things that are different. That is, incomposite entities into which no further differentiation is possible. These must exist if things are different. It is their separation by disbonding that is the movement of decay and dissolution, and ultimately destruction.

Division into lesser units till an ultimately irreducible unit, from whose aggregation of such units comes to be the material existents (material "macrosystems") of the world, is the means of destruction and perishing. There are indivisible bits whence all the actual beings of the universe are ultimately composed, and because there are we can look upon destruction as the segregation of those bits by disintegrative, disbonding, forces. These impervious bits are not extensions of space, wave vibrations. They are the imporous irreducible infinitesimal bulks that cannot be further divided and from which the composition of material existents ultimately must issue.

Destruction, i.e., is not some transference of wave vibrations to a different level or different levels. Destruction is the actual decomposition into smaller units of reality till their division is no longer possible. What exists is not simply a system of wave frequencies, but an entity composed of inert, impassable units that go to constitute the universe and into whose reduction consists the decay of all aggregations of such units.

If this is so, then we have clearly established the grounds for arguing that if an entity exists without matter in any way its decomposition, what it means and what it entails, becomes a topic of serious discussion. If decomposition into smaller units is the pathway to perishing, does an entity whose reality involves an aspect of the immaterial, of what is without matter, have a reality that is not totally decomposable, is not what can completely perish? If, when we die, we are nothing but our bodies, then death is the end to everything we are. If nothing but matter exists, and our bodies are the aggregation of numberless bits of matter, bodily death means there is no more to us.

Indivisible bits of imporous intertia, which is what the ultimately irreducible components of a material being must involve if our argument regarding the possibility of things being separate or different is valid, are not "points." Points are without extension. The indivisible and that which is without extension are not the same. Something can be indivisible without being extenseless, but what is without extension, is extenseless, is necessarily indivisible. Were all indivisibility without extension, nothing could be made of indivisible bits because irrespective of their aggregation they would never take up space.

Indivisible bits are indestructible because they cannot be divided further. What makes them indivisible is not that they are without extension. It is that each is the first length of extension such that reduced any further extension would cease. Points are not spatial. These bits are those whose annihilation would mean replacement by space. In this sense, then, they take up space with minimalist extension.

Under the microscope (as we have observed already), the world appears far different than to the unaided eye. The greater its power, the greater the difference that appears. We encounter a universe composed mostly of space. These "bits," however, that we have just established as existing, and which result ultimately in the shape of different gross structures, exist in that "space." We can allow, then, that space does occupy a material reality's existent. Space, though, is not that by which the material existent comes to be. It is by the bits, the inert, impassable potions whose existence we established above, by whose aggregation a material existent becomes "matter" to us.

With each "tinier" bit that has been "discovered" (or reasoned to) comes a new name, and the nomenclature of the sub-atomic world tells us just how populated the universe is at the minutest level with these bits. But between them, on a proportionate scale, to elaborate the quantum position further, is a distance, a space that the electron microscope tells us goes to comprise each reality that we encounter. The microscope whose components are from this world tell us that. Powered to what the most sophisticated microscope can capture we "see" space as the primary "occupant," the primary component, actually, of any entity's reality in the universe. The evidence the microscope makes available tells us that the universe, at its core, is primarily in each entity emptiness. The quantum world, that is, is primarily without content.

In this emptiness, however, are those constituent bits that are directly opposite to this emptiness. They are "solid," without any space between them. Emptiness is totally absent from their constitution. Whatever the "bit," the impenetrability of the unit makes it almost eternal in itself. It appears, indeed, that what goes on in the decomposition of every entity is, at bottom, these bits. "Matter can be neither created nor destroyed by ordinary means."

Waves are energy fields in motion (their presence is known more by the effects to which we must reason their existence than observation) and we have been told that matter itself is a form of energy. Matter in fact when it achieves the square of the speed of light is energy. Energy becomes matter upon matter's destruction, which occurs at this velocity. Matter and energy are two sides of the same coin, two aspects of reality, one would want to advance. The Plank constants, to proceed somewhat further on this, are a centerpiece of quantum physics. They describe the minimal slice of space/time attainable. In them, matter is spoken of in terms of frequency vibrations; and formulated one gets $E = mc^2$ is the same as the Plank constant times frequency.

Neither equation, though, avoids the absolute requirement of a minimalist unit we have stated that goes ultimately to constitute the beginning of each material being. We have reached the reality of such a unit by noting that without it there could be no differences among things since separateness requires at some juncture a dissimilarity in what goes to make up one thing versus that from which it is different.

Any physics, our point is, that understands all reality in the end as wave patterns does not reach the ontological conditions that each corruptible reality, upon reflection, shows itself to require. That is its status as being composed of ultimately irreducible components, trillions upon trillions, that congeal and intra-aggregate by way of a sustaining organizing principle which is responsible for the ultimate form, structure, and condition of that reality. The reality that we encounter every day, at its core, is not "bitless." It is constituted by "bits," whatever their extension, and this is the world that we call "material."

There is another aspect to reality, though, that is not susceptible to this classification. It is a realty to which we have already referred, that is, as we call it, "bitless." As "bitless," it is a reality not susceptible to decay, decomposition, dissolution, destruction, or perishing. If all realty decomposes by way of the breakdown of constituent parts, if any existent is dissoluble only because it possesses parts into which it can decompose, absence of parts one would think might provide for a realty that cannot decompose. If having parts is how things are susceptible to destruction, we need to see if absence of parts insures against destruction. First, though, we want to see if there is any entity that shows it is without parts.

It helps, first, to separate the term "part" from other terms that usually substitute for it.[3] A "part," for our purposes of exactitude, is not an "ingredient," "component," "factor," "segment," "section," of something. Consciousness, e.g., has different powers in its reality, factors by which it achieves, or through which it interacts with, its world. But this does not mean consciousness has "parts" as we are using the term. We can use for "part" terms such as "piece," "fragment," "bit," as its alternatives because they all identify one basic reality: spatial separability from that with which it was previously one.

A part, for our purposes of precision, will convey extension, spatiality (extension in space) as essential to its reality. Concomitant with that reality is its status as that which results when division takes place in that which was previously one and is now two. The parts of a thing can be homogeneous (as in salt) or heterogeneous (as in a house). What matters for our purposes here is the fact that their dismemberment or diremption is how their loss of existence comes about, how the loss of anything that has parts results in its perishing.

A branch that was one does not have an actual part until it has been cut, separated, divided. The branch is an extended reality that by means of an instrument of severance applied to it with force loses that unity. The instrument of severance must, by virtue of its thinness (e.g., a blade), have a force that accompanies it in the right direction for the partition to occur. The partition, though, is the end of unity. The branch, now two, has lost its identity as what it once was. Once it was six inches; now it is three.

Applied continuously, the severance of each succeeding part will result in a branch that has pretty much lost all of its "branchness." It becomes at some moment to us no longer a "branch," or "piece of branch," but a "particle of wood." Something has happened to it that destroyed its "branchness." Continual and unremitting severance of the small piece of wood into ever smaller "pieces" gives us minute "particles," and finally sawdust. Our "branch" is gone. All that remains is the "woodness" that is its ultimate natural "component." However, not all the time in the world will enable one to take all that "woodness," all the granulates of wood, and make it the branch that it once was. Something has forever perished from that assemblage of dust, of wooden "dust." It is that bonding of woodness throughout what was once a branch. An axe, or a knife, has had the power to end the organizing force, bring it to non-existence. Separability has yielded its ultimate law: non-existence for that which is separable, partible, within itself.

A principle of organization occurs in a complex where within are movements, notes, moments, and drives that can be at odds with each other individually, but when seen as a cohesive reality lose these characteristics. We use the term "principle" because for the reality to have any possibility of being there must be that from which it begins. This is the "principle." "Principle" is that which, prior to the being's existence, means that being does not yet exist. The principle can be transmitted from a prior existent or can be totally and spontaneously new. Each first member of a species was such. Subsequent to that, it was by receiving being from a prior member of that species that all that it eventually became came to be.

Part of what it came to be was the vitality that limited the opposing ionizations, charges, and instabilities of atomic composition. This is the force that we spoke about, e.g., in the branch. What enabled it to continue growing on the tree? What enabled it to interact with the air, the moisture of the surrounding climate, and the like while all the opposing charges within its atomic and subatomic constituency interacted and acted against and with each other charge? Were there only one such entity in existence it is conceivable that "it just so happened" that the atomic constituency yields the stability and permanence of the entity in question. We are led to believe, however, that since this stability is a property[4] throughout the numberless beings that have come to be and pass away, and that it happens on all variations and levels of atomic constituency (and not just branches), that an organizing factor in each instance must abide for the entity that is atomistically structured.

The universe that confronts us does so as one composed of beings that come to be and pass away. Accretion of parts signifies growth; reduction of parts, or their diminution, signifies, decay. All of this occurs by the occupation of or exiting from space. Berkeley, of course, did not think of space as anything "visible," knowledge of it being more a product of comparison among our own sensations. Clearly, however, our own experience tells us that exhaustion from walking a long "distance" did not result from the eye's, or the mind's, activity of "comparison." Space does exist not as some "line endwise to the eye," and it is a relation among objects that gives the mind one means of awareness of both their magnitude and proportion to one another. Physical exhaustion and lethargy are another means by which "space" comes to our awareness as an actual reality.

What exists is in its place This place is an occupation of that very space in the limits of the entity it encloses without being in any way part of that entity.

Taking up space as a thing grows is not the removal of that space "taken." It still is there. Emptiness has now fit within its extension the bounds of a density that does not move the extension away but becomes that extension. The space which density leaves becomes the extension that was formerly the density. Not however as a thing or substance does space become that density. It becomes it by taking on what it has allowed to enter it.

The amount of space in the galaxy is not infinite. Were half the galaxy to be taken up by one continuous density, and then the entire galaxy taken up by it, there would be no possibility of the density increasing. The amount of emptiness, space, is fixed so that once the emptiness became the entirety of a body equal to the emptiness the body would not be able to expand any further.[5]

Finite space (curved on itself or not), and limits to the size an entity can be as one integrated unit, give us the outermost possibilities of what any material body can be. We know between its components, whether on the microscopic scale, or on the galactic, lies a proportionately expanded emptiness. As we argued earlier in this regard, it may be that the electron microscope gives us only one half of one percent of all the cosmos, but it is only what it can tell us with which we have to and can argue. It may be that instruments that are available from the other nine-nine point five percent of the universe may tell us a different story. However, it is only this half of one percent world that our microscopes of the "infinitesimal" give us from which we can discourse about the constituents of the entities before us.

Allowing for that, we can note that the instruments of electron microscopy show that most of the material body is empty. Reason tells us what holds the constituent bits in unity is an organizing principle that accounts for how atomic interaction and reaction occur in the trillions of cases that it does without destruction to the entity. There are the minimalist forces and the exacting attractive/repellant mechanisms that see to the orderly conduct of the constituents "parts."

Accretion and separation, joining and severance, are the processes of growth and destruction that occur before our eyes every day. In rare instances, the severance of parts can have a regrowth of the severed entity, as in certain reptilian forms. It will not take place, though, if force is applied to stop the regrowth. The severance, in that case, will be the beginning of the reptilian form's destruction.

It would appear, accordingly, that composition by matter is a sure sign of destructibility. Whatever the minimalist bit, proceeding from being an entity that is composed of these bits in the millions of shapes and varieties organization of those bits can take, having come into existence through their accretion and conjunction means that the being so made will some day decompose into the disaggregated bits that comprised its ultimate constituency. And it does so in space.

Some existents that we encounter show themselves to have a capacity which other existents in our experience do not. Self-determination, self-aggrandizement, self-sustenance are what immediately come to mind. A comparison of the objects of our experience shows that beings divide along lines of certain capacities which at some point give them an independence and freedom not found in other beings. These beings have an ability to move without the assistance of an outside cause. They show an ability by which, in cooperation with their environment, they grow. Here, while there is not an independence that we can cite, the growth in question separates them from an entire class of existents.

Independence is that state of being wherein the occurrence of an event lies totally with one existent. The existent is not hampered by a "something" without which the event would not have occurred. Nothing except that entity's very being is determinative in what has come about. What has come about is "independent" of anything else.

In the existent that can move of itself, grow through interaction with its surroundings, independence constitutes for it the highest form of existence. The excellence of existence is not the number of effects an entity can bring about. The excellence is also determined by whether those effects are determined by that existent to the exclusion of everything else. We may call this excellence "life," which takes on higher grades the more complicated the excellence becomes.

That greater complexity begins in the activity of cognition, awareness. In a way, granted, both are dependent on what is known for their actual state. However, what provides for that awareness is not external to the entity possessed of it. It is a principle intrinsic to the conscious being, to the being that knows. Consciousness is a principle by which the agent possessed of it deals with the world in a particular way, in a way superior to the vegetative and movent forms of independence.

Cognition is a higher form of consciousness in that it reaches the universal in its activity. Cognition does not reflect total independence unless through it one reaches what is totally free. The *intuitus* of the Divine[6] for Thomas Aquinas is what sets one's being free, but our discussion here is with respect to earthly conditions. And in this regard what constitutes life to its fullest would be the capacity at self-origination, self-determination. This means of self-determination is the basis for the relative independence from others the living being can have. Absolute independence, where nothing from without can affect a being, where any level of interaction with any other being is its own doing, does not exist in living being.

Life, not just non-living matter, also undergoes destruction when ingredient to its occurrence is material constituency. Through chemical processes not yet understood, the atomic/sub-atomic bonding (covalence/valence) of the submicroscopic "bits" does not hold in perpetuity. Friction, of which there are a number of kinds, is often cited as partly responsible for decay. Without entering into the debate on its corrosive activity, and whether all systems are tendencies towards breakdown, disorder, we know there is nothing about life materially composed that provides for unending continuance as that life.

The "other" to consciousness, as both lifeless and living, it appears shows no evidence of perduring destruction. We have just given its two manners of existing in the above paragraphs, arguing that in both cases ultimately the "other" which confronts us everyday is a destructible entity because matter is basic to its constitution. While in destruction, of course, remnants of the entity decomposing remain, what the entity was is gone and for the living being our language is "it did not survive." Animal and human, once lifeless, appear totally bereft of any of the characteristics that marked them as "living." This total bereftment of all in what was once life gives us the opportunity to take a brief aside and look at the question of purpose and its structure in death.

DEATH AND PURPOSE

To the human being, meditation on the possibility of the moment of one's complete lifelessness is a sure pathway to the experience of dread. However the mind collects its memories, and however their meaning emerges in those moments of meditation, meditation upon death is meditation upon emptiness. However the death comes about—through relentless cancer and its accompanying suffering, through the heart that is stopped permanently with a searing pain, through an accident at sea or simply a failure to awake from one's bed—the blackness of death in one's meditation has no corollary in the vibrant living of everyday activity and encounter. What makes death possible in the human being is his material composition, the fact that he is made of extensions of solidity which, in their course, sever and separate one from the other in a process that moves ineluctably athwart science's capacity to in any way stop it. Matter gives the body part of its stature in life; and is a factor totally ingredient to the body's degradation.

This "dread" of death of which we speak may be an indication that there is something about death that is wrong for the human person. The survival instinct indicates to us, surely, that death is not that for the sake of which we came to be. The human person, one might take from this look at dread and instinct, was not born to die. "Being born to die," as we remarked in the opening pages, indicates almost purposelessness in the act of birth because death is the defeat of birth. More though, birth is the direct contradiction of death. That death would be the goal of birth is almost as if seeded into birth itself is that which will completely undo it, be its contradiction. We are saying, as we go further than our previous remarks, birth was meant for its contradiction if by being born we were meant to die.

Why there is a time element for what is supposed to perish after coming to be, then, becomes a problem. If death is the pre-ordained state for all that comes to be, [following the law of entropy (all things are falling into their own disorder)], the element of time as stretching out that process of decay becomes a problem inasmuch as we know that Nature, when it does anything, does it efficiently and with the absolute minimum of steps. If what comes to be has as its original goal its own perishing, it is clear that stretching out the process through a decay over time, as we see endlessly, is not an act of efficiency.

If Nature acts efficiently, and allowing a process of decay to take place over time rather than instantly indicates inefficiency (for the more quickly something is done the more efficient is the process involved), then it may not be the case that death is the purpose of birth. It seems that it is, if something comes to be and only perishes after having existed a while. If it is going to perish, why should it have come to be in the first place, as we asked above? If we opt for the outlook that in fact Nature is not inefficient, then since instantaneous death would fulfill the requirements of efficiency for anything whose purpose is to cease to exist after having come to be, and Nature is efficient, we would have to conclude that passing away is not the purpose for something coming to be. Otherwise, in Nature (which is efficient), it would have happened immediately. This is what efficiency means, after all.

The argument is important, even though it may seem recondite. Looking at the issue as we have just done may make it, though, what is only too obvious. If Nature is efficient, and death is the purpose of birth, death should come about quickly, for this is ingredient to any operation that is efficient. Since it does not, perhaps it is not the case, even though at first it seems, that birth's' purpose is death. This means that what comes to life does not have as its purpose death. It is not, inasmuch as we have addressed a case where it seems total purposelessness governs existence if whatever comes to be is only going to pass away anyway. We have shown by argument regarding Nature as an efficient agent that what comes to be does not have as its purpose passing away.

Then why do things pass away? And further, is the passing away of whatever comes to be an end to the totality of their existence? The question of meaning comes up here once more. If death is total nothingness, how can that which is totally of nothingness have any meaning? Meaning implies content, and death as total nothingness must be without content, and thus meaning.[1]

INDIVISBILE SENSATION AND "ZOMBIE" THEORY

Physio-chemically, we know how things pass away. Physical chemistry and physics gives us the "process" to the extent that it is able. We already saw that insight into the mechanics of passing away is limited inasmuch as we are not able to grasp how bonding effectuates, through the many laws that govern force etc., the organization of trillions of bits in what is actually primarily empty space between them. The figure of a one hundred by thirty yard football field as the empty space with a post at one end, a post in the middle, and a post at the other gets the picture across as to how material reality, in accepted physical theory, is constituted. It is primarily emptiness. In the end, whether that theory is correct, it is a theory whose currency requires our addressing it further than we already have. It is not so much that one can question whether reality is composed in an atomistic way, i.e., that infinitesimally sized bits go to make up the things of experience. It is the question of the spatiality to which modern physics attributes each individual building block of any material body. We are given to believe that almost all of existence is emptiness. Yet, if the tools from materials secured from that portion of the cosmos to which quantum mechanics denies us access were used and available, would those tools point us to, show us, a universe whose constituents after all were not primarily space?

Resistance gives us the sense that what we encounter is not empty. "Resistance" is another word for "solidity." It appears without much possible dispute that what we think is "solid" (totally impenetrable, imporous) actually is not simply the result of one action, but many. What we experience as "solid" results from the infinitesimal bits that go to make up our "material" body and the charges among and between them in "contact" with an entity of similar physical properties. There is a law of organization by which the two bodies do not suddenly, upon contact, meld into or interpenetrate one another. The atomic and sub-atomic bonding governing one human body does not suddenly, upon contact with another such body, dissipate into that body and the like. There is something that prohibits it. If it happens in each case of contact that the two bodies upon contact do not collapse into one another, it would appear that some organizational power or dynamic is operant to prevent that collapse, some imperative to which adherence by the atoms and sub-atomic particles stops from happening.

This law is not the "form" or "essence" of the entity in question. Considered by Hume and others to be simply "occult powers" that explained nothing, the essence or form of an entity gives it its intelligibility and what now makes it be. This "form" is not a rule of proportions among all the "bits" and their bonding processes in the individual entity. What the mind knows when it grasps a being is not proportions or rules. It knows "content," which no rule or proportion can be. To say that knowledge of a person is actually knowledge of the proportions that go to make him or her up is perhaps the height of depersonalizaton. The "form" is that by which material beings have something in common and because of which material beings appear to us as being in a "class."

It is not the "form" that is the organizational dynamic in each being that keeps its covalence and bondings at the measure which they kept. It is existence as a principle of the unity of any material being's components that does. The structure of the bits in the entity comes about through the actuating form. What secures the structure is existence as the synthesizing union of the form and material components. The "other" is not merely a "formal" reality, but an "existing" one.

The infinitesimal material bits, imperceptible to our awareness, exist in current physics; but not as the "other" in our awareness. The structure that activates these bits into a knowable reality, into the "other," it exists, but not as we perceive. We do not perceive an entity's "structure." What we perceive is an actually existing unity of numberless parts, which cannot exist except through the synthesizing operations of existence that makes the "other" an existing reality before us.

We know the "other" we encounter is not a "formal" reality, a thought of ours, but what we counter as not being us by its acting as a resistant being, as solid, as impervious. We cannot be resistant to ourselves. We conclude, on reflection, that the entity we encounter non-inferentially as "real," as not "me," actually, as the etymology of the word *ex-ists* suggests, "stands outside of me." It is not "me." We return to the basic fact that the universe and I are not identical. Something exists other than I. If it has the same features as I do, and is not the non-living matter of this heavy earth, we are seeking to ascertain if it too can possess "an existence beyond."

Does anything about living beings avoid composition by parts, or is every reality about them divisible? Since whatever comes to be, living or non living, is multi-composed, we have the opportunity to ask does anything about the living avoid partiblity, composition by parts? This is not the same as asking whether there is anything about them independent of partibility. Consciousness may possess impartible (incomposable) features, but this does not mean it can occur without partibility in some way.

Does consciousness possess features that do not make it a partible reality, but one that is incomposite? Can consciousness first be shown to be without parts, not just "other" than that which has parts? And can it be shown in its actuality e.g., as being "of color," "of sound," to be partless and without dimensions in those very percepts? Finally, can the occurrence of the percept, any act of consciousness, point us to that which partible, divisible, being does not have? If the percept is an occurrence that does not resemble those events which occasion it, does it show a factor it possesses that is not possessed by what occasions it (what occurs along with it)? I.e., does it show itself to necessarily be other than that which occasions it? If so, does it show itself to be immaterial, just as other aspects of it may?

We alluded in an earlier chapter to an aspect of our consciousness that sharply differentiates it from the material. We have established as highly reasonable that there is an "objective" occurrence called "the percept red": it is my consciousness of "red." The color red cannot be located in consciousness. It cannot be measured. It is without any dimension. One cannot touch it. It does not move from place to place. Increasing its size in one's awareness does not add to its inherent hue. Reducing it in size does not decrease it, either. One cannot pick it up. One cannot, for that matter, throw it, or catch it. It actually is not a "thing," like a circumscribed three-dimensional object is. But it is with such objects that one's experience is filled, brimming, happening.

Further differentiating consciousness from that about which it takes place is that no physical property or existent has the character "about" which consciousness has. "Red" does not have the characteristic "aboutness," "of-ness." Nor does "desk," "pen," "house"—whatever the material existent you choose. They are never "about" things. Consciousness, however, is in its reality as intentionality. Material existents, whether dependent on consciousness (as in the percept "red") or not (as in the object "desk"), their objectivity grounded in their reality as in some way being "caused" to consciousness, as being, i.e., "other" than consciousness, are not intentional in their being.

Materialism, the view that nothing but matter exists or that everything is explicable in terms of or reducible to it, says that whatever is true or factual about the color "red" must be material, must be explicable in physical terms. Anything beyond that constitutes inaccuracy. The physical properties of whatever it is that are involved in having the percept "red" suffice to account for the percept.

A similar argument materialism will lodge against how one speaks about pain. A toothache on x-ray will show a tooth that has anatomical/physiological abnormalities. But the "ache" is not in the tooth which feels the pain. It is the individual who does. And does so because nerve endings, bone structure, are conduits for sending signals of abnormality to the brain which then register to it as "pain."

The difficulty, however, is that the pain one has looks nothing like abnormalities in the tooth. It cannot, in fact, be seen. Nothing physically or materially correlates with this sensation I call "pain." If pain is the object of any of the sense receptors it is difficult to know which one. The pressure of touch, e.g., which some may want to associate with pain in the tooth, feels completely different at other times in the tooth. That is, it is not accompanied by pain at those times. The sense receptors would therefore not appear to be the locus of the ache.

The experience of pleasure is a far more intricate issue, inasmuch as it comes under many different guises. It is never extended, is without depth, has no size or weight. In some instances it gives a sense of completion while in others, as in the anticipation of something wonderful, it is obviously a sense of the incomplete.

In none of these cases is the conscious experience, the percept, equatable with the bodily, the physical, the material, the divisible. There are no parts in the percept which we can break off and have less of a percept. There is no part that we can break off and by successive reduction bring the percept to an end. It is not subject to diminution or aggrandizement. It cannot be reshaped or stretched. Nor can it be heated or cooled. Surface is absent in all percepts, as is resistance. Unlike the existence that we call matter, we can never push up against a percept. Nor can it ever act as a weight: gravity exercises no pull on it.

It does not help to say that if we replaced certain brain structures with others of a different material, but of the same organization, that we could have the same percepts and therefore that bodily composition is of no consequence to the debate. It doesn't matter, that is, so one may aver, that percepts can be non-bodily and therefore this may indicate indestructibility. Because we can imagine an organizational entity structured the same as the neuronal network of the brain that accomplished what the bodily neuronal network does. If we can do that, what importance does neuronal composition have to the debate? It is bodily, but not essential to having a percept.

It is not clear, however, how this avoids the question at issue, sc., material composition. No matter what organizational structure you choose to replace the neuronal, we are still left with something that is extended, in place, and therefore susceptible to division and partition.

Then, to the contrary, it is perfectly conceivable that we could have this organizational structure that mimics the neuronal to the last detail and it might not give the "percept" when stimulated. No percept may arise where the creature in question resembles us in every way. Wounding it or attacking it may yield no sensation of pain.

This is the so-called "zombie" argument. In this case the argument about bodily composition (and hence whether that composition is by "parts") is no longer a factor in our argument because we have a body identical in composition to the human, but without the possibility of percept. If it can decompose but not have a percept, the argument that bodily composition or parts is a precondition to the percept fails, the zombie advocates want to argue.

Postulating a bodily structure identical in every way to the human, but which may never have a percept, while a conceivable reality, does not serve as an effective argument against what we are discussing, though. We are looking at the bodily structure, the neuronal composition, in which there occurs the percept, not one in that, however identical to our body, it does not. To say that parts are not essential to the body's composition (and thus the percept) because bodily composition may not provide for the percept, as in the case of the zombie, does not answer how the percept occurs in the presence of that composition. If it occurs in the case of the body which is made up of parts, if it does not when the body is decomposed requires we answer whether the body's composition was a precondition for the percept. If it was, it would follow that without the precondition the percept would not come to be. That, though, would equate the human body with the zombie body. That our body is not the zombie body should suffice as a response to the zombie argument.[1]

COHERENCE, PERCEPT, *QUALIA*

Our inquiry is: if the conscious agent can have a percept, while bodily composed, does the non-bodily status of the percept indicate that bodily dissolution may not be the precondition for eliminating the possibility of a percept? Is the body of the human being the necessary condition for a percept? If the percept differs in structure from the body, and the body decomposes, does consciousness in having access to the percept have access to that which is non-bodily? Said otherwise: if the percept is immaterial, must the agent possessed of it have some immateriality about him?

We are not simply asking about the conceivability of a percept *sans* body, the so-named "modal argument." In it, if something is not self-contradictory, what claims the materialist makes against survival of bodily decomposition will need to be so persuasive that even if a percept without a body is not self-contradictory materialism will have amassed the evidence necessary to discredit any claim of immortality despite the conceivability of a percept *sans* a material brain. Materialism, or reductionism, we will argue, amasses no such evidence in any format, and in fact cannot. Underlying the belief that a percept is possible *sans* a material brain is the assumed equivalence of a neuroelectric firing with a percept, and that that neuroelectric firing can be replicated in the absence of a suitably complex cortex. That in fine is our just reviewed zombie case. You can have a zombie state mimicking consciousness, but the claim's difficulty is that what you have is a percept in the first place. The moon's reflection in a lake mimics the moon: but it is not the moon.

Take, e.g., impairments of conscious states. Can this support the thesis that a neuroelectric charge mimicking the percept is equivalent to the percept? In impaired "conscious states" unity and coherence of percept are absent to a degree, such as in cortical lesion failings, that result in different forms of apperceptive agnosia [e.g., asterognosia, disjunctive agnosia, autotopagnosia]).[1] This has resulted in one neurophilosophic postulate that what accounts indeed for the coherence in the first place is that deep in the background against which our percepts emerge, occurs a "rhythmic dance of neuronal discharges and oscillations."[2] These neurons are arguably hundreds of billions in number, and their electrical interaction and reaction create, almost dialectically it seems, the unity that is the percept. A "field," perhaps more accurately a "space," of neurons is an intensity of opposing charges and countercharges. For the percept to occur seamlessly united these charges have to be subsumed, sublated, continuously so that all differences and contradictions are absent, yielding only what we achieve in the percept: harmony, continuity, and stability. This occurs by achieving precisely the correct balance between diversity of neuroelectric input and synthesis of output.

More so, the model of the "standing-context loop" shows how all this is possible. Within milliseconds of electrical inputs and outputs different inputs are referred back to prior, are held *in situ*, as an ever larger "context" comes about in the milliseconds of neuro-processing. There is also the possibility that synchrony of neuronal firings, such as those resulting in gamma band oscillations, can account for our unity and cohesion of percept. The so-called "feature binding" (all the different aspects of the object, its color, width, depth, length, etc.) is the work of firings that create a network of neurons that represent the single object.

When cortical impairments occur, as in above, that neuronal space lacks all the equipment essential for this sublation and subsumption, and impedes this loop-back model so that, as in asterognosia, I lack the ability to recognize what I touch, or in disjunctive agnosia, the inability to integrate what is seen with what is heard.

The theory that synchrony of firings is multitudinous enough (hundreds of billions of neurons in a networked pattern) to be the reason for an object's cohesion in the percept is equivalent to saying that the neuronal firings are the percept. Electrical firings, however, do not have the quality of the object in question, much less resemble in any way the object as it in the percept. We know quite clearly what differentiates a spark firing from the color in my vision, or the smell wafting past my nostrils. To say that my claim that this electrical charge that differs from any quality or quantity in my percept is possible only because neuronal synchrony's work has already provided for my having the percept (which, according to the synchrony theory is actually an "electrical charge") appears to presuppose what is at question—that awareness is by way of neuronal synchrony. The neuronal synchrony theory does not get us to the quality of what it is that constitutes the percept's content, the quality of sound, of color, of feel. None of these has the characteristic of an electrical charge.

The millisecond loop-back theory of consciousness, another possibility offered of how it is that we have "coherence of the percept," has one grave setback to it. The oscillations and firings of neurons occur without external stimulus, in the absence of any object present to the brain. The brain, in other words, does not appear to have a dependence on any particular object for its excitations. While excitations do occur in the presence of objects, neuronal excitations also occur in their absence.

The percept's presence, being so contradictory to what is supposed to have occasioned it, makes the causal argument of the materialists totally ineffectual. If a percept is coherent, unitary, balanced, and harmonious in its actuality, the materialist event that is supposed to be its substratum, sc., the disaggregated, chaotic, atomistic electro-chemical disturbances, could not possibly effectuate the percept. Causality argues nothing in the effect that is not in the cause. The realty of the percept, as we have just described it, rules out any causation by way of the neuroelectro-chemical events that are supposed to be its precondition, occasion, or cause because those events contain nothing in them that the percept does.

Accordingly, if the percept is not the neuroelectric charge in the body, it cannot be the charge *sans* the body. I.e., one cannot take a software program intricately enough that mimics the intricacies of the theory of neural synchrony and at some level declare that we have achieved a percept, even though the body is not where the percept has occurred but instead it has occurred through a software program.

Paul Churchland's reasoning is probably the most pronounced for the equation of neural event and consciousness. Neural and C-fiber activity in the brain set in process by external sense-stimuli compliant with the neural topography of a material substrate suitably disposed totally accounts for sensation according to Churchland. Consciousness is the activity of matter suitably organized. Consciousness is totally explicable in terms of the bodily matter called the brain (the cortex).

Churchland's thesis will not hold. If consciousness, or the percept, derives from neuroelectric activity in the brain (in concert with the intricately innervated system throughout the sensing body), it is either a replication of the composite object activating the neural disturbances in the brain; or it is not. The percept as a neural disturbance cannot be a material reproduction of the object. The neural event exhibits none of the features of the percept: integrity, cohesion, order, proportion, stability. The neural-electrical disturbances in the brain are a chaos of cacophonic, out of sequence, out of balance, sporadic charges composed of unpredictable vectors of electrical direction. Even if what the percept carries in no wise resembles what we call the "original object," and we assume that the "original object" itself outside the brain is the same cacophony of disturbances and unpredictable electrical charges stimulating the sensory system, we have to ask how the percept comes to be as it is. What can give the cohesion and stability to a state of affairs except that which itself provides for such cohesion and stability? But the brain possesses no such capacity. We know it strictly as that which involves chaotic, unpredictable, chance-filled charges that have no permanence or pattern. The electrical charges in the brain are constantly discontinuous and intermittent, in no way resembling the percept's continuity. They cannot provide for the singleness and unity the percept manifests.

Churchland's position, and that of other reductionists, also suffers from the inability to "quantify" this reality about ourselves which we call "subjectivity." The point receives best wording in Nagel's famous essay, "What is it like to be a bat?"[3] Subjectivity is not something that one weighs, puts on a range of spectral extensions, and the like and at a specific point identifies "where" it occurs. Yet, it does occur. In sensation there is awareness of differences from what it is like to experience "blue," in contrast to what it is like to experience "sound," "taste," "pungency." There is in experience something that differs from what the experience is about. The experience is not an event of one thing. It is an event that includes the thing and that to whom the experience occurs.

I can legitimately ask of someone "What was it like for you to experience that?" The answer may different from what it was like for me to have that experience. There is a locus of all these unquantifiable consciousnesses, these percepts, these conscious events, about which locus nothing can quantify, give a number. The event that I experience can have a mathematical formula placed on it. One can specify it in terms of megaherz and the like. But that formula is not what it is like for me to have that experience. Something else is involved, something more than a mathematical calculation, or an algebraic expression of quantity. It is the non-mathematicable, to coin a word. It escapes partibility, divisibility, locatability. For sure it is concurrent with the body of the "subject" that experiences. But this is not to specify a location for the percept, the unquantifiable we have just noted.

This unquantifiable is "subjectivity." If we say it is through the whole body, we are saying it is extended, which gives us the problem of why an experience cannot be cut in two, but subjectivity (if it is throughout the body, and thus extended) in this case can be. Subjectivity, as *my* consciousness, as the consciousness of each sentient being *in persona propria*, says what the sentient being experiences is that sentient being's experience, and no other's. What subjectivity is cannot be counted. It cannot be put to measure. It defies arithmetic classification. It is not, to use Descartes' term applied to another setting, a *res extensa*.

Subjectivity is the reality that each experience is private to the one having the experience. "Every subjective phenomenon is essentially connected with a single point of view," a point of view no other individual has.[4] It means that the experience is not a formula that one can pick out of a grid, place it in a body, and say "there's the subjectivity of seeing blue in that beach in that inlet, off that island, which is surrounded by these bodies of water, etc." There is an impenetrability to having the experience that subjectivity specifies. It is a reality that does not admit of number in the same way that "one" is not a number, but is that by which we number. Subjectivity is not an experience; it is that by which we experience.

There are, that is, "first person" events that do not come within the realm of public observation, that are not accessible to anyone except the individual subject. Materialism is the postulate that there is nothing except what "third person" access provides. No description of reality is other than what occurs from the third person point of view. No other vantage point captures what is real. The only valid expression of experience can be given from a third person standpoint. That statement, however, one cannot reach from a third person standpoint. It itself is from a first person perspective. Were it not, how could *I* know it in the first place?

Subjectivity to the human percipient entails an awareness of his or her own unity as that to which all his or her awareness occurs. Subjectivity is the rejection of the atomistic formula that each individual is merely a successive heap of experiences so closely linked together as to escape their separateness one from the other to us who reflect on our self.[5] Subjectivity is the status of being the center in its continuity of all that happens to my awareness, as being that awareness to which no other awareness can lay claim or participation. It is that about my awareness which is totally inviolate.[6]

As inviolate, it is a unity. Only what is a unity, is without parts, is incapable of trespass. Subjectivity, which is "me," does not admit of incursion by any other consciousness. My consciousness cannot be the consciousness of any other individual, and vice-versa. No individual other than me can become my consciousness, can take on my consciousness. What is a unity does not admit of entrance from any other entity. For that would require a possibility of partitioning, which no intrinsic unity can have.

The unity that consciousness constitutes raises its truth in the simple experiment of taking the consciousness that you are and placing it in two bodies by division. You have two new individuals, presumably conscious in fact, from the one consciousness divided in two. But it is not the original consciousness. One thing cannot be the same as two other things. Otherwise they would not be different. But in being divided they are different. Consciousness, then, has a unity about it, an identity to it through that unity that differentiates it from every other consciousness. This is clear from Bernard Williams' thought experiment[7] where a consciousness is divided in two, Part A and Part B. One is to be rewarded upon the division, the other tortured. But it is you, who divided, are both A and B. You cannot, however, be both tortured and rewarded at the same time. You cannot, as a unity, be A and B, or AB.

Kant, of course, thought that the segregation of the "soul" into smaller material bits could not be undergone. Yet, he postulated the case of the conscious self qualitatively losing existence, as something that apparently could fade so that eventually its existence was gone, just as a sound diminishes the further we walk from its origin to the point where it no longer is hard. Parts, the points is, were not necessary to consciousness for it to diminish and just pass away.

Kant believed his position was correct only because he believed something was capable of more or less existence.[8] It is a position for which no argument by Kant was ever made. Chisolm summarizes the view perfectly:

> It is as though [Kant] thought that there is a path between being and nonbeing, so that one day you may set out from nonbeing and head in the direction toward being with the result that the father you go in that direction the more being you will have. But surely there is no mean between being and nonbeing. If something *is* on a path, then that something *is*. Or if it *isn't* yet, then it can't be on a path between being and nonbeing.[9]

In the language of contemporary theory of mind, the private or subjective state of awareness correlates with the term *qualia*. These are those events in our sensation, consciousness, awareness that appear to have no explanation in physical materialist terms. "Eliminative materialism," such as espoused by Dennet, a stance asserting all terms such as "consciousness," "will," "experience" will, as science progresses give way to more "scientific" (i.e., non-descriptive quantifiers) terms,[10] simply deny they exist, while also, it appears denying they are explicable which for him may be the same as denying their existence.[11]

To advance how it is that a material substrate can have, if we admit their existence, *qualia*, admittedly non-material events, one school, the property dualist, has suggested that *qualia* can inhere in the material substrate, the mind. The mind can be a material entity with non-material inherence.

Their solution is a response to the problem of Cartesian dualism which essentially asks how can a non-material entity, mind, act on, interact with, that which is material.[12] Apparently, the *qualia* are not acted upon, or not in interaction with, the material substrate in property dualism. They possess an inherence for which the material substrate provides as being the experience of the particular individual who has that substrate. In each case, in each sentient being, the material substrate is different. The *qualia*, when an actual unit of experience, is known to be of a certain person or sentient being because the *qualia* is inhering in the material substrate of the being in question, and no other sentient being's material substrate.

If all experience is explicable only in materialist terms, or a materialist framework, one has to account for how the percept exists. One need not, however, comply with the materialist doctrine that all experience is explicable in only materialist terms, There is a presupposition in the claim of materialism. If we cannot explain a phenomenon in terms of current materialist orthodoxy, we must assume the orthodoxy is not wide enough. But that supposition can only be true if all experience is explicable only materialistically.

That by and by, to argue that a percept can be an unextended, first-person, event in a third-person, material substrate does not answer how it is that the material substrate can have within it something that has neither place nor space. If a phenomenon is indivisible, which the percept is, it cannot be said to inhere in a piece of matter. It is never "*in*." What is indivisible cannot have a place. Place is always extended. "*In*" however is speech about place. Whatever the percept is, place is not one of its features or characteristics. Precisely on account of this "property dualism" appears to raise more problems than solve as a theory of consciousness.

As does the charge that interaction between a divisible and indivisible entity (body and mind) is impossible. On the materialist view, there must be a locus for the interaction. All events require a starting place, after all. In the theory that an immaterial entity acts on a material one, thus accounting for all sensation and emotion, there is no locatable point evident for the interaction. The reason there is none, the materialist objection runs, is because the immaterial cannot act on the material. Extension and inextension cannot interact.

If all interaction and effect is by way of mass, and only mass, the materialist rejection of mind-body interaction has merit. It is, however, first of all not clear at all what argument the materialist can advance for his assertion of interaction only by mass. It seems to assume from the outset only one kind of interaction—mass on (or through) mass.

If that is the case, the assertion of a beginning to the universe becomes problematic for a science that denies any interaction except mass on mass. If one denies a universe that came into existence from nothing, but was eternally some "point" that suddenly erupted into the galaxies we know today, there is the hard pressing issue of "where" this eternally existing "point" could have been the aeons that it has been infinitely compressed, waiting to erupt. There is no "where" that it was during these aeons because space did not exist.

Conversely, if it is granted that the universe did not eternally exist, but came into being, did we have the activity of an immaterial entity effectuating the coming into existence? If so, we have a situation where an immaterial entity in the absence of a material entity brought into being that entity—and conserves it.[13] This was not an instance of "mass on mass." But that is precisely what the materialist is seeking to claim is the only form of interaction possible.

More than simply a particular philosophy of mind appears operant in the rejection of mind-body interaction. There is a claim, without any proof, that something can occur only by way of "mass on mass." Mind-body interaction is not an instance of mass on mass. Thus it must be ruled out.

Some have argued that this is a powerful impediment to the assertion of the existence of an immaterial activity in a sentient being. Yet, it is not clear how powerful this can be when it starts with a premise that only "mass on mass" is the way anything occurs. There simply is no evidence at all to support the assertion, unless you assume everything occurring is already simply "mass on mass." Assuming a proposition's truth, however, is not proving it. Proving it is what the philosopher requires.

This is a difficulty we find similarly in eliminative materialism, which we briefly mentioned above. For it, all talk of "self," "feeling," "awareness of red," "scent of lavender," are actually terms from an almost troglodytic past. Sophistication and science now have brought us perhaps to realize that these are only "folk" terms for what is actually occurring in our brain states. This position, that "consciousness," "feeling," "hoping," and the like are "benign user-illusion(s)"[14] Dennet, whom we have already mentioned, holds with the Churchlands. Patricia Churchland elaborates the view in her *Neurophilosophy*, though the eliminative materialists seem cautious in that they offer this approach as more an "alternative" (rather than an apodictic substitute) to the way in which the "the common man," "the folk people," couch these terms of their scientific insight.[15]

If the percept we have cannot issue, as we have argued, from the body's neural machinery, the eliminativists' word caution is a peculiar one. In fact, their view will not be able to prevail if what we have argued the empirical facts about the neural apparatus prevails. That is, the grounds the eliminative materialist, the "folk psychology" critics, need for distinguishing between neural and mental events derive from an impossibility. It is the impossibility of neural occurrences causing of themselves those events, which impossibility has led mankind to come up with the classification "mental." Neural occurrences cannot produce what we have labeled as mental, and it is that which validates the distinction between neural and mental. It is the events themselves that require the distinction.[16]

Without the distinction one and the same term, "neural," would apply equally to a contrary state of affairs. "Neural" would be that which is momentary, discrete, chaotic, as well as coherent and uniform. One and the same term, however, cannot have contrary meanings for the same event. The features themselves, about which we are writing here, e.g., chaotic versus coherent, force the distinction between "neural" and "mental"—terms linked to which (e.g., mind, mentation, consciousness, will, desire) the detractors (the eliminative materialists) of "folk psychology" reject. Our ordinary speech, our "folk patois," is not the cause of the distinction, the dualism, which objectors to folk psychology's classification deride and believe to be groundless. Folk psychology, the manner of everyday people speaking about states of consciousness, is grounded in the distinction present in the events themselves in which this derided folk psychology has made the distinction it has. The percept has grounds other than those which neural occurrences can provide.

Eliminative materialism, to look further into its stance, has objected, however, that it is not the events themselves, but rather the current framework (what Peter Watson in *New Scientist* has called "prescientific")[17] of discourse which is the impediment to accurate speech. This framework is the less than enlightened way of knowing not suffered by eliminative materialism, if you will, in which we operate at the misguided everyday level of speech. It is this that has bred the distinction between the neural and the mental.

Churchland's arguments for this appear in her chapters entitled "Reduction and the Mind-Body Problem" and "Mental States Irreducible to Neurobiological States."[18] One is that the high degree of similarity between human behavior and physical bodies allows for the eliminative description in terms of quantifiers and the like which replace the ordinary language that everyone uses (misguidedly) to discuss their states of mind, their affections, their pains, and the like. Physical descriptions in terms of mass and motion, e.g., explain the movement of an inanimate object. So, Churchland opines, one can shift to using the same quantifications in expressions about the human body moving (for all consciousness is simply a "motion.") Instead of saying "Howard moved to the couch to comfort his grieving wife," eliminative materialism would do away with such expressions in favor of how "mass x" and "mass y" through "force z" came to rest at "place a."

This is supposedly an equivalent and satisfactory explanation of what Howard did. Obviously, it is not. We do not learn that Howard is grieving or that his wife is either. In terms of courts and the law it is hard to see how eliminative materialism would have a role in jurisprudence since the core of jurisprudence, sc., motive, simply is discarded in a quantification process of "mental" events.[19]

Choice, or the freedom to do or not to do, seems beyond the court's jurisdiction also. In the eliminative framework, freedom is the absence of opposing force to a synchrony of neurocircuitry initiating muscular and bone activity towards a place or end. It is not the "ability" to not be moved by an object that one finds alluring, etc. Involuntary and voluntary are not terms actually indicative of behavior so much as force on mass and direction are.

That is because involuntary and voluntary are events of the mind, and "mental" is an old fashioned term for the new language that calls all such processes "neural." New understanding brings new words.[20] This is true. However, new understanding cannot discard the permanence of what we know to be factual, and this eliminative materialism does in its attempt to assert "non-*qualia*" classifications as binding and folk psychology as a language of centuries where the common man has been wrong and misled in the underlying realities of what his consciousness actually entails. Passion, e.g., is a neural event that only mathematics accurately describes. This assertion, though, eliminates the subjectivity ("inner experience") that mathematics (the "third person" standpoint) is unable to locate inasmuch as mathematics is without the tools for its location, just as subjectivity is in telling a navigator what coordinates are necessary to reach destination "x."[21]

In discarding "*qualia*" for these algebraic niceties, as it were, one may want to pose the question to the eliminativists, How much does the activity in my brain "weigh" (given mathematics is the new key to what is going on there), or how many yards, maybe miles, would my "thoughts"(neural excitations at Hrz32, e.g.) stretch out laid end to end? Would their length have something at all to do with anything that I am about? Or where do we put a stop to the mathematical quantification format? And how does one know where to stop it? What criterion serves as its endpoint?

And what exactly is to be measured? What neural circumstance tells us what we call "consciousness" has started or is occurring, or that a percept of such and such has just arisen? More fascinating is that no inward look into ourselves shows any neuroelectric activity or neurochemcal transmission. Indeed, these electrical excitations we never "feel," though the percept (e.g., as in touch) we can.[22]

The average neuron consists of one hundred thousand molecules, and is eighty percent water. One cannot fathom the number of neurons the brain houses, but we are safe in suggesting it exceeds one hundred million. That would mean 10^{15} molecules also. Each neuron has about ten thousand connections from other neurons. Within an average lifespan the neuronal DNA replaces the molecules in the unchanging neuronal cell ten thousand times. Yet nothing is lost in the *qualia*, the feel, the inner experience, as the molecular make-up comes into being and passes away.

This complicates the problem for eliminative materialism. Dennet in his *Kinds of Minds*[23] calls neurons "billions of crude intentional systems." I don't actually "feel" like buying ice cream, he will tell me. It is a morass of neuronal "intenders" amassed and "systemed" in a way that quantifies for me motions that lead to the ice cream parlor. Now, in this classification of the eliminativist, I am left as one without initiative because the "I" is not actually an experiencer that folk psychology terms. What we have, instead, is an arithmetic vector somehow pivoting to the ice cream parlor 'midst all the brainy gelatinous matter and water to "satisfy" what is not really "hunger" but a chemical imbalance, which how it came about it is difficult to see. Unless it is the synchrony of impulses somehow come in uniformity, a synchrony that is without any basis in the individual except in the substrate called the cortex that seemingly has these impulses for ice cream that "desire" cannot "scientifically" explain. And cannot because it is a term of folk psychology.

We are seeing obvious difficulties with this derisive term "folk psychology." There is an absurdity about denying it as an accurate and veridical conveyance of states of human perception. The difficulties we have shown in denying it as a tool of meaning and fact in the account of human consciousness leads one to believe that it was coined to conceal a problem that eliminativism has rather than offer a solution to a scientific problem, the nature of consciousness. Denying private awareness, first person subjectivity, requires these "coinages,"[24] these substitute terms of the eliminativists for awareness. The reasons for this Eric Harth's *The Creative Loop* makes clear:

> We would want to know in every millisecond (the time it takes a neuron to fire) which of the 100 billion or so neurons are active and which are not. If we denote activity by a "1" and inactivity by a "0," this would require a string of 100 billion zeros and ones every millisecond or 100 trillion every second. To give a running account of the true neural state, I would have to produce in every second something like 110 million books, each containing a million symbols. This awesome record is to be compared with my mental states as they occur.[25]

This is not the end of the issue, however. The body is continuously in change; it is never unchanging, even at death, as any coroner will tell you. Change courses throughout the network of the brain, ever new, ever different, ever distinct neurochemical synapses and charges. Ionzation build up, decline; macromolecular permutations and exchanges—continuously, unrelentingly, never at pause, never at surcease. Each is a different neural state. Perhaps some trillion over a lifetime that one must multiply with our Harth calculation above. This tells the actual tale of Dennet and Churchland, and eliminative materialism. If it is in any way possibly true, there would be no way to verify it. The numbers are too staggering, if not nigh unimaginable, for science to even begin to get a hold of what eliminative materialism actually requires to meet its *onus probandi*. And without a possible means of verification, it is difficult to see how anyone calls the eliminative materialist hypothesis "scientific." For essential to science is verification. Without it, science is lifeless, as the human body without blood is.[26]

OTHER DIFFICULTIES FOR NEUROPHILOSO-PHY

There is the famous Botvinick-Cohen rubber ball illusion[1] where one comes to believe that a stroked rubber ball is actually his own hand. With this has come the suggestion that perhaps the brain creates the whole of the self, a self that constitutes world, in the same way that it created the illusion of the rubber ball as my hand. "Representational content," apparently, replaces the ontological self in this illusion.[2] The suggestion takes up more imaginative skill and power to even begin to grasp than Descartes' theory of the *malin génie*. It is, arguably, the most peculiar expression of a theory that there is no world outside of consciousness. The theory we have shown needs to be addressed if we are to establish our contention that there is an existence beyond me awaiting my habitation at death. We have proceeded quite far in that direction. In this chapter we believe we make it a safe and secure belief that what you call a world outside you actually is what you think it is. Examining the Botvinick-Cohen experiment in detail opens the way to that belief, an experiment that up till now we have only mentioned. It needed to wait for our other arguments about the reality of the "other" to be set forth so that this "illusion" that it frames could be better appreciated, and its implications done with. This allows us to show further, which we take up subsequently in this chapter, why consciousness cannot only not be the brain, but why the brain cannot be matter.

How the Botvinick-Cohen model of consciousness implies what it does to its adherents is of especial interest given that we actually have no understanding of electrical positive and negative charges, except how to use and harness them. Reading any claim to understanding of neuroelectric activity and how this activity unfolds in brain events should be very cautious, then; if not cautious, at least set out with some similitude to the scientific method. This means carefulness to avoid expressions that are not testable by that method, or which can have as many different understandings applied to them as there are readers of those expressions .

There is in the Botvinick-Cohen event no self *per se*, only content. There is no self that experiences the world. There is only experience. Such experience the brain builds up. The brain creates content, anchored as it is in what we believe, mistakenly (according to various neurophilosophy proponents), are bodily feelings and sensations separate from an organ called "brain." It is this representational content that actually is what we, in our chapter on consciousness, delineated as the correlate of "my point of view." Accordingly, because there is no content other than what the brain has fashioned, there is no "correlate" to brain.

The self, then, is the content of a simulation in one's brain. It is not something that is ever an object of introspection. It is a manner in which you see, feel, taste, emote, and the like. There is no "one" who sees. There is only seeing, a form that the brain takes on. There is no tasting; only a form that the brain takes on. Whenever the organism needs to control and plan behavior, the brain activates this illusory ego, this point of view. Ego and point of view are not realities outside the brain. They are for the brain's purposes and predilections as a biological agent embedded with a filtering sensory system that never reaches the world.

This Botvinick-Cohen architectonic will have it that all experience, or what we call experience, can take place inside the brain while at the same time providing us with the feeling of experiencing a world that is "out there." All sensory content is, in theory, determinable only by the brain in concert with the neuronal networks throughout what folk psychology would call the "body." The model is that the two thousand glomeruli in the olfactory lobe (organ of smell) can be selectively stimulated so that say receptor cells 13, 19, 29, 40, and 142 when simultaneously excited yield the smell of lavender. These correlates of the experience of lavender give us the smell of lavender without the actual presence of the lavender stimulant that we believed was "out there."

It is this that has also, therefore, done away with that private, incommunicable nature we want to ascribe to subjectivity. If neural correlates can give an experience, there is no private or select point of view to any human organism. We can in fact drive this architectonic further and say that all states of experience (fear, happiness, calm) are resultant from the structure of inner living neuronal networks that the brain can activate. To one who believes there is a reality outside the brain, he would compare these activations to what electrodes can do. But electrodes are from the outside; the brain mechanism, for activation would be internal. And there is no "outside." Just as there is no self, no point of view, no external world. Only the brain with the power of selectively activating what you think is your contact with an outside world (even electrodes) but which could just as easily be the brain developed over one's lifetime gradually becoming increasingly adept and sophisticated through trial and error at making "your world."[3]

The theory is a variant of those arguing that the world we experience is one of the brain's creation. We already noted the contention that the atom is essentially space, more an electrical vibrational phenomenon than a solid. The 3D existents we claim populate the world outside our mind are really frequency fields. The theory follows from Fourier's work on a mathematical system that converts patterns into simple waveforms and back again. This is how television, which a world where only the brain is reality could never contain, came about: pictures are converted into electromagnetic frequencies and then the television apparatus converts the frequencies to pictures.

The brain is like the TV screen we believe is in the real world: it "decodes" frequency fields into our seemingly solid world. Access to these frequency fields is by way of what we cal the five sense organs. They transform the frequency fields into electrical signals, which the brain then resets into the world we call "reality." In this respect, too, the body and brain are only illusions inasmuch as they are frequency occurrences that pass through the decoding system of the neuronal matrix which makes them appear as they do to us. Brain and body (with all its features and 'parts'), i.e., are simply frequency fields decoded into the same three dimensionality as the rest of our world. In the end, then, brain is not so much "tissue" (which we thought it was) but a vibrational matrix. Seemingly, in Botvinick-Cohen it would not need, or would be without, a center.

Vision, then, is light (energy frequency field) converted into electrical signals at the site of the ocular apparatus transmitted to the brain which then sees a three dimensional world via the encoding in the visual cortex (matrix vibrations of various "lengths"). Or the brain, via that encoding, takes on this form of "seeing." It becomes seeing. There is no individual that "sees."

Because, as we saw, our senses provide access to only a very narrow, thin frequency wave oscillation, the world we "sense" is not the world in its fullness or plenitude by the slightest degree. All that we experience is the work of a decoding brain that has transformed empty space into a virtual solidity.[4]

This outlook surely is the most extravagant thesis in neurophilosophy, where stimulation of neural correlates replaces the actual experience we, as individual selves, claim we have. If possible in theory, why not in actual fact? Why have a paradigm of a consciousness interacting with its world when maybe, someday, we will be able to give an account of (what folk psychology calls) "consciousness," as we just have in this chapter's opening paragraphs? If the model is right, there is no "outside world" towards which consciousness tends as an intentional reality at all. If there is no "outside world," all this talk of "matter," "partibility," "decomposition," and the like as arguments preparatory for advancing the immortality of consciousness are ineffectual, if not simply useless.

The implications in the Bovinick-Cohen model certainly circumvent the problem that the percept must resemble the "object out there." That argument showed a pattern of electrical discharges certainly could not be the percept since the electrical charges in no way resemble what our percept conveys. If what is in our percept does not resemble electrical charges then the percept is not its creation but is in fact something other than those charges. Presumably, those charges are internal to the brain; and if the brain's activity is only electrical, the percept emerges as something not brain originated. That was because electrical events n the brain appeared as disaggregated, chaotic, and the like. If, however, there is no "outside world." We need not worry about the percept and the issue of resemblance. There is nothing for which the percept in the brain needs to resemble outside. Furthermore, though, if all events are brain concoctions, brain realities, what we called disaggregated, atomistic, and chaotic electrical charges may not have anything to do with percepts after all. They may simply be brain occurrences not in need of reconciling with the problem of the coherence of percepts. They are brain events strictly outside the electrical discharges neuroscientists claim they measure in brain activity. Those neuroscientists, however, are merely events of our brain if one can create one's own world. Such creating is exactly what extrapolating from the rubber ball illusion affords as a possible explanation for some of what "consciousness" is. If self, which is innermost to me, is an illusion, how can anything "further" from me be any more real than self, which the rubber ball illusion, has made room to think is simply itself an illusion? If I cannot be certain of that which is closest to me as being real, all the less that which is further.

Along these lines, apperception of the "now" in some quarters of neurophilosophy appears to be a tool that the brain (this matrix of variously situated oscillations, vibrations) has devised for dealing with our world. There is no present moment in actuality, according to this theory. What we call the "now" is an artifice, elaborated over aeons by the brain, for the purposes of righting our contacts with our neuro-world. The brain creates the "now," which accounts for our experience as slow, fast, drawn out. It is a medium which we cannot perceive, but is that by which we perceive—more exactly, that by which the brain "events" each experience it, the brain, becomes. The matrix of oscillations changes and this is how we have "changing experiences." As such the "now" is transparent. It is a medium the brain has set for itself by which it deals with the electrical stimulations that course through the seemingly infinitely intricate matrix that makes for, through such coursing, what we call "experience."

Such a position, that there is no actual "now," rules out causality and its effect as being one, of course. An effect cannot be delayed from a cause if something that makes it be has a gap where the object is neither the cause nor the effect. That is what denial of a present, of a "now," in the real fact world entails.

That aside, if the brain creates this "now," *when* does it create it? Is it simultaneous with our experience of it? If so, how is it that there is no time delay in the experience of it but there needs to be one, as some neurophilosohers have argued, in the excitations from the stimuli to the neural network?

To get to its doctrine that the brain creates our percept, that in fact what we are in touch with is not the world, but what the brain has made of "objects out there," the neurophilosopher has come up with the model of the brain as a material (striated) construct of higher order electro-representations. These touch in, upon, and move away from each other in a time pattern of incredible speed that intentionally surpasses our ability to experience the succession of these representations one into and out of the other. The striated construct that the brain is is endlessly bombarded with electro stimuli. This enables the neurophilosopher to avoid the claim that the brain already contains the material (electro-content) whence it will create its world. If the brain did, the neurophilosopher would have to admit the brain already had in some way the experience that he claims it actually puts together from the electro data. One reason, according to neuro-theoreticians using this model, that we believe we are in touch with an "external world," an "observer-independent" world, is on account of the speed of neural-processing of the electro data that come from "without" the brain. At the level the brain permits one to experience, one cannot actually discover or verify the origin of the stimulations. At other levels [("higher consciousness") when permitted by the brain], this of course would not be a problem. We believe in an external world because the brain does not give us access to its own machinery of how it makes the world, a world that comes from within.

Remember, it is the fact that we seem to be able to create a percept of a hand that is not there, as we noted in the "rubber ball" experiment discussed in the opening lines of our chapter, that gave impetus to the theory that perhaps this is the way consciousness is adequately explained: the brain creates what is there. The computer and speed of light transmission of electro-bits through its semi-conductors makes the perfect model for suggesting the brain apparatus along these lines. And just as the computer is self-less, i.e., there is no ego separate from the computer experiencing this, but simply the computer activity being the electro-bits processing and nothing separate from it, nothing that can step back from the activity of processing, so with us. There is no brain separate from the processes of higher order electro-integration, representation, and the like. Rather, it is in fact all those processes as a substrate for their occurrence, and not separate from their occurrence. The brain does not use the brain, just as the computer does not use the computer. The notion of an ego using the brain is an add-on that explains nothing of how we have our percept.

Constancy over a time that the brain creates, after all, cannot be the verification one needs for a self continuant through the changes we experience if the source of time, the "now," is a way of transparent representation created by this brain which we never see (and are constitutionally unable to see). Transparency is not "constancy," irrespective of whether one holds the brain fashions our awareness of "now" as a means of our dealing with the world and all that occurs to the individual experiencing that world.

To say that constancy is a sense that the brain creates through the mechanism of the "now," a "now" through which the "present" is a transparency only, and not what we view as that in which we live and which, when gone, means the end of each individual, seems to create difficulty, however, for the Botvinick-Cohen model. It is that death, which happens in the "now," might also simply be a product of the brain, and not what actually happens to the individual in this world.

This creation of "time" zones, of "temporal wholes,"[5] if you will, some claim to see in the experiments of what Dennett called the "cutaneous rabbit" and Libet.[6] In Dennet's "cutaneous rabbit"[7] the subject's arm rests cushioned on a table, and mechanical tappers are placed at two or three locations along the arm, up to a foot apart. A rhythmic series of taps follows, e.g. five at the wrist followed by two near the elbow and three more on the upper arm, in intervals between 50 and 200 milliseconds. The subject, however, feels the taps traveling in regular sequence over equidistant points up the arm. The intervals are not regular, however. The brain experiences a tap at the elbow before it happens, which is not supposed to be possible. Another example are two alternately flashing lights in a dark room, separated by a distance not too large. The subject perceives them as *one* single, rapid moving dot. If the lights have different colors, it seems to the subject that there is a change in color in the middle of the move (although the second light is not yet shining at this very moment). This reversal of time cannot be a physical event, so we must conclude the brain again has a part to play in the experience of time, if not in fact is what creates time.

Benjamin Libet's experimental findings of neural delays, retrograde stimulus masking, and subjective referral backwards in time, is more controversial.[8] The comparison between an electrical stimulus applied to the hand and a stimulus applied directly to the corresponding cortex area demonstrates that we perceive the hand but not the cortex stimulus 0,5 seconds later. However, we do not realize this delay, because our brain shifts it back into the past. There seems to be, accordingly, a double illusion: our experience of time is, contrary to common sense, pretty much behind the events. We are not able to realize this because our temporal frame of reference is also shifted. Libet's experiments and others have also shown that unconscious brain processes (marked by a "readiness potential") occur at least 0,35 seconds before the conscious intention to act, although it seems to us that our intention causes our action. Again, time seems to be the work of the brain and not an external phenomenon, one independent of a subject.

It may very well be, however, that the brain is not so much in this creating time. Instead, it has blocked out a time interval from outside its flow, its internal time experience, because of the anticipation factor in these experiments. We very well know that the mind, in anticipation, will disregard or overlook certain minutiae. It will seek to economize on what it already expects in order to get to the point it anticipates. One wonders why this cannot be the case here. Instead of saying the mind has in some way "made" time, it seems just as reasonable to suggest that it blocked out time (an actual quantity numbering actual motion) that comes to its awareness as a flow because of how it will respond in the state of anticipation to events.

Consider the Libet case where brain processes normally associated with an event occur before the event does. What "time" has the mind created? Did neural correlates receive some stimulation unknown by which the processes that occur usually *with* an event occurred *before*? Take the Libet case where apparently we are not in a state of anticipation. This is the experiment where a cortical stimulus and hand stimulus are at half-second intervals. The hand stimulus is first felt, and then only later (0.5 seconds) the cortical area associated with the hand stimulus shows a reaction. The reaction, in other words, lags the movement of the hand, which seems to place the effect before the cause.

The experiments of Libet on the human brain....show that direct stimulation of the somaesthetic cortex results in a conscious experience after a delay as long as 0.5s for weak stimulation, and similar delay is observed for a sharp, but weak, peripheral skin stimulus....Although there is this delay in experiencing the peripheral stimulus, it is actually judged to be much earlier, at about the time of cortical arrival of the afferent output....This antedating procedure does not seem to be explicable by any neurophysiologic process.[9]

> The cortical activities evoked by some sharp stimulus to the hand in conscious human subjects took as long as half a second to build up to the level for giving consciousness; yet the subject antedated it in its experience to a time which was the time of the arrival of the message from the periphery on to the cerebral cortex, which may be almost half a second earlier. This is an extraordinary happening, and there is no way in which this can be explained by the operation of the neural machinery.[10]

Some, it is obvious, have interpreted this as evidence that the brain does not control bodily movement, but as evidence an agency "external" to, free of, it does. This agency would be the non-material self. And, indeed, this is a possible interpretation. Simultaneously this interpretation rids us of the "time creation" interpretation that has been the wont of some in neurophilosophy.

We want to look more closely at the Libet experiment. Libet's results show that sensations from stimuli applied simultaneously to body parts responsible for the same sensation (here an electrode to the cortex region associated with brain sensation and another to the hand part associated with that cortex region) were not indicating a disassociation of sensation and physical stimulus. They should have both occurred at the same time were stimulus (neurochemical change) and sensation identical. That they were not synchronous implies sensation and stimulus (the electrode's application to the cortex, which effects simultaneously a neural change) are not reducible to each other, and therefore the sensation might not be wholly neurophysiologic.

The difference in the timing (0.5 second) of the sensation would suggest severance of neurophysiologic change (i.e., the stimulus) from the conscious event (the sensation). The reductionist equation of the two, and thus of consciousness with materiality, encounters in Libet's work an empirical instance that does not allow for the equation to be drawn. One, because simultaneity is absent, thus disidentifying stimulus with consciousness. And two, because of that absence, the stimulus' causal role would emerge as problematic given the simultaneity that cause and effect require.[11]

Dennet and Churchland[12] for their part have challenged Libet in the length of the antedating time interval (Churchland declaring it, from the work with other participants, to be less). That, however, sidesteps Libet's implication that any lag in reporting invites explanation by means other than materialist (reductionist), given the simultaneity of cause and effect. The time interval is the point at issue, while between cause and effect no time can elapse if an effect is coterminous, cotemporaneous, with its cause. Dennet, in this regard, has suggested that there may be different neural "times," say "cortical" versus "limbic" (for the hand), each with its own threshold requirements or "neuronal" adequacies for awareness. Perhaps, he seems to be opining, there are different awareness build-up periods neuronally pre-set that explain the time disparities.

That would argue for identical sensations being generated though different time spans with the same stimulus. That, however, is a case of equal effects issuing from different causes (namely, different time periods), differing factors (those time periods) causing identical results (the sensation of hand tingling). Different causes, however, do not generate identical effects, just as different premises do not yield identical conclusions. That reading of Dennet would put to question his suggestion on limbic versus cortical time. The suggestion does not explain how the sensation is caused. Libet's, findings, surely however brief the antedating interval appears, remains, then, still an unanswered challenge to reductionism.

Botvinick-Cohen has emboldened neurophilosophy in its hypothesis that we can actually posit the world as the GNCC, the global neural correlate. Intricately complex, endlessly detailed, the global neural correlate is that whose multi-excitation at neuronal levels descending and ascending one into and out of the other in the physical brain (whether striated flesh or vibrational matrix) that constitutes the world as to the window to it—but never the world itself.

The Libet antedating phenomenon does not permit to the GNCC thesis that consciousness and brain might be two different realities. The results and findings of Libet's experiment clearly imply they are, though. It is clearly absurd to say that the GNCC is responsible for the Libet findings, because the Libet experiments invalidates it. The GNCC thesis is, by Libet then, in peril. Immediately, given Libet's findings, that would sever consciousness from any inextricable tie with the brain. The GNCC, which in today's neurophilosophic discussions constitutes what and how the brain brings what "folk psychology" calls "consciousness" cannot be the means by which this separable consciousness takes on its reality, its existence. The brain cannot bring something to be which is independent of or underived from it. But this is precisely what Libet's experiments imply—that consciousness and brain matter are not the same.

To argue for the non-reality of folk psychology's "consciousness," the superfluity of it as a hypothesis for explaining brain activity, neurophilosophy has sought, as one would expect from the Botvinick-Cohen paradigm, to argue the close approximation (if not identity) of brain function/processing with the computer. If the computer can bring about and fashion the images and sounds it does, is it not only a matter of time before we come upon that as yet unidentified particle or solution that finally severs us from the "ghost in the machine" model[13] and reduces all awareness to what it actually is—electrochemical events of a suitable organized matter? Somewhere along the way, the claim that the neuroelectric charge and percept (as we saw) differ, thus not allowing for the reduction of consciousness to electrochemical activity, will be overcome. The claim that they do not resemble one another and thus cannot be the same will succumb to mathematical formulae explaining away the concern about their non-resemblance. We will have a one source solution to the activity of awareness: it is totally materially derived. The partition from that which is not material (such as "self," "mind") will fall by the way, just as in the manner of geocentrism. It was the "folk" view of the world in relation to the universe, till science "disproved" it and placed the earth where it actually belongs.

That a computer can serve as a model for some of the brain's activities, however, does not necessitate that the brain and the computer are simply the same phenomenon, one made of flesh, the other of steel and silicon, or electromagnetic fields. Human mentation, done with (but not through) the human brain, has a difference from computational systems in that it does not arrive at all reality computationally (if it ever did, in the first place), or, said otherwise, algorithmically.

In neuroscience, research into biological computers is well underway. A study at the University of Florida (Gainesville), summarized by the editor of *Frontiers in Neurobiotics*, Dr. Thomas DeMarse,[14] (in the so-called "brain in a dish" experiment, 24 October 2004) took twenty-five thousand neural cells from a rat embryo and taught their arrangement to manipulate (operate) an F22 jet simulator. The cells were suspended in a specialized life sustaining liquid, and then placed across a grid of sixty electrodes. Under the microscope they appeared at first to be grains of sand, but in the liquid they quickly connected to form "a live computational device." The scientists involved then connected the rat brain cells through a desktop computer to the jet simulator and they were programmed to fly a plane. In the beginning the plane repeatedly crashed. The neural network, however, slowly adapted as the brain learned to control the pitch and roll of the aircraft so that it achieved a straight and level trajectory. Eventually, without any human help, the rat cells were able to control the aircraft even in hurricane-force winds. The neural network without external input took on a task that exhibits planning and design.

Binary numerics operate every computer. Experiments have shown that when the correct electrical current passes through the living cell membrane, its gates and channels open. Absent the current, they close. This is identical to the binary system in a computer. Using "zero" and "one" provides the absence and presence, respectively, of a current or voltage. The University of Colorado's Professor Randall O'Reilly points out that the region of the brain critical to human intellectual abilities functions much like our computers. Computers operate by turning electrical signals into binary "on and off" states. "The neurons in the prefrontal cortex are binary. They have two states, either active or inactive. The basal ganglia is essentially a big switch that allows you to dynamically turn on and off different parts of the prefrontal cortex."[15] In other words, the neuronal cell membrane acts like a silicon chip. All cell membranes, in fact, do. Electrical impulses in the cells acting as "open" and "close" instructions to the DNA gates provide for cell stability, and in the neuronal stability with the world encountered.

But there is more than simply a binary operation. Guosong Liu, a neuroscientist at MIT's Picower Center for Learning and Memory, writes in *Nature Neuroscience* of the brain's trinary code. The neuronal cell uses the "numbers" "nought," "one," and "minus one." Two signals can add together or cancel each other out, or different pieces of information can link up or try to override one another. This allows the brain to ignore information when necessary, which the binary (as in the computer) does not.

Liu discovered an important element of how brain circuits work. It involves wiring the correct positive, or "excitatory" wires, with the correct negative, or "inhibitory" wires. His work, anticipated twenty years earlier by Tomaso Poggio (who held neurons use an excitatory/inhibitory form to process information), demonstrates that brain cells contain many individual processing modules, that each collects a set number of excitatory and inhibitory inputs. Liu, by demonstrating the existence of tiny excitation/inhibition modules within brain cells, confirmed Poggio's thesis When the two types of inputs are correctly connected together, powerful processing can occur at each module.

Liu's work also addressed a basic issue in neuroscience: What is the brain's transistor, or fundamental processing unit? Once all the modules have completed their processing, they funnel signals to the cell body, where all of the signals are integrated and passed on. "With cells composed of so many smaller computational parts, the complexity attributed to the nervous system begins to make more sense," Liu said at the announcement of his trinary code.

Liu found that these microprocessors automatically form all along the surface of the cell as the brain develops. The modules also have their own built-in intelligence that seems to allow them to accommodate defects in the wiring or electrical storms in the circuitry: if any of the connections break, new ones automatically form to replace the old ones. If the positive, "excitatory," connections are overloading, new negative, "inhibitory," connections quickly form to balance out the signaling, immediately restoring the capacity to transmit information.[16]

Liu's work, by showing that each cell is built from hundreds of tiny modules, each of which computes independently, has added to a growing orthodoxy that there might be something even smaller than the cell at the heart of computation, a "natural nanotechnology," "quantum computing." Professor Drew Endy in biological engineering at MIT says that soon we will be able to write DNA—perhaps even building and coding living organisms capable of conducting work for us on the nano-scale. It will result in the possibility of "scripting" DNA, and usher in the era of synthetic biology, leveraging natural structures as a way of building things on the molecular scale. "If you can write DNA, you're no longer limited to 'what is,' but to what you could make," Endy suggests. "The science you get out of that is more than 'Here's this gene and what it does.' It's 'What are the physical limitations of biological systems?'" "Synthetic biology" offers the possibility that our computers within two, three decades might be able to observe what we do all day, understand what is important to us, and act as a virtual assistant which helps us on a second-by-second basis. Some envision wearable computers and their applications progressing to the point where everyone has a virtual personal assistant with innumerable capabilities.[17]

All of these operations just noted proceed by way of algorithm. It is difficult to imagine any operation that does not so proceed. Examination of the neuronal activity as in Liu's work gives more than enough data to allow us to confirm that electrical signaling, "coding" by ionization, valence, impulse, is an actual fact of both human and artificial intelligence.

Not all awareness or mental events come under that process, however. Gödel's theorem has shown us that the human being comes to awareness non-algorithmically in the "incompleteness theorem." Mathematics, the theorem states, cannot verify itself. It is not a self-verifying system. No algorithm leads us to that insight, and yet we know it is true. In fact, there is no process of time that it takes to see the truth of this theorem. Once the variables for it are understood, the understanding comes immediately. It is not processed through a series of steps leading up to it. The steps are not in any way what give us, produce, the insight.[18]

To enlarge, as we must: assume Gödel's theorem is false (which it would be were there no indemonstrable truth.) We would know this only by algorithm or insight (non-algorithmically). In the former that would be a process of reasoning (series of calculations); in the latter, independently of any such process or steps in thought. Knowledge only comes about indirectly (as by an algorithm, or series of steps) or directly (this we call "insight" or "intuition"). If we know it by the latter (direct acquaintance with the reality in question) we are exercising an intellective capacity the computer (Artificial Intelligence [AI]) is known not to have. If by the former, how do we know that algorithm to be true and adequate to disprove Gödel's theorem, to prove, in effect, that there are no indemonstrable truths? (Here, recall that our claimed indemonstrable truth is, "No mathematical system is self-verifying")? If all human thought, like a computer's calculative operations, is by an algorithm, then it is by an algorithm only that we can discern the truth or falsity of any assertion.

If we say it is by an algorithm's practical application, i.e., by the results its usage bring about in actual empirical circumstances in contrast to those in abstract models, that we can discern its truth and adequacy, how do we know that practical application suffices as a criterion? If, in response, we say by an algorithm, we then have to ask how we know that the algorithm is sufficient to defend the usage of practical algorithm as a criterion. By another algorithm? The same problem slides us into an infinite regress.

To suggest, on the other hand, self-evidence as the criterion for an algorithm's adequacy as an answer to this conundrum is to admit to an indemonstrable truth; for the self-evident is not demonstrable. The regress, then, can be broken only by granting that some truths are known indemonstrably, i.e., without an algorithm. To assert in the face of all these difficulties that there are still no indemonstrable truths requires for that assertion acceptance of at least one. For since the assertion is not self-evident, it would have to be proven. Proof, though, requires for it at some juncture a proposition which itself is not susceptible to proof, a proposition which is true on its own. Otherwise, proof could never begin.

Accordingly, to disprove or deny Gödel's theorem of the presence of an indemonstrable truth in order to maintain reductionism's equivalence of AI (com-

puter computation) with human thought requires accepting as true what one denies. While that does not prove that what is being denied is true, it does prevent
the equation of Artificial Intelligence with human thought. Their identity cannot
be shown to be true by its advocates because it cannot be shown, nor known,
that there are no indemonstrable truths. Only if it could, could the identity of
human thought with AI, with computational processing, be maintained.

The fact , though, that Gödel's theorem is true directly rules out the identity.
Human thought is not reducible to the computer processing of data. Contained
within human intellection is the capacity to see, without need of algorithm, the
truth of certain relations or statements. The computer is without that ability, and
that differentiates the being of its calculative processes from that of human intellection. Materiality of human thought, therefore, cannot be shown by comparing
it to computer algorithm. The two are not identical.

Gödel's theorem's assertion has a correlate in Aristotle's doctrine that not
everything can be proven.[19] There must be an indemonstrable premise whence a
demonstration can flow. Otherwise, we could never start the demonstration. It is
not an assertion that one can "prove." No means of formulation gets us to the
insight. To use a formula is itself a matter of proof. Thus, we cannot "demonstrate" what we know inevitably to be a requirement of a syllogistic process. We
do know, though, as we have just proven, that it does not come by way of algorithm.

Because both these assertions (Gödel's and Aristotle's) are indemonstrably
true, and hence show the mind as a non-computational entity in at least some of
its operations, one has to inquire as to what licenses the neurophilosopher to
suggest that the brain is a computational process (beyond any speed of our prehension) and by its many levels of computational intricacy and electrical sophistication it comes to a world that it identifies as the world I experience? One can
quite well suggest that there is a possible analogue by which experience unfolds,
the analogue of computational speed. Is there a sense to the computer (on the
smallest bit of space imaginable) that gives it what subjectivists call a "feel" that
identifies to the computer that what it is processing is uniquely its and nothing
else's? Simply, can a computer "feel," "sense" its processes or the like?

We can return to this neural correlates (GNCC or NCC)[20] model discussed
above. This held that for every "conscious" experience we claim we can find (or
will find, eventually) a neural correlate that actually is the conscious event. It
will be our backdrop for discussing the upcoming famous shade of blue problem
in Hume.[21] Can it account for how we come to the awareness that there is, on
the scale of blue, a shade missing? If it cannot, then we can suggest that the
NCC model of consciousness itself is insufficient as a model for explaining consciousness or the awareness of a world.

Hume recognized that in the process of looking over the successive shad-
ings of blue that are possible, we may note a shade that is actually missing from
the shade scale before us. It is conceivable on a first look at the shade scale that I
detect the missing shade. Concomitantly (to bring Hume's quandary to the pitch
scale), one may detect a sound in the pitch scale that does not belong there. One

just knows it does not. How account for this if the conscious world is a neural correlate product by which stimulation of neural correlates in the topography of the brain generates the world I experience?

Some appear to argue that we simply can charge that this "percept" (my awareness of the "missing shade of blue") might be a neural correlate after all, but a neural correlate by which we come to judge other neural correlates for similar mental percepts. As such no stimulation of it will give us the correlate because it is a "that by which" correlates in its universe are known to be correlates. Just as a mirror is "that by which" something is reflected (but is not as "pure," as "precise," as the original), but which reflection is not the mirror but that by which the reflection occurs, so also in these supposed "missing shades" along a scale. The reason I come across it, but it does not reach me when other neural correlates of blue receive electro-stimulation and which give me my experience of "blue," is because the missing shade of blue in question is the measure for all other shades. Thus it is that by which the correlates are measured as to their blueness. That by which something is measured cannot be that which is measured, and hence why we miss the shade of blue in question.

Analogs seem to be the tool of the neurophilosopher, and as in other instances, here they do not work either. The "missing shade of blue" cannot be a "that by which" other shades are compared or contrasted because in every case of blue we encounter it can be contrasted or compared. There is nothing about any shade of blue that stops the contrasting and comparison. The missing shade of blue demonstrates the NCC theory is not an apt replacement, analog, for consciousness.

That, again, e.g., NCC seem to establish a lawful relationship between REM states and awake states[22] does not tell us that neural correlates can substitute, or provide a lawful domain of, when electro-stimulated, for the outside percept. Mapping the entire astronomy of the NCC (viewed as a constellation of endless amount of neuronal points) and arguing stimulation of those points can substitute for the percept we choose does not tell us how the unwanted percept comes into consciousness; or how the wanted one does not. The importance of this failure cannot be over-emphasized. NCC theory does not account for or, explain, what is immediate to each conscious being: his or her not expecting or wanting a percept that he or she does have. What correlates of the NCC grid generate the "not wanted, but suddenly experienced without warning, percept of fire?" If suddenly I burn my hand, what neural correlate of consciousness do I invoke that gives me the "not wanted burned hand percept"?

It seems not less than obvious that a certain framework for discussion is operant in neurophilosophy where the outcome is predetermined. One catches it in Wolf Singer's categorical claim that the "binding" feature we observe in the percept, that feature by which we have a coherence, cohesion, and singleness to it, seems "a problem" inasmuch as the brain "lacks a single convergence center" in which the results of its parallel processing of billions upon billons of info-bits (to coin a term) can receive coherent valuation. It appears that if there is a uniformity to our percept, and the underlying assumption is that chaos and sheer unrelated atomism of electrical charges are the substrate of its emergence, and in the brain which is the producer of the percept nothing can be found that effectuates this constancy, we have in the percept then evidence that the brain may not be the total originator of our percept after all. Singer, however, opts for a doctrine of synchrony of oscillating rhythmic patterns of neurons. "Synchronized oscillatory discharges in the visual cortex" increasingly suggest itself as what binds together the percept so that we experience as we do.

Singer, and the point is essential, does not explain how he can hold this position as reflective of the percept's emergence when absolutely nothing in oscillatory reverberations of electrical charges have the features of the qualities in percepts.[23] No electrical input or charge has the feature of the thousands of objects that become the percept. The indimidiate problem for neurophilosophy is the inexplicable change of, from, electrical charge to what we experience, to what the percept gives us in consciousness. It does not give us an electrical charge. Nor an intercommunion of such charges, billions per nano-second each, though one may want to postulate this. What we have is a world where none of what Singer or neurophilosophy wants to claim appears: a world that can be compared to those electrical charges and which world shows no similarity at all to them. We ourselves can assemble a billion of those charges at one time in any arrangement we choose and cause the charge to occur in a millisecond. We will not see, or come across, the percept that the subject, that consciousness, has.

If one wishes to opt for the theory of sensation where awareness is caused by a series of excitations or stimuli upon the sense apparatus of the conscious being, how it is that these excitations, electrical and chemical in nature, change over into a totally non-electrical setting, a totally non-electrical appearance? It has no neurophilosophic account. To suggest that cohesion in the percept is occasioned by a system of higher order integrations, as suggested above, does not tell us how the percept occurs as it does. It occurs as a being that is totally unlike anything contained in these higher order integrations. Synchrony, neuronal firings in balance, in complementarity of podes and valences—all have one thing in common: they are electrical in nature. The percept is simply not.

Singer himself admits that how these electrical "moments" in the brain become subjective states of emotion, color, sound, and the like will be a "conundrum" for quite some time. It is a "conundrum" if one's starting point is an assumption that neuronal patterns and activities are the path to subjective states of awareness, that correlation is an indication of causation.

It is clear that neurophilosophy takes as a working axiom that correlation and causation are two sides of the same coin. Correlation equals causation. Our percepts as they are do not exhibit any materiality about them. Accordingly, an approach that argues all experience is explicable exclusively in terms of matter will have an impediment to any progress if in this case of the percept and the brain's activity one cannot see correlation as a necessary feature of causality, and not as the same as it, as identical to it. In correlation is absent what causation contains. That is the difference that neurohilosophy does not admit.

What advance neurophilosophy has made in the argument against immateriality seems checked and brought up short in the instance of hydrocephalus. Individuals suffering from it, the case of a profoundly diminished brain tissue, have succeeded both academically and socially, as Robert Lewin's *Science* article pointed out.[24] In such cases, these individuals have a grossly reduced cerebral mantle; ventricle expansion fills ninety-five percent of the cranium, which is filled mainly with cerebrospinal fluid. Normal brain tissue associated with sense-input has been compromised in these individuals, forcing doubt about the accuracy of neural mapping. If consciousness is associated with neural reverberations in one brain area, and these reverberations cannot occur with the compromised brain tissue of the hydrocephalic, it is clear that the neural activity in that area, when uncompromised, does not "produce" (cause) consciousness. Nor is it consciousness. For there is normal awareness in these hydrocephalic humans while their brain tissue, whose different areas are supposed to be the sites of consciousness, has been compromised. This, though, violates current neurophysiologic doctrine which holds that impaired brain sites should mean impaired intellection and functioning.

Even granting redundancy of brain tissue, where one healthy area of the brain is hypothesized to take up the neural functioning of a damaged area, the problem is not resolved. Left unanswered is the absence of such redundancy in the remaining areas of hydrocephalus. To say in cases where hydrocephalus does not have its devastating effects that redundancy of brain tissue is the reason it does not, and in cases where it does that there is no redundancy, is not explanatory at all.

The redundancy thesis could be useful only if it could account for why redundancy did not occur in those cases in which it did not The reply cannot be that in those cases something in the brain tissue inhibited redundancy from occurring. One would then have to ask what it is about redundancy that would make it inoperant in those cases. By definition, though, redundancy means that those factors which should make particular brain areas ineffective as the site of consciousness have been overcome. We should not have to ask, then, what it is about brain tissue that would prevent redundancy from occurring. Redundancy is the theory meant to explain why the failure to possess normal consciousness—which the brain tissue prevention of redundancy would cause—does not occur.

So-called "split-brain" experiments also muddle the materialist hypothesis. Severing the corpus callosum (known as cerebral commisneurotomy) to relieve epileptic distress involves disconnecting neural fibers relating the right and left hemispheres of the brain. In the journal *Neurology*[25] Donald Wilson and others reported the case of a patient who, upon recovery from this surgery, exhibited two "consciousnesses." The left hemisphere had likes and goals totally different from the right. In sum, the left hemisphere was sufficient for awareness, an awareness coinciding with its goals and views, and the right likewise.

Consciousness in this case seems to need only half a brain such that redundancy of brain tissue is not an operant explanation. No brain areas were removed

save possibly remnants of nerve fiber from the severance of the corpus callosum. In this circumstance of bicameral splitting there are two sets of awareness,
each with far less brain tissue than was present in the original awareness.

From this clinical case the question surfaces as to precisely what the quantity of brain tissue must be for consciousness; or if there is any relationship to
tissue quantity at all. As the instances of bicameral splitting and hydrocephalus
indicate, the relationship between brain tissue and consciousness is much less
certain than the materialist doctrine has allowed.

In the case of impaired brain tissue, how is the adjustment made so that
consciousness remains unimpeded? Is it by way of some brain mechanism, some
neural activity? Is there some neuroreceptor mechanism which is an interaction
with all brain areas and through neural electrical messages it receives or fails to
receive from different brain areas, brain tissue impairment is detected, with subsequent messages to other brain areas sent to compensate for this impairment?
Were there, the difficulty the question of brain tissue quantity presents to the
materialist interpretation would lose force. With a neuroreceptor mechanism
explaining how brain tissue impairment is overcome, the materialist interpretation of consciousness could still claim plausibility, whatever the outcome of the
question of tissue quantity, since this neuroreceptor mechanism would be material in nature.

It has a difficulty, however. It is a variation of the one we saw in the redundancy thesis. If the ability to overcome brain tissue impairment is said to be part
of the individual's brain composition, to say in the cases that do not overcome
this impairment that that brain's neurocapacity was insufficient, is uninforma-
tive. It has not been demonstrated that it is the brain's composition that gives
consciousness. That is what must be demonstrated if the insufficiency of physical brain composition is to be explanatory in the cases of impaired consciousness.

There is, further, the issue of brain/mind interaction. Not all interaction is
by way of the model of billiard ball hitting the second ball. That is, contact (the
absence of intervening medium) is not the only means for "interaction." To say
it is assumes what one cannot prove. That on a gross level we see interaction
occur that way does not mean it occurs no other way. Descartes sought to offer a
pineal conjunction as the site of brain/mind commerce.[26] This is, however, matter on matter. How does the mind, indivisible and without extension, get sited at
a locus where only matter, extension exists? The issue of consciousness is, pa-
ramountly, more than one of location at a bodiy site.

The non-corporeal status of mind, which Descartes accepted, but could not
explain, finds further evidence in recent study of human behavior disorders. Particular behavior disorders linked to brain disorders took correction over time
through non-pharmacological intervention. The disorders diminished greatly or
completely.

Drugs and chemicals did not effectuate the change. We appear to be free of
the "mass on mass paradigm, in other words. Rethinking one's desires and
goals, repetition of such rethinking, e.g., in the case of obsessive-compulsive

disorder, gave way to the elimination of its extremes. Neuralplasticity took re-shaping not through surgical attack or medical suffusion On one's own, neural circuits generative of a path to the disorder gradually became useless as one ac-tivated those that were productive of a more fruitful and balanced behavior. In-stead of washing one's hands repeatedly, a neural pathway towards perhaps fo-cusing on the flight of sparrows, or the wisps of a rose's scent, or the pleasures of knitting, gradually became the choice of those engaged in changing their ob-sessive behavior.

Meditative therapy, as reported by UCLA psychiatrist Jeffrey Schwartz, showed, on the PET scan, resultant changes in the causate, orbital frontal cortex, and the right hemisphere thalamus of the patients who employed its curative effects. They had, by this approach, changed their brain. Through non-neuronal effort they had caused synaptic readjustment to where clearly predatory and harmful behavior, through meditative access, redirected neuronal signaling. Concomitant with these findings, Antoine Lutz, Lawrence L. Greischar, Nancy B. Rawlings, Mathieu Ricard and Richard J. Davidson reported that meditation thickens cortical areas that actually thin with age.[27]

This changeover, reported in Jeffrey Schwartz and Sharon Begley's *The Mind and the Brain: Neuralplasticity and the Power of Mental Force*,[28] and elu-cidated in Mario Beauregard and Denyse O'Leary's *The Spiritual Brain: A Neu-roscientist's Case for the Existence of the Soul*[29] is not the sole evidence of hu-man mentation as exercising change or directionality of neural circuitry. Clinical examination of brain activity in sexual arousal photographs showed that, upon choice, the brain areas held as correlating with the arousal (the limbic and para-limbic areas) in the case of refusing the arousal react. The activity they show in arousal is non-existent in the choice to not be aroused. Arousal is not automatic. Intervention has occurred that is neither medicinal nor from an external threat.[30]

Brass and Hagard[31] have opined an explanation on change in behavior: in-hibition of volitional acts stems from unconscious acts in the anterior median cortex. This part of the brain is what would account, maybe, for these new "neu-ral pathways" inhibitory to behavior disorders noted above. The material brain, i.e., is, Brass and Hagard want to declare, explanatory after all.

The explanation, however, does not fit because, as we saw, the conscious agent in the case of eliminating behavioral oddity has consciously deployed other images and incentives to initiate his change in outlook and behavior. Addi-tionally, it is not clear how unconscious acts (acts by definition not known) could be summoned forth as explanatory of any behavior.

Placebo effects, *The Spiritual Brain* authors recount, where one does not take a medicine [but thinks one is, in our discussion here it is a saline injection], but relief or even cure takes place, is well known in the study of Parkinsons. A profound dopamine disorder of the brain, evidence has come forth that in some of these cases of saline injection Parkinsons tremors ceased. On PET scan ob-servation it was clear that dopamine had been re-triggered (through activation of the damaged nigrostriatal dopamine apparatus), but that was not supposed to happen.[32]

Similar placebo treatment showed an effect on brain-response regions through an fMRI (functional magnetic resonance imaging). Jaw-injured patients received saline solution and subsequently they reported relief. No pain relief drug was administered, however.[33]

What causes these changes in neural topography, or inhibits them, if the material brain is the center and point of all action, reaction, and interaction of human behavior? The brain is not acting the way reductionism has proposed it must. In the changeover from obsessive-compulsive disorders there has been evinced actual tissue changes. Neural topography is different in the PET scan pre-and-post meditative therapy. What portion of the brain changed the brain striation causing the disorder of the person to a calmer and more settled behavior? We see the correlation of the changed behavior with a neural change. But we see no brain area effectuating the change from pre-to-post. The change, however, occurred. In the case of erotic arousal, what should have been involuntary bodily response has not occurred; and the correlation in the brain has been demonstrated.

We have demonstration that change in behavior has no material inducement, no physical cause. Psychiatrist Michael Storm's *The Anatomy of Evil* reports similarly:

> [I]t is a long and tortuous road from enzymes to evil. None of the unfavorable genes, frontal lobe abnormalities, limbic system irregularities, neurotransmitter peculiarities and the like mark out a clear and predictable path toward evil actions. Instead of neat and unmistakable causes, we must settle for factors such as the ones we have been looking at [environment, parental and societal influences, and Nature] that heighten the risk for someone committing the kinds of acts that so affect the 'collective conscience.'[34]

How does the "agency" productive of these non-material influences act on an organism itself extended, while it is not? Picturing the two instrumentalities as "things," impedes understanding because we are trying in the one instance to visualize an immaterial efficacy as a "thing" in the same way we picture any material composite of our experience. We are left with an image of two entities knocking (hitting, bumping up) against each other, as it were. To do so is to assume a status of the efficacies involved that we have not shown to be how they are to be conceived.

Might one suggest that the interaction occurs through power from the being that the self is? The being that the self is is not a "thing," but a power that is limited only by the dimensions of that body through which it actuates every parcel, however, minute, exercises its force and operationality for the bodily person possessed of that self. In each instance the self differs in entirety from any other self that has existed, exists, or will exist. The being that the self is exercises a non-tangible power through each and every bodily cell. The power comes about through proportionality. In each case, we are suggesting as a solution, the cell is so proportioned as to be effectible by the being of the self. The very proportionality of dynamism in each cell is that power, that presence, for how all efficacy, to the degree it takes place, does so; that degree being on the level of powering the totally integrated proportionality and organization to knowledge, to desire, to emotions, to affectations.

That power is not a "thing." It is a proportionality that the dynamic synthesis of being exercises in each cell through a presence which alone can account for the organization and sustainability of the changes that the cells and the body undergo. The very way proportion occurs in the cell makes for being's power through it. The power is not something that "touches" the innermost environs of each bodily cell. There is no "touch" here (of thing on thing, "mass on mass"), simply a presence of the self by a proportion (its presence) commensurate with the capacity of each cell for such a proportionality of presence. The power to change or renew or direct comes by that presence, the proportion of efficacy operant throughout each component of the body to the extent the proportion occurs.

CONCEPTUALIZATION, MEMORY, IMMATE-RIALITY

Discussion of the Botvinick-Cohen model should make clear how modern day theoreticians of the brain in their postulates rule out a possibility of an afterlife. *In extremis*, the rubber ball illusion allows for the suggestion that brain creates more than self. It can create its own world, and in fact be that world. There is no separation of subject from object in such a setting. All that occurs are awarenesses through the production of brain waves in different frequencies and valences. Without establishing the problems the model presents for itself and others as we did in the preceding chapter, we cannot seriously take on the subject of immortality. While we had proceeded in previous chapters to establish the reasonableness of asserting that there is more to existence than just *my* consciousness, it was important to discuss Botvinick-Cohen to demonstrate to the reader how far theories of brain have gone in our day. In effectively eliminating "object" in awareness modern day neuroepistemologists leave the individual with a theory of awareness that in the end cannot look for its causes inasmuch as all awareness for these theoreticians are self-originating brain events. The casual reader is totally unaware of how far neuroepistemology has gone in this day to fashion models of what we call consciousness that are at distances from what we in our everyday could not possibly recognize as what explains consciousness to us. We have argued that consciousness cannot be an electrical event, or a material occurrence. We have given many reasons why. The simplest appears to be that you cannot break down the percept, the conscious event, into electrical sparks or atoms or electrons. If you cannot break it down into them, it appears impossible to bring the percept or conscious event out of electrons, electrical charges, and the like. The percept's constituency is not electrical.

Modern day neurophilosophy seems bent on establishing a model where electrical valences and the like give what nothing in our experience validates. Hypothesizing brain models because electrical events and phenomena occur in the cortical substrate amongst its densely packed histology—seeking to reduce all awareness to a histology of electrical conjunctions while not addressing how it is that no percept in any way resembles these conjunctions, seems more a process of trying to force an interpretation for which no evidence can vouch or is forthcoming. One wonders what frame of mind makes one insist on an approach, such as in some neurophilosophic circles, where every round ball of perception it comes across it tries to fit into its square peg of electrical phenomena and occurrence. It appears to be an attempt at explaining what is itself obscure by what is equally obscure, sc., the models of neurophilosophy. One does not explain light, however, by shadows.

Frequently there is the possibility that one may frame an argument in terms of a theory opposed to what one holds. We believe that neurophilosophy has demonstrated enough fault lines in its reasoning that continuation of a discussion on immortal consciousness should return to the grounds of where adherence to the facts, rather than "electro modelings," and the like guide a discussion seeking to avoid errors, if not also to attain truth.

We have noted the complete difference, otherness, of neuroelectric disturbances from the actual experience or percept that one has. It is puzzling that this difference plays no role in neurophilosophy's position save for the use of the word "conundrum" it applies to this complete "otherness" or difference. If water is totally other than fire, is that a "conundrum" that we will eventually solve? That was the force of Singer's comment in the last chapter on how neuroelectric patterns had cohesion and the "conundrum" of subjectivity it evoked. That conundrum is the fact that experience is nothing like electrical charges, but for neurophilosophy this difference will eventually be solved. The nature of electrical charges (atomic bonding, valence, and the like) is totally other than the nature of the percept in consciousness wherein are no electrons, protons, or quarks. Neurophilosophy does not appear to accept what is obvious, sc., their irreducibility, just as water is irreducible to fire.

Consciousness, we seem to have arrived at, is not reducible to a material substrate. Just as water and fire are not reducible one to the other, electrical charge putatively my percept say, of water, not in any way reducible or equivalent to the experience I have of that water, so consciousness is not reducible to matter, to extended, spatial existence. Consciousness emerges as non-material.

We can proceed with further evidence on this if we look at the prehension of "universals" and the existence of memory. The doctrine of the universal is that the mind has concepts which are of things that in all features except one are different. It has a prehension of what is the same throughout a multiplicity of objects which differ in all other features.

The doctrine is fatal to a materialist philosophy of mentation. We noted in the argument of the nominalists Berkeley and Hume that their claim that universals are a matter of convention already accepts what they deny, sc., the existence of universals. We can now point to the relevance of this to the issue of the mind's make-up. "Triangularity" is a feature we grasp in shapes that differ in length, positioning, angularity, and hypotenuse. The shapes are in no wise identical, they differ in many respects, and yet we see in the differences something all the shaped entities exhibit together, exhibit in common: they are "triangles." This is an instance of what our "universal" is.

Since all material things are singular, were the awareness, e.g., of triangularity material, then our knowledge of it would be of one singular thing because whatever is material is single. Were triangularity material it too would be singular. It could not be in any other thing without being different because each material thing is singular. However, triangularity is the same in all things where it is prehended. The universal does not differ in any way where it is found, not even numerically, from thing to thing in which it inheres. There are not many universals of "triangle." There is only one. There are, however, many material things that are triangular. The universal and the material differ.

The pre-nominalist position,[1] originated in Aristotle and repeated in the Schoolmen of the High Middle Ages, offers an account of how the universal comes to our awareness. What makes a thing be what it is and answers to the question "what is it?" is the thing's form (εἶδος), It is in virtue of reaching the form that the mind comes to a prehension of something universal in things. Each has the same form that makes them in some way the same, This takes presence in the mind as what is universal, or the same, throughout objects that are otherwise not the same. Were this "universal" matter (physical extended stuff, material), once the universal "triangle," e.g., came to be, the matter that it became could not appear in another entity because that other entity is already matter. Since the universal is endlessly replicable, it for this reason cannot, again, be matter. There is a difference between the two.

This inability to be matter applies, the pre-nominalist position argues, to the intellect. Inasmuch as the intellect can take on many different awarenessess,[2] can know many different things, it cannot be matter. Were it, how would it come to know mathematical truths? These clearly are not material in any way.

The mind must be unlike what it knows. If knowledge is to take on what was previously not known, were something exactly like the mind the mind obviously could not take it on. The mind therefore cannot be material. It must be unlike matter.

It differs further from matter in that a material thing cannot take on another form, shape, without ceasing to be the material thing it was. The statue of Cletus, when it takes on a new shape, say of "ball," ceases to be the statue of Cletus. It is now a round ball. The material thing has changed.

The mind, however, does not change as the capacity to become the cognitional content that it takes on. That it is just such a capacity is clear from the fact that it grasps a cognitional content not previously possessed, which it could not were it incapable, were it not a capacity, to do just that. The mind remains the same whatever the content it grasps in the act of knowledge. Were it not, then we could never have understanding, knowledge since we would need a different mind for each act of knowledge we achieved.[3]

The argument from concept formation, from awareness of the universal, as evidence for an immaterial capacity in the person is not abstruse. To prehend what is not singular, but universal (and therefore what is not material), the mind must have a capacity for it. The capacity, when actualized, means that which has the capacity for the not-material is in a state that is actually not-material. Therefore, there is a component of the individual knower, the individual human being, that is actually not material. And if the material is alone that which corrupts, which can perish because of its partibility, the mind would appear to not suffer from that same fate.

We argued that this argument is self-verifying. To deny it, one needs (or tacitly admits) the universal which is being denied. If different individuals hold the same objection (here, to the doctrine of universal), I could not identify the objection as the same in them unless I had the ability to conceptualize that sameness. What is that ability but grasping what is the same in individuals (here, various forms of the argument holding one view in general, sc., there are no universal) otherwise different? Here we cannot say it is by convention that we call their argument the same. We cannot say I have imposed a sameness in the discussion of those who deny universals. That sameness issues from them. It is they, not I, who hold their denial "in common," "together."

The assertion of an immaterial capacity in the human emerges also from a study of memory. Memory's reality is undeniable. Denying it requires the capacity to which the term "memory" refers. We must remember what it is we are denying when denying it. Its value to the individual is clearly known when one considers what personal existence without it would be like.

This actuality, memory, must likewise be self-verifying. To doubt memory's veracity requires memory, which is precisely what we are doubting when the hypothesis is that memory is not self-verifying. Descartes' charge of memory's deceitfulness entangles him in a vicious circle of sorts, then. What he chooses to view as deceitful he must first remember as being deceitful, and what is doing the remembering, of course, is memory.[4]

Memory requires a continuity over time to the one that remembers. If event A occurs to individual X at time B, at time B + 1 event A can only be a memory, experienced as past, to individual X if individual X existed previously for the event A to have occurred to him. I.e., it was the same individual to whom the event occurred as a present reality. He must exist longer than event A in order to have an experience of it later as that which happened to him previously. That is what memory constitutes—an event past now re-presented as past. The continuity over time which it shows must obtain for its occurrence is selfhood at its minimum.

The experience of this continuity gives individual selfhood its reality as subject, as "incapable of being no other, and no other capable of being me." In its irreducible reality it is the entirety of the individual's actions/reactions as unique to the one knowing them. And remembering them. Without memory, a crucial component of one's uniqueness—the fact that no one else has one's memories—would be non-existent.

This uniqueness constitutes awareness to the individual of his identity. Through that identity selfhood is known. By selfhood identity powers through the individual's growth, an individuality that only selfhood identifies as a conscious being in this body, in this space, in this moment.

For one to say that the individual having a memory need not be the same as the individual to whom what is being remembered occurred requires the individual making the claim not be different during the course of making it. Otherwise, we simply have successive instances, one after the other, of sequentially different individuals over the span it takes to speak a sentence, each saying a different word or syllable than the prior individual in the span. We are left not with an individual making a claim, but a series of words or syllables that no one individual uttered, but simply a succession of individuals who uttered—each not remembering what the previous individual in this span uttered as a syllable or word. No claim was ever made, then: only a succession of utterances from a number of successively different sources. Yet for one to know that, he has to remain the same throughout the succession of words or syllables that the aforementioned succession of individuals uttered.

Concomitant with consciousness, then, we have a self, a self with memories. "I" am in all my memories: either as participant in what is being remembered, or as the one who is remembering. I may be right in the thick of the memory, or one aware of oneself as observing, taking everything in. Perhaps, alternately, I am at a distance from what is being remembered. Again, are there not memories that can come and go, almost instantly, as if they just hit me? They seem without sequence with respect to what was occurring in my awareness before or after. I am in them too as the one aware, as being the one to whom this "sudden" memory occurs. Too, I may be the one who is remembered, and remembered in ways eventful, complementary, derogatorily, or with conviction that is toneless, deadening, or unseeming. As nuanced as what is being remembered so is the capacity for and actuality of the memory.

The capacity for, and actuality of, memories indicates an immaterial aspect of consciousness, and of the individual with them. If the actuality of the event is factual, the capacity for it is also. Neurochemical make-up or activity is insufficient as an explanation for long-term memory. The evidence, therefore, is lacking that a breakdown in neural composition and neural structures in bodily demise is the end of that memory. This is our position, for which we now proceed with argument.

Memory is the capacity for an event, or reality, to be present beyond when it has occurred, appeared. Mind makes the presence possible, and actual. Mind is not some abyssopelagic or hadalpelagic electro process. We have already noted that mentation cannot be a physical phenomenon. Theories of synchrony of electro bits and charges, we have found, paint only pictures that fade more and more as the light of reasoning shines on them. Mind as a reality, and not simply some folk psychology misnomer, will come forth now in our findings on the nonspatial status of memory. This further separates any theory of consciousness seeking its actual status from theories insistently stopping at the edge of the materialist terrain. These leave one always short of the threshold of consciousness' entranceway.

Memory is the capacity for, and activity of, an event or existent to be mentally present to us for longer than an instant, or the duration of its occurrence as happening "now." In memory the event takes on a permanence that its original occurrence does not give. There it is fleeting. The mind, in the act of memory, conveys on the event or the reality that appeared a new existence, a different existence: an existence as "being kept in mind." This conveyance, however, is not one of a mere repetition, mere imagistic copy,[5] of what has occurred. In memory the past becomes present[6] *in propria persona* (to the one remembering it and only to that one, in each and every case of that remembering) through what is "being kept in mind."

A *memorius focus* is present to the remembering consciousness, around which fades of lesser remembrances come and go, collate and relate. Imbrications of one "past" with another take place, as no memory is without borders by which the mind regresses further back or trespasses further forward, further from the past that is being remembered or closer to the future that terminates in the present in which the remembering takes place.

I can remember my own remembering,[7] furthermore; just as I can forget my own forgetting. At times, too, I may remember to forget, just as I can forget to remember.

In memory "time" does not have the dynamism of the forceful movements all around me. There is succession, progression, regression, ingression, egression, just as in active time. I, however, in memory have a capacity over the time swirling about me. I am aware that it does not have the charge over me that encountering the present has. There can be a gulf between me and what I am remembering that the ever present now does not permit me. At every moment in lived time I stand at the lip, the edge, of whatever is accelerating or flowing towards me. In memory time has no such control.

Memory both stores, and recollects.[8] Nothing passive, then, is it. It can be compositive, distinguishing sharply from it being simply retentive.[9] It can "refresh" how we once viewed an attitude or event. It can renew feelings long gone. In such renewal it also seems able to have qualities of its own: one's memory may be "hardened" with respect to something that has happened. Alternatively, it may take on a softness or ease.

Events trigger its search in recollection, a search that is at the discretion of the mind, or can be involuntary. I may not want to remember something, but external forces put upon me the demand to recollect. A moment of reverie[10] may solicit a search for something calming that I once knew.

Spinoza's comment, then, that memory is simply an associate mechanism or tribunal,[11] echoed by Hume,[12] goes totally contrary, it would appear, to what everyone who has a memory knows to be true about the capacity of memory. Kant's *Critique*, giving it apparently a role as the "reproductive imagination," bestows a more active dimension on it.[13] His term, however, diminishes from its richness and depth as what actually gives to the individual self an identity of being so essential to awareness of one's uniqueness.

"Memory within a memory" is a capacity of this self. Time, however, can partition no "time within time." Occurrences in the present, that is, cannot be rearranged in the way memory can take liberty with the past. In the past one is not tied to the present. Memory offers that severance from the inevitable. The present confronts us with a determinism that no past requires us to fear or accept. Memory makes us of different creatureliness than the present does. It frees us.

Memory seems to take on differing dimensions, contingent upon how near to the event remembered it is. In the car, on the way home from a baseball game just completed, it seems some of the events remembered blend right into my present: the taste of the mustard on the hot dog, the ice in my cola, the glaring sun in my way of sight, the lush green texture of the grass on which I walked only moments ago on the way out of the ball park, the blare of the loudspeaker. These all seem to persist into, be continuous with, my present in the car in which I am remembering as I drive, even though the event is just past. What is of interest, also, is that this event being remembered involves all the senses taken together and seems almost, as it were, that they are still under a stimulus which is not yet faded.

William James[14] speaks of this phenomenon as "the rearward portion of the present space of time." However, the further into the past memory moves, the less "actual," the less "present," is what occurs to the one who remembers. Memory, that is, appears related to "time."

In terms of neuroelectric discussion, i.e., the materialist or reductionist model, does one feel that time "wears away" the electro charges that for reductionists constitute the percept in the memory? How does one account for the role of time on the percept? Time reduces it in richness, dimension, texture, feel. We know that a battery that repeatedly distributes electrical charges over time, as the battery wears down, loses its ability to generate the same power of charge. In the case of memory, what wears away? Does memory over time lose its ability to "recharge"? Does memory "tire?"

Reproducing a copy constitutes one model of how memory takes place. How does the copy fade? Is it the reproducing power that loses vitality that causes a faded image? Why is it that I cannot recall the past of a year ago with the same vibrance that shows in James' "rearward portion of the present space of time"? Is there something to this reductionist idea of memory and mental events somehow being an "electro charge" after all?

Memory "fades" as it has increasingly more to do with time than that which is remembered. As time becomes a greater component of what is remembered, that event or actuality that is remembered seems to recede more and more as time takes on a greater portion. Does detail in the reality or event give way to a time component? Does time, so to speak, in taking a greater portion of what is remembered, reduce that which is remembered so it appears to be increasingly less distinct? In this model, memory is not like battery charger at all. Its "charge" does not diminish because it is a material component that is wearing down. On the contrary, what has occurred is that time has become a greater factor in recall. As such, what does get recalled is less of the detail and more of the time that has passed—a time that emerges as, can be likened to, a blank cement or wooden block, so to speak, separating the past from the present without content, diversity, or occurrence in between.

We then do not have a "battery" model of memory, a model that would clearly refer back to a materialist paradigm for understanding it. Other factors in the study of the neurology of memory make the materialist paradigm additionally of less use in understanding memory.

Broadly, the capacity for memory has two opposing explanations. The first is the excitatory: memory traces to excitation of certain neuronal structures "where" it is located. This further divides into memory as a (a) macromolecular reality, or (b) a neuronal "trace." The second is the non-physical: memory is without a material cause or component.

If the second is true, and yet memory is ingredient to individual reality, is intrinsic to *this* private consciousness and no other, a critical reality of the individual human being is not material. If memory is not corporeal in being, the reality living with it is not totally corporeal. By use of analogy, can we deny it to whatever sentient organism (any animal other than man) is possessed of it? "Pictorial" memory, which is the memory we are debating here, as opposed to "short-term" or "habit" memory—if it has non-spatial "depth" in man, what prevents the same from being said of all animals likewise possessed?

"Place" of pictorial or long-term memory is the critical term we first encounter in looking at our debate whether memory is or is not a material event. It was with the neurosurgical practice of Dr. Wilder Penfield that data came forth about the experimental and clinical inability to specify a place for such memory in the brain.

There is nothing Pickwickian about this term "place" here. It has its everyday pedestrian meaning. Place specifies the presence of an entity by way of co-ordinates indicating "distance from" and "distance near" and "distance at," etc.

Penfield found that the memory, the remembered, that we draw upon in moments of recall and review—long-term memory, as distinct from the rote memory of habit and repetition—is not any "where" in the brain. There is no store where the brain "places" it. Memory of this nature has no "where" in the brain. No location specifies it.

This facet of long-term memory focuses neurological evidence against the reductionist equation of human individual with neural tissue. Penfield dealt extensively with correcting epileptic conditions in patients. Before the development of electro-encephalography and electrocorticography, electrical exploration—direct electrode stimulation of brain tissue—was the neurological procedure to identify the problem site of epilepsy in the brain. Through incision the scalp was drawn back and electrode stimulation (Penfield used galvanic current to outline motor and sensory areas, and a faradic coil to reproduce features of a seizure; also, a thyratron stimulator with unilateral or bipolar electrodes consisting of a platinum wire in a glass holder) begun to pinpoint the epileptic fault site.[15] Once pinpointed, the procedure was surgical excision with the aim of eliminating the cause of epileptic seizure.

In the course of surgical treatment of patients suffering from temporal lobe seizures....we stumbled upon the fact that electrical stimulation of the interpretative area of the cortex occasionally produces....activations of the sequential record of consciousness, a record that had been laid down during the patient's earlier experience. The patient 'relived' all that he had been aware of till that earlier period....as in a.... 'flashback.'[16]

Electrode stimulation of neural mass brought forth memories in the patient's life, involuntarily retrieved through this stimulation. The quality of the memories:

A mother told me she was suddenly aware, as my electrode touched the cortex, of being ill in her kitchen listening to the voice of her little boy who was playing outside in the yard. She was aware of the neighborhood noises, such as passing motor cars, that might mean danger to him.

A young man stated he was sitting at a baseball game in a small town and watching a little boy crawl under the fence to join the audience. Another was in a concert hall listening to music. 'An orchestration,' he explained. He could hear the different instruments. All these were unimportant events, but recalled with complete detail.[17]

Penfield goes on to present the clinical case of one patient where eighteen points of her brain's right hemisphere were electro-touched in looking for the causal site of her epileptic trauma.

The succeeding responses from the temporal lobe were 'psychical' instead of sensory or motor. They were activations of the stream of consciousness from the past....(Site 11)— 'I think I heard a mother calling her little boy somewhere. It seemed to be something that happened years ago.' (Site 18a)—'I had a little memory—a scene in a play—they were talking and I could see it—I was just seeing it in my memory.'

I was more astonished each time my electrode brought forth such a response. How could it be? This had to do with the mind! I called such a response 'experiential' and waited for more evidence.[18]

Penfield's surprise resulted from what happened with his original intent to simply map out the sensory, the motor, and the speech areas of the human cortex. (1) It was discovered that cortical responses to electrode cartography—this mapping out procedure—included recall of past experiences, as in the examples noted. (2) Beyond that, it was found in the surgical excision of known causal sites of epilepsy in the brain's temporal lobes the memories elicited by electrode stimulation of those sites remained intact. The patient still had the memory he (she) reported when the tissue site was first stimulated, but which site was now removed.[19] The site, then, did not contain the memory.

Postulate of a duplicate site where it was contained, and thus explaining recall upon removal of the original excitatory site, seemingly advances no explanation. What would prevent a duplicate recall (recalling duplicately) if it was thus duplicated? And why stop at a duplicate site? What theoretical difference is there between a duplicate or quintlicate (five locations) site of a memory in the brain tissue?

Nor could stimulation of any other area of requisite complexity (sufficient intricacy so as to be neurologically credible as a site of memory, given memory's own intricacy of composition) be found to stimulate the memory first discovered by the initial cortical electro-stimulation. In repeated such cases with other patients, surgical excision of a cortical site whose electro-stimulation aroused a memory, did not remove the memory.

In cases other than Penfield's report, such as injury to the hippocampus[20] or mesial thalamus—brain areas believed to be shown formative in long-term memories—memories formed prior to those injuries were not destroyed. In these traumas, while it is clinically certain that the patient cannot form new memories, his past memories are not extinguished. Brain areas neuroclinically established as instrumental to the creation of long-term memories, are not in their preservation. The neurological findings, the scientific results, from the method of electro-exploration is that brain mass does not qualify as the repository of the individual's memory, the ability at pictorial recall.

The results of this work, reported by Penfield in *The Mystery of the Mind* and with those of Phaner Parot,[21] as well as those of Sir John Eccles,[22] and Jacques Barbizet,[23] Michael Marsh's *A Matter of Personal Survival: Life After Death*[24] deftly furthers. Could memory, Marsh asks, be situated in, stored as, a neural groove imprinted by experience—a groove that escapes the excision procedures curative of epilepsy? E. Roy John, as Director of New York University's Brain Research Lab, in a 1980 paper published findings from the research undertaken to confirm or deny the neural groove hypothesis.

Countless experiments with animals, destroying or removing parts of their brain, as John is cited in the Marsh study, failed to locate the site of any pathway responsible for memory. Additionally, John's paper advanced empirical evidence increasing the hypothesis' implausibility. Brain neurons, John states, often fire spontaneously, e.g., in the absence of any stimulus. They respond unpredictably to any given stimulus, showing no tendency toward sameness of response regardless of the stimulus. They will also respond in the same way to a stimulus sent by different sense organs.

Given such variability of neuronal activity, neuronal activity in memory could frequently be different. On one occasion it might be a groove formation, another not. The groove hypothesis would then be invalidated. And given science's requirement for predictability, its absence here would disqualify the neural groove hypothesis as science.

Also in support of his rejection of the groove hypothesis John noted that because so many neurons are affected in sense-experience, it is difficult to see how any neural groove could remain unaltered—which it must if it is to be the memory store—from the innumerable excitations each sense-experience would cause.

Pressing the analysis further, Marsh argues that the fact of a past event's recall after a number of years makes the storage theory of memory unsatisfactory. It is difficult to see how, e.g., in the recollection of an event forty years past that recollection is possible without repeated mental reference to it and constant reinforcement over the years. With the brain's neurological structure constantly subject to all kinds of stimuli and chemical processes, the claim that the brain could hold a memory over so many years with no change in content from what is being remembered is not easily credible.[25]

Depth psychiatry, Marsh points out, does note in this regard that many of our long-term memories are retrieved in their original perceptual form. Think of the time you accidentally drank a mixed drink at a summer barbeque when you were a child instead of the lemonade that you thought was in the glass. The actual percept, though of thirty-five years past, is immediate to mind. Yet my awareness of that past event as past, which my awareness of that event is, rules out, Marsh shows, the memory as some storage trace in the brain. The imagery recall we achieve in long-term memory has no analogue to the notion of "trace." "The bear's footprint is his trace," Marsh notes, "but it offers no picture of the bear." In long-term memory, however, the content is pictorial, as in the case of the summer barbeque, redolent with detail.

Nor can the "trace" hypothesis explain our awareness of past as past. The awareness cannot come from the memory's content, for we have seen from depth psychiatry that it frequently has the perceptuality, the presentness, of the original event. In our bear footprint analogy, the footprint does not generate an awareness of the trace as trace. Our awareness is of the footprint as the trace of an original. Trace as trace does not contain the original. The original, however, is that which is past. Trace as trace, then, and our awareness of such, does not contain the past. Additionally, Marsh continues, the trace itself—the footprint—has nothing of the original's content, while our long-term memories quite clearly do.

The "trace" theory of memory, that an event is preserved neurally as a trace, also fails, Marsh argues, in accounting for the difference in feeling that a long-term memory may have from the original event. Were memory a trace phenomenon, a neural trace reactivation, my recollection of past suffering would have necessarily a feeling of that suffering. Deactivating the trace, then, would be deactivating the memory. However, I can have the memory of an injury without a semblance of injury to myself. The suffering component has been deactivated without extinguishing the memory. This invalidates the trace hypothesis as the neural memory store, for the semblance of suffering is not retained. If memory cannot be a trace of the original, it cannot be recollected by neural trace activation.[26]

Removal of brain tissue, whose electro-stimulation elicited reports of long-term memories from the patients involved, does not remove those memories. They remain, but the brain tissue does not. And memory as a neural pathway—whether one calls it a "groove" or a "trace"—has been shown to explain nothing of memory's existence.

Moving to a smaller—or more micro scale, if one wishes—than these larger components of brain matter, advocates of the physical basis of memory's preservation have advanced the suggestion that RNA/DNA events in the cell show this possibility. Memory, that is, has a material substrate.

A. R. Luria, a leading proponent of this view, summarized the hypothesis in *The Working Brain*:[27]

> The quest for a solution to the problem of the material basis of memory took a new turn as a result of the work of Hyden (1960; 1962; 1964) who showed that retention of a trace from previous excitation is associated with a last change in the ribonucleic acid and who found a lasting increase in the RNA/DNA content in nuclei subjected to intensive excitation. In both places RNA/DNA molecules....play the decisive role....in the retention of traces from previous experience during the life of the individual. At the moment of excitation the RNA level in the neuron rises while that of the surrounding glia falls; whereas in the after-period (evidently connected with trace retention) it falls sharply in the neuron but rises equally sharply and remains high for a long time in the glia. The hypothesis that the glia is concerned in the retention of memory traces is unquestionably one of the most important discoveries in neurophysiology.

Holger Hyden working at the University of Göteborg, developed a quite precise microminiaturized method for analyzing the nucleic content of nerve and glial cells. In his experiments Hyden isolated Deiters cells—very large neurons—out of the rat (rhodent family) medulla and subjected them to a heavy barrage of nerve impulses. He then compared their RNA content with that of a control group of cells. Subsequently, having shown that this was possible, Hyden presented young rats with the difficulty of traversing a thin tight wire to get to their food source. When they had learned how to negotiate it, he compared the RNA content of their Deiters cells with those of control animals that had not learned this tight wire maneuver. The RNA content of the control group was measurably less than the non-control group. Also, the base sequence of the RNA in the control group differed from the non-control group.

Similarly, with planaria (flatworms) the base composition of their cerebral RNA changed upon learning a conditioned response: the quantity of adenine diminished and of guanine increased. Furthermore, the changed RNA was extracted from the conditioned planaria and injected into other flatworms. Their behavior changed as though the conditioned response taught to the first group had been transferred.[28]

The change in the molecular structure of neuronal glial cells in the laboratory animals upon their conditioning, or learning, serves for this line of reasoning as evidence of chemical basis for memory. A change in behavior upon introduction of a stimulus presumably involves a macrochemically-made recall capacity in the organism in that, once the behavior is acquired, it need not be relearned. It is now part of the organism's chemistry, its neural composition.

Problematic with this line of reasoning is that it seeks to extrapolate from the activity of behavior modification a thesis that it could then equally apply to an entirely different phenomenon, long-term memory. While behavior modification is a change in behavior due to a certain stimulus, long-term memory involves no behavior modification. But it was behavior modification that the chemical changes in neuronal cells was supposed to explain. If long-term memory is not a behavior modification, the chemical changes involved to explain behavior modification have nothing to do with long-term memory. Citing those changes accordingly, in the case of long-term memory does nothing to advance our understanding of how long-term memory might be formed. The changes are irrelevant to an inquiry into how long-term memory comes about.

Even should we grant that behavioral modification has a chemical basis, that has not been made evident by those advancing it. If impartial reasoning is how one reaches truth, and impartial reasoning means the avoidance of assumptions in favor of letting the data speak for themselves, it is clear that the chemical hypothesis of learned behavior has not proceeded this way.

For example, two changes occurring together, as in the case of neuronal RNA and behavior, do not necessitate that one is the cause of the other. That one is, however, (in the absence of any evidence to the contrary) must be assumed if the chemical hypothesis is to have any force. At best, only a correlation between the two can be established. A change in neuronal RNA, as in the case of the rats after crossing a tight wire, is not evidence that it was the process of learning the tight wire that caused the change. One can equally ask how did the rat first cross the tight wire prior to the RNA change? If the RNA change explains how it learned the tight wire crossing, what explains how it first crossed it? For "to learn" means "to come to know how."

To assert that RNA change explains the subsequent and evident facility with which the rat crosses the tight wire after first doing it—or after a number of times—requires that the RNA change be viewed as a cause for quickly, adroitly, crossing the tight wire. A modification in behavior is linked to a chemical change: once the change occurs, the modification follows.

The position has difficulties. If (similarity of conditions each time holding) a cause is responsible for the sameness of result each time it is operant, exceptions to that result have to be explained. One would expect that the rat's behavior each time in crossing the tight wire should be the same if it is chemically induced. That, unimpeded, for example, it should take the same number of steps, effect the same bodily movements, cross at the same speed

It does not, though, which leaves one uncertain as to what kind of causality the RNA change is supposed to effect. How does neuronal RNA explain behavior when the behavior in question frequently differs? When is the behavior suffi-ciently different—or the same—so that one can distinguish between pre- and post-neuronal RNA change, or assert that it is post-neuronal RNA that explains the behavior? Requests for such delineation have not been readily answered by defenders of the chemical hypothesis of behavior.

Applying these canons of evidence to the instance of tissue transplantation and planaria behavior involves similar difficulties. To posit that the RNA tissue transplant from a planarian with behavior X is responsible, after transplantation, for a second planarian's new behavioral trait, is it not necessary to show that the second planarian could behave in no way other than which the RNA change is held to cause? In cases of causality we know that certain effects are not possible from a cause, that instead only one effect is possible. In the case of the planarian we do not know what effects are involved because we have no way of knowing if another behavior, other than the one observed, is possible. And we do not know this because we do not know whether it is the tissue transplant that ac-counts for the behavior. In this case, we would have to prove that no other be-havior, other than the one associated with the RNA tissue transplant, was possi-ble. That would satisfy a claim of causality in this case.

No such proof is possible, though while it is proof that is required to con-vince one that changes in behavior are RNA-explained. At most, one can only suggest from the evidence that RNA neuronal change might be instrumental to the change in behavior, not causative of it.

Some causality is required in a learning change. That is admitted. And that causality could be material. Since a learning change has no connection with long-term memory, that materiality would have no impact, however, on the ar-gument for long-term memory's non-materiality. That notwithstanding, it has not been proven that the material agency causing learning changes is RNA.[29]

Difficulties similar to those besetting the materialist reasoning process that drew conclusions from experiments without data for such conclusions appear in a suggestion from the same quarter: neuronal synaptic changes may be causative of behavioral changes and memory preservation. It is known in neuroscience that the neuronal cell synthesizes those substances that travel down the axon to the nerve synapse. So in Hyden's findings and others', e.g., Edward Glassman's, since neuronal RNA changes in the presence of a new behavior, it follows that a change in the synaptic conjunction among neuronal cells occurred. In fact, this was shown to be the case in electron micrograph studies carried out by Brian Cragg in London.[30] The anatomical change in the synapse is evidence of a mate-rial substrate accounting for memory functioning since, the materialist hypothe-sis maintains, upon acquiring new behavior the synaptic structure changes one way and no further.

The difficulty with this hypothesis is two-fold. (1) In Cragg's work, rats were reared in the dark for the first two weeks of their lives and then exposed to laboratory light for three hours before they were killed.[31] Cragg found that changes occurred in both the size and number of synapses in the visual cortex, lateral geniculate, and retinae of these animals.

These synaptic changes, however, do not show that learning involves them. They are, in fact, changes one would expect in the presence of new stimuli, given the obvious neurochemical changes that occur in sensation. No connection with learning can be made here unless (2) it is assumed that the synaptic change in neuronal cells that occurs in behavior modification is the basis of an organism's new behavior.

It is the assumption that one must watch. Too much is assumed, too much not proven, in the conclusions that follow from it. As we saw before, if neuronal changes account for a new behavior, how are to explain the behavior of the rat in first crossing the tight wire? How did it learn this feat initially? The neuronal change held to affect learning, behavior, had not yet occurred.

If it is because the rat crossed the tight wire more easily after the neuronal RNA change that the RNA change is now deemed causal, it is being assumed that without the RNA change the new found agility would not have arisen. And that has to be proven. It is just as plausible that the rat's learning to cross the tight wire caused the RNA's recomposition. That position becomes objectionable only on the assumption that learning and behavior change are chemically caused. And that is the point—that they are chemically caused has to be proven, not assumed.

The point in this review of the scientific claim of a material basis for memory is that this claim has not been demonstrated. An unproved assumption underlies the claim, which we have seen to be the case in other clams advancing a materialist explanation for living existence.

The issue here can be further focused. Learned habits—which is the example scientists advancing a material nature for memory use—are not, as we already commented, in any manner like the long-term memories whose material basis they sought to establish in their behavior modification experiments with animals. Acquired habits can be lost through lack of reinforcement. Long-term memories need no reinforcement for their retention Skill at a certain task, in a certain habit, can be improved. A long-term memory cannot. The basis required for comparison, sc., similarity, between short-term memory (habit, behavior modification) and long-term is clearly not proven. Their difference is one of essence.

Even dismissing these problems with the scientific claims of a chemical structure to memory, there are improbabilities in their own thesis. If we assume that memories are molecular phenomena, what kind of brain molecules could serve as their basis? They would have to be complex, and thus large enough, to accommodate the high complexity of differences contained in the wide variety of memories we have. The macromolecules within the nerve cell which we could select for this memory role are limited, They would have to be, on the materialist's own grounds, either proteins or the nucleic acid themselves—DNA, or RNA, the ribonucleic acid that bears the gene's DNA message and builds the protein molecules. It is these that are the constituents of the nerve cells, what physically comprise them.

Here, again, the molecular thesis runs into difficulty. All three candidates for memory production use logically equivalent codes. The amino acids' series in a protein processes information exactly parallel to, indeed identical with, the sequence of bases in RNA on which it grew. And that sequence is simply a translation of the base sequence in the DNA gene. It is much like stating the sequence in Braille, Fortran, and script.

If memory is molecular, each new memory would need a wholly unique protein or RNA molecule to be made so that it could be stored. That, however, would require a synthesis of a totally new DNA sequence in the neuronal gene. Since memories are continuously being formed, the change in the DNA sequence would concomitantly have to be continuous. There is no evidence, though, that the DNA of nerve cells is constantly changing. Quite the contrary; it is scientific fact that DNA is not continuously being replaced. Just the opposite: it manifests extraordinary persistence and imperviousness to change.[32]

The molecular basis theory of memory falls, then, on its own requirements. The component cited for memory formation, that is, the molecule—the basic structure of all cellularity—is empirically known to be inadmissible. Neuronal gene DNA, which would have to be the neurological agent in a molecular theory of memory, functions exactly opposite to what the theory requires.

As the core agency of all neuronal molecularity, production of memory tissue would require that its own sequence of nucleic acids alter for each new memory-specific molecule. To account for the differences each human memory contains, no memory molecule could be the same as another. Otherwise, the memories would be the same. The difference among our memories, their variation in complexity, imagery, information, and structure would require each a molecule precisely fitted for those differences; as well as the necessary permutations in the sequence of DNA arrangement productive of that molecular fitting. It is those permutations, however, which do not occur, and is known scientifically not to. Memory, accordingly, emerges as unable to be molecular. The conditions necessary to that molecularity are scientifically known not to exist.

A brain-tissue basis of memory, then, is not supportable on the evidence From the levels of gross tissue excision to the molecular, the reductionist case has not been demonstrated. This means that tissue such as the aforementioned hippocampus or mesial thalamus known to be necessary to the formation of memory could not be productive of it. The fact that such tissue is DNA-based shows this.

The past in its details cannot be stored as a molecule; we just saw that. To produce memory is to store the past, with its details, such that it can be recalled to awareness. The action of DNA—its constancy of chain sequence—makes clear that brain tissue cannot contain it. Each new memory requires a different RNA so that it can be molecularly contained. The permanence of DNA's sequence means that the RNA required to fulfill this task is not being produced; and thus the brain molecule is not.

That DNA does not change or, said else wise, the neuronal cells remain undifferentiated one from another, puts to serious test theories postulating that

memory exists in bits stored over various brain sites and assembled for our recall in or by the hippocampus when we wish to remember. Each cell or neuronal
cluster would have to change with each bit of memory that it was supposed to
encode or encapsulate since each memory-bit itself would be different for different memories. DNA's sameness of neuronal cell production, however, makes
that thesis untenable. All memories would have to be the same.

Further, assemblage of memory-bits assumes prehension of the whole that
the parts to be assembled are to comprise. That which is to be remembered is
already present to mind, thus eliminating the need for assembly of its constituents. Memory, then, is not preserved in this disaggregated condition among neural clusters. Neurological sites may be physically active in the activity of memory but, clearly, they are not its constituents.

Memory, accordingly, is not reducible to a brain molecule. Memory is the
storage of the past in its detail, a storage, though, that cannot be neurocellular.
No brain tissue can produce it, therefore, since to store the past with its details
(of events and all therein) is to produce memory. (Remembering is to draw from
that store into the present what is past.)

This means that the necessity of the hippocampus or mesial thalamus to
memory's emergence cannot be causative. This holds for any brain tissue whose
absence would prevent the formation of memories. If their absence prevents the
formation of new memories, it does not follow that those tissues form new
memories. Absence of part followed by absence of an event does not mean that
the part is causal to, or suffices for, the occurrence of the event. As necessary to
storage of the past they must be instrumental in memory's formation, not causative of it. The causality is ruled out because they are governed by DNA.

Brain tissue's instrumentality may be conceived of as that by which the individual missing such tissue could not form any memory as his, and thus not
form any memory, because memory always belongs to someone. That by which
he would form a memory as his would be missing and thus would be unable to
form a new memory. It is in this that brain tissue's instrumentality to memory's
formation can be suggested. It is the instrument for the memory's being *mine*
(because, for example the mesial thalamus is mine), and therefore for the memory occurring. Parts such as the hippocampus and mesial thalamus are instruments by which an event is prepared for storage such that what is stored
uniquely and individually for each person could not be so without these brain
parts. The actual storage—what causes the event to be preserved, what preserves
it—is beyond their instrumentality. The evidence is that it is not a material process.

This leaves one remaining hypothesis to consider. It is the hologram theory
of brain. Can the hologram theory find a place for memory in the brain tissue?

The hologram model of brain received its impetus in neuroscience from
Karl Pribam, experimental psychologist at Stanford University, and Christopher-
Longuet Higgins of the University of Edinburgh.[33] Essentially, a hologram is a
photographic plate whose image data can be resurrected and reconstructed three
dimensionally by laser light at any point on that plate. The image-forming prop-

erty is dispersed throughout the plate, such that the image can be reconstructed more or less from any part broken off the plate.

Such a construct, Pribam, suggested, might explain the fact that memories are not extinguished despite the destruction of brain areas whose electrode stimulation were known to have previously evoked them. Memory, the holo-gram argument runs, is distributed over the brain as a whole in much the way the image of the hologram is enfolded in all of its parts in accord with the principle behind the hologram: all of the whole is contained in any of its parts.

The suggestion has drawbacks. It requires that the brain tissue be shown to have those physical properties which make it holographic in the way the photo-graphic plate is when struck by laser light. Is it only a laser light that can gener-ate such a property? If not, what is the analogue for that light in the brain? More directly, how do we show that the analogue can accomplish that for which it is the analogue?

The hologram thesis requires the use of analogical conception to have ex-planatory power given the differences between the media, namely, the photo-graphic plate and brain tissue involved in the thesis. Between the two there must be some analogue by which these differences are overcome so that there be a similarity remaining that makes intelligible or workable the thesis as it applies to brain tissue.

Beyond that, the analogue, to have serviceability, must be shown to oper-ate similarly in the case of both media. The analogue would have to be "the power of enfoldment" or its equivalent. That precise power in the brain, equiva-lent to the action of laser on plate, would require that the tissue it act on respond in a fashion similar to that of the photographic plate to laser. The tissue must have similarity enough to the plate's constituency (for this is what analogy re-quires) to respond holographically.

For this requirement we have the physical datum by which to judge the analogy's usefulness. It is the brain tissue itself. Composed ultimately of DNA, RNA, and proteins, it is difficult to fathom how they would exercise properties similar to a photographic plate's components when the photographic plate con-tains none of the brain's cellular make-up. If the properties of the photographic plate are required in the neurons so that it react holographically, the neuron would have to be so composed that it could exhibit those properties.

Empirically, however, we know those properties to occur only through pho-tographic constituency. If there is an agency in the brain by which in connection, in interaction, with the neuron(s) it could act in a power of enfoldment, and thus the neuron(s) exhibit the properties of the photographic plate, we have no evi-dence for it.

Holonomic theory, i.e., that wave interferences form holographic patterns throughout the brain's cortex, that the cortex, more exactly, is the environment of multi-dimensional holographic like processes accounting for memory, gives us a regress problem that Draisma has noted:

In holography the stored image is "read out" by illumination with an appropriate beam and projected in a quasi-space in front of or behind the storage medium. Subsequently, the viewer observes this projection. Pribam's holographic memory theory states that the stored images are projected outside the storage medium (the brain) and from there absorbed into consciousness....How can the memory perceive the projected images without duplicating the whole procedure? Human consciousness as a reading-out of the hologram in the head, Arbib wrote, may lead to the homunculus fallacy.[34]

Pribam's account would have ever smaller homunculi (each in a successively reduced portion of an ever decreasing hologram) needing to watch each successively smaller homunculus look at ever smaller parts containing the ever receding whole in all its parts And a power working on tissue whose molecules cannot contain memories (unlike the photographic plate, which in its parts has at least the whole [however contained]), and yet still is supposed to be able to produce memories in the way of holographic reproduction, appears to be a totally unworkable hypothesis.

The hologram theory, in fine, is a variant of that which postulates a neural substratum that contains redundancy to the point that memory can appear anywhere once the right activation (however that occurs) takes place. But this appears to require we ask what prohibits the activation occurring at any time so that we could have two identical memories differing only by their number and in no other way; or any number of the same memories at any time.

Our misgivings here on the materialist interpretation of memory lead us to reiterate the position that there is no evidence that long-term memory is a physical result, or occurrence. No scientific experimentation shows it to be equatable with a neurochemical, a biological, component. Long-term memory is not reducible to brain issue or brain space.

The evidence that memories are retained after brain tissue, whose electrode stimulation evoked these memories, is removed impairs the brain-storage explanation of memory. The evidence that a more substantial removal leaves memories intact further reduces its plausibility. Clinical removal of suitably complex tissue with memory unaffected argues that memory has no place, no location, in the human brain.

Removal of the hippocampal region, as we noted, prevents further memories from being formed. That, though, would simply show that brain region to be instrumental in memory formation. And this no one questions. The memories the person already has, however, the evidence suggests, reside someway other than in the brain tissue. The brain, from what can be empirically shown, is not causal to the memories formed. The notion that the whole is somehow present in the part, and thus memory preservation may be possible that way, requires that our memory be contained in the brain in the first place. Neuromolecularity, however, makes plain that memory cannot be molecular.

Regions of the brain possibly not explored in clinical treatment will be shown not to contain memory, for their molecularity requires neuronal DNA, in which regions it plays the same role as in the remaining brain. Examination of the information provided by neuroscience, therefore, as well as its assumptions, rules out memory being in any part of the brain. It exists without place.

This preservation of one's past in one's cognitive apparatus appears to have no plausibility as a material process. Its preservation, rather, emerges as immaterial.

It is worth restating how this assertion comes about. To preserve the past from one's life requires an activity for the one remembering that is not constricted to place. Bodily make-up—histological structure and content—is not whence the re-presented past is drawn. The past does not stay in the body, does not persist in a material state and then, upon the individual's election, enter awareness.

The responsibility for bodily function is cellular: bodily life is cellularly controlled and based. The past recollected is not cellular. Neuronal DNA's biochemical identity—its sameness of chemical coding and thus cellular production—over the life of the brain eliminates a cellular/molecular role in memory. That precludes retention of the past as a material process at the most constitutive level of the brain, the level of DNA. The most constitutive level of an organism is responsible for what results in or from the organism at any other level when no other factor intervenes. Science has found no other factor of such importance in the cell's constitution for its growth than DNA. Since DNA cannot account for memory, that would rule out a cellular (material) explanation or basis for it.

Neuroelectric activity as a possible factor in memory somehow would have to alter the composition of the molecule if the molecule is to be the store for memory. Since the molecular composition of the neuron does not alter (neuronal DNA being established as the sole agent of neuronal composition), a neuroelectric role in memory appears excluded. Neuroelectric activity would have to be able to alter a (macro) molecule, exercise the same causality DNA can. It is known, however, not to (that is, it provides no cellular code.) The known spontaneity and randomness of such changes would equally eliminate them as a role in memory. Memory does not happen sporadically, suddenly; thus it could not be a neuroelectric circumstance.

If memory has no place, then it is not necessary for what exists to have place. To think it must is gratuitous, to assume what cannot be proven. Our entire material world of being exits in place; and much, if not all, of what we remember is of that world. It is not extraordinary, then, that we come to think of all existence as placed, and only as such. Nor, given man's proclivity to habit—of thought, as well as of action—that he would find dubious the notion of existence without place. In most thought processes sense-image is the most serviceable vehicle, and that image generally carries with it the representation, content, of place.[35]

If place is a boundary around that which is in it (but not part of what is bounded),[36] to think of memory as not in place is to think of it as having no boundary, of not being contained. To so think it is not to conceive it as infinite. Absence of physical boundaries simply means the content of an existent, or the existent itself, does not require place. An infinite existent would require a content that is infinite, as well as absence of physical constraints. Memory does not exist in that way; its content is always finite but, we are saying, not in place.

Though we do not in our everyday thinking picture to ourselves such existence, it is not for that reason unintelligible to us. The absence of sense-imagery in thought processes, e.g., has not been all impedimental to convergence theory in mathematics,[37] or the mathematics of Lobaschevskian geometry within a Euclidean framework.[38] In the latter, especially, a mental representation of the unbounded appears as a conceptual apparatus.

Thought in the absence of sense-imagery conveying physical containment is, of course, not a commonplace but is operant when thought penetrates to formalization, as in mathematics. Conceptualizing memory in a non-bounded way reaches a similar level of abstraction. If that level be serviceable in mathematics, ruling it out in how we think about memory appears unwarranted.

Thinking of memory in non-bounded terms, therefore, is not an exception that stands out alone in human thought processes. The thesis that long-term memory is an existence not susceptible to material containment, physical boundary, does not lead to an unconceptualizeability. Memory can be so conceived. The thesis does not conflict with other thought processes, and has a cognate in areas of mathematics.

That thesis, so formulated, means that human existence appears to possess a capacity not limited to this world of space-time; not everything human has the constraints of materiality. One objection to immortality has stemmed from the requirement that survival of death be existence as we know it in this space-time. If existence after death, so the objection went, is not life as we know it while living, post-mortem existence must be rejected.

From all the research, though, memory does not appear emplaced. The objection that post-mortem existence has no validity because it must, like life, be spatio-temporal, assumes something for which it does not have evidence, to wit: that human capacity in this life is only spatio-temporal. The argument from memory should make clear that it need not be. By eliminating the materialist candidates for its explanation at every cellular level of brain tissue, the case for memory's immateriality takes on serious considerability.

It would be a demonstration of that immateriality were the method of excluding possibilities demonstrative in force.[39] In the case of concept formation, (achievement of the universal [knowledge of that which is same in many despite everything else, every other feature of the objects in question, being different]) the principle of excluded middle allowed us to demonstrate the concept's immateriality because the alternative to its materiality was not a variety of other possibilities, but only one, that is, immateriality. In the instance of memory, materialists can suggest some terra incognita that the method of exclusion has not considered. While our procedure of examining all levels of neuronal cellularity has excluded those levels as possible stores for memory, it can be argued that it is not inconceivable that some as yet undiscovered neuronal material or structure may surface to account for the place of long-term memory in the human brain.

To that extent, the immateriality of memory is not established. Its likelihood, though, has been established if no cellular agent exists overriding and replacing DNA's role in the neuronal gene. DNA in such a circumstance would relinquish its role as the basis of cellularity. To the extent that that is unlikely, the immortalist can argue that memory's immateriality is not.

ANECDOTAL OR EVIDENTIAL?

Materialism and immaterialism have come to the question of endless life with particular starting points. Materialism's principal one seems to be that certain assumptions need not be proven. One can use them to reach predetermined conclusions, conclusions already contained in the assumption. For it, all consciousness is reducible to material explanation for there is no possibility of a realm that is immaterial. Once the assumption is made, a whole area of conclusions becomes impossible. One of them is endless life.

With immaterialism the procedure is different. It can, as in religion, postulate an immaterial possibility. However, it cannot get to it from arguing that no material explanation for what occurs is possible, therefore there must be immaterial. It has argued from an observation that in the world we know, albeit within only the frequency that we stated experience registers, a being comes to an end through the severance of its parts. We call it "break-up," corruption," "dissolution." If corruption only occurs this way, by partibility, does that mean that which is without parts cannot corrupt?

We have already argued for why the universe must be composed from "irreducible bits," and why everything in it is composed that way. Our universe, irrespective of the findings of quantum mechanics that the universe our senses register is only a minute portion of the cosmos, comes to be through the aggregation of these bits. Quantum mechanics' statements about the "rest of the cosmos" does not affect the account of our experiences in this world. We do not experience in the "rest of the cosmos." We can only argue for what we can scientifically establish, and we clearly know that we do not have any knowledge of the rest of the cosmos that quantum theory claims exists. We argued that quantum theory's tools, in coming from the universe that is only a minute portion of the cosmos, is on relatively unsteady ground in its assertions for that reason. It is, to be scientific, only about this universe that our senses register that we can discourse. And that universe tells us that at points in the coming to be in everything in it are irreducibilities, "irreducible bits," whose separation means the end of the thing they composed. To move beyond these "irreducibilities" is to move into nothingness.

On what is it that organizes those irreducible bits into the entities they become we have already briefly touched.[1] We are interested here now more in knowing if consciousness in the body of personhood can be viewed as that which. because not bodily, partible, can escape corruption.

We have so far concluded that bodily decomposition does not necessitate the extinction of consciousness, the end of individual personhood. Why is it that the body appears as it does at death? If we take the quantum doctrine of vibrational fields as a hypothesis, can we suggest that in decomposition is entrance into another frequency? Our five senses, it is indisputable, have an incapability of registering on that frequency. However, this does not get us to what we are seeking. Animals have different sense images than we do. Is it because their senses are attuned differently, have access to different "frequencies"? One need only look at the way bats navigate their airway flights, or the way fish in the great deep of the ocean move, to understand how sense powers convey different sense objects. Perhaps different sense capacities mean reaching differing "electrical fields."

Is it possible the dead are entered into a frequency inaccessible to our consciousness that can only use the sense organs proportioned to the wavelengths we noted in our earlier chapter on this subject? This would possibly explain why we do not see in the casket the "person" anymore that we once knew. Our senses are so constructed that they do not allow us access beyond the heartbreak of the death of a loved one. That does not mean the loved one is without consciousness or existence as a person. It is just that we do not, because of how we come by evidence in this frequency that quantum mechanics has hypothesized, have that evidence we need to confirm the person is not gone, but simply move on to a realm not within our ken. If vitality, "life," can occur on frequencies to which quantum's hypothesis has opened the door but not confirmed by tools beyond this realm of experience, this wavelength in which we experience and live, we cannot rule out this hypothesis of decomposition as entrance into a different frequency. In those frequencies, if we want to use the language of "form," "essence," we can say the sense power becomes the sensation in question, in virtue of the "form" wherein the frequency attains the level of coherence and order that all sensation manifests.

Does the NDE (near-death experience), or the OBE (out-of-body experience), have any evidentiary value to the one seeking the answer to what happens after death? Here no frequency level other than the one in which we now experience seems to be operant. Does either the NDE or OBE, which we encounter on the frequency level to which alone quantum mechanics says we have access, say anything conclusive? Or are both on account of some yet to be explained physiologic process demonstrated to have no bearing on this most serous of question, the question of life after death? Are these processes, the OBE and NDE, strictly corporeal and in now wise evidence of trans-corporeal bearing?

The OBE and NDE comprise a topic more familiar to the populace at large than what we have gone through in the previous chapters. We have already puzzled as to why the subject of mortality is not genuinely all consuming, Would not a reality of this magnitude, the size of death, the total end of one's world, not impel everyone to examine and ponder and do all one could to achieve a breakthrough of understanding in this, ones' final moment?

The question is pressed: if one is immortal, why is it that no one knows it, as one knows his own name, or his own surroundings? Why is it that the grave appears to me as it does? Why do I not have certainty that the grave is not my end, my finality, my extinction? Why is not immortality "obvious" to me? Is it because immortality is not part of the human constitution? Is it that I am not immortal because I was not born immortal? After all, were I born immortal, I would not have to worry about thinking how I prove it: to be human is to be immortal should be quite clear to the one born that way.

We asked earlier if it made sense that to come into being was only on account of perishing? One comes to be in order to perish. That does not appear to make sense to the thinker. Yet, because we have no prima facie evidence of immortality, it seems, claiming immortality appears to be more a leap of hope than a hard-eyed look at what will actually befall every human who has come to be or will.

The NDE and OBE are considered "anecdotal." They do not, some argue, hold up to the rigors of scientific inquiry. Anecdotes, however, when of similar content distributed over a large population sample (i.e., experienced by many) have something about them that skepticism cannot simply dismiss by the term "anecdote." One, two, maybe even a dozen, surely do not give us a feel of "science." Over many different individuals in many different settings at many different times speaking many different language with thought patterns not always identical in each language may tell us that "repeatability"—cardinal to all scientific endeavor—in fact has been achieved. In this country, a 1991 Gallup poll has recorded millions as claiming an NDE.[2]

Observability, though? Has it been achieved? The scientist wants whatever is called "evidence" to be publicly available, publicly accessible. If it is not, what one reports cannot count as evidence as science set out.

Does the individual who states he has had an experience such as the OBE speak then "without evidence?" If he says at some moment in his struggle to survive and beat death while his body appeared to have totally ceased operating something occurred to him, he saw something, he heard something—is this just the situation of a mistake that has fed a hope in something that cannot possibly have perdurance? Is it not just that the person reporting it will also die, as everyone else is going to?

One has to wonder, however, if so many people have had the NDE and OBE, why that does not in a way fulfill the criterion of "publicly accessible?" True, it is individual (special) to each one who has it, but when so many have the "same" or "similar" experience, it ceases in actuality to be "private" any more. To object and say it remains "private," is to give a new meaning to the word. *My* NDE is private to me; yes. But that does not mean the NDE is private. When something is private, no one else has access to it. In the case of the millions Gallup reports, it is as private as the next person having it.

Advances in death prevention and resuscitation have brought this NDE and OBE issue to the fore in the past three decades. Beginning with Raymond Moody, and then moving on with the work of Kenneth Ring and Martin Sabom,[3] the marked role of data and verification, to the extent it is possible, have been characteristic of inquiries addressing what it is that the patient near death and in many cases given up for dead has reported he went through at the time of his near-death trauma.

What they report is unique for that moment. The near-death experience has no cognate in the person's life. The NDE correlates very heavily with what has been described as heavenly, paradisiacal, transcendent; for some who report it, even inexpressible. Those who have had an NDE, in compelling numbers, have spoken of what they assert can only be termed non-worldly, but yet very real and in no way hallucinatory. For them the phenomenon is a real human experience, a genuine—as opposed to imagined—event. Indeed, the frequent feeling of passivity in the NDE, as those who have had it relate, would argue against a subjective initiation of the event, This suggests the need for a more careful explanation.[4] The individual's affirmation of it as an experienced reality brings it to the concrete.

At the crisis of near-death, where the coronary victim has suffered from a failed heart, the suicide attempt been almost successful, the accident victim returned from the edge of death, arises a constellation of moments that whispers of a supernal country:

> A feeling of easeful peace and a sense of well-being....a sense of overwhelming joy and happiness. The ecstatic tone....tends to persist as a constant emotional ground as other features of the experience begin to unfold. At this point, the person is aware he feels no pain nor does he have any other bodily sensations....These cues suggest to him that he is either in the process of dying or has already 'died.'

> He may then be aware of a transitory buzzing or a wind like sound....he finds himself looking down on his physical body, as though he were viewing it from some external vantage point....aware of the actions and conversations taking place in the physical environment [as] a passive, detached spectator. All this seems very real—even quite natural to him; it does not seem at all like a dream or an hallucination.

> At some point he may find himself in a state of dual awareness....aware of 'another reality' and feel himself being drawn into it....The experience here is predominantly peaceful and serene.

> The presence....stimulates him to review his life and asks him to decide whether he wants to live or die....He has no awareness of space and time. Neither is he identified any longer with his body. Only the mind is present.

Sometimes, however, the decisional crisis occurs later or is altogether absent, and the individual undergoes further experiences. He may, for example, continue to float through the dark void towards a magnetic brilliant golden light, from which remains a feeling of love, warms, and total acceptance. Or he may enter into a 'world of light' and preternatural beauty, to be (temporarily) reunited with deceased loved ones before being told, in effect, that it is not yet his time and that he has to return to life.[5]

Ring's summary draws questions. How does one reach "easeful peace"? Exactly what is this condition? Is it a condition of mind, of the body? Of both? Of both as one, or separately but mingled in the separation in a way (as water and wine) that is not experienced in this existence? Just as wine and water in water are not one, yet are not separate, is this the way the "at oneness" with mind and body comes about? An "at oneness" that preserves identity but in a way that conflict is gone, just as the water and wine in the goblet are not at conflict, but blend to bring abut a new existent while not losing their own?

In this near-death condition what can one mean that the traumatized patient, with paddles hard at his chest, or perhaps needles firing stimulants to his heart, or frenetic fists pounding at his chest, experiences "peace?" Is it a peace of resignation? How can one have such a peace on the battlefield in Viet Nam with limbs torn off and terror one's only understanding, or the mother dying holding her child close to her heart in a desolate underground tunnel in turn of the century Armenia? How is it that with dread and fear presenting themselves as they do to the one dying, suddenly it all vanishes and everything settles, everything comes to rest?

How can absolute horror become joy? What has happened in the near-death consciousness that happiness is now one's condition and being? What can the patient reporting such sense of felicity mean? Is what he feels in any way like the "happiness" that one is said to have in various moments as an embodied soul? Or is the happiness mentioned something that means a totally different state than earthly? And does one mean here only a state of mind, a state of consciousness? How can one have happiness if one with the NDE has been a battle wounded soldier and the body is so completely torn up, so compromised? Is consciousness in the NDE state blocking out the reality of the body it inhabited? Surely the body's condition cannot be the occasion of restful contentment. Has consciousness reached a state of awareness where physical dismemberment becomes insignificant? But how can such dismemberment become insignificant if part of the realty of personhood is this body?

And what does the body mean to the person "near death"? Is the body this primarily space filled existent that quantum physics (the frailty of its tools we discussed notwithstanding) claims it is? And is this how the individual near death is come to understand what in the existence he is leaving he understood and experienced to be a resistant, solid, rigorous construct that at some time in his life attracted someone to marry him and promise to be with him always?

All sensation is gone. The individual in the NDE is no longer at its mercy. He can move beyond the bodily sense-apparatus in a way that the near-death sufferer seems yet to have made clear. Sensation would end, of course, if life has stopped. Nothing powers the sense organs to receive and transmit. They have become themselves lifeless. Yet the NDE can "see" his body below him as he "rises" above it. He can even "hear" what is around "his" body from the voices of those seeking to restore it, to aid it. How can this occur if the senses are the only means to having contact with these sense stimuli, but they are now shut down?

In this condition, the individual suddenly has his consciousness in that state altered to an alertness to some entity soliciting, calling, compelling him to move towards it. In what does this "movement" consist? Surely it cannot be a place change. Is the transcendent where our patient hovers one that has extension? If it does, how does it differ from ordinary existence where we have the extension of space?

This turning to the presence or voice that calls to the individual: how is the individual made aware of it? Is the "movement" voluntary? Is it a moment where what beckons is so overwhelming in persuasion, as it were, that the individual has no choice but to acquiesce and "move towards" it, move towards this "light"?

Of significance that is immediate and perhaps critical to the individual "near death" is that he reported accurately on persons in his NDE who had once lived but whom he could not have possibly known. These instances seem too varied for one explanation.

This is the inchoate form of the full NDE, with some possible questions on the one who reads of it. In *Heading Towards Omega*, Kenneth Ring, to quote him again, has neatly delineated the features of the core NDE:

> There is no time in these experiences. ('It was eternity....It's like I was always there.'), there is a certain feeling of progression....We remember (1) the incredible speed and sense of acceleration as one approaches (2) the light that (3) glows with an overwhelming brilliance and yet (4) does not hurt one's eyes....One feels in the presence of light (5) pure love, (6) total acceptance, (7) forgiving of sins, and (8) a sense of homecoming, that (9) communication with the light is instantaneous and nonverbal and that the light (10) imparts knowledge of a universal nature as well as (11) enables one to see or understand his entire life so that (12) it is clear what truly matters....One may be aware of (13) transcendental music, (14) paradisiacal environments, and (15) cities of light as one progresses further into the experience....Finally (16) once having encountered the light, one yearns to be with it forever.[6]

We have encountered this importance of light in studying earlier on the process of vision. Because our visual apparatus is limited, much of the universe cannot be seen. Light, which we need, is in terrible dearth. We have no light with which to see the rest of the universe because the electromagnetic radiation at the frequencies in which the rest of the universe would be made manifest (if ever it is) our eyes cannot register. We do not know, for that reason whether the rest of the universe would resemble what we think the universe to be, solid moving, warm, cold, and the like.

In the NDE we encounter again the light phenomenon. However, light here is not a means by which something is seen. It appears rather to be something personal, guiding, an individual. It is not at all easy to argue whether this "light" is strictly an excitation of the visual cortex, or some temporal lobe occurrence. In those cases one would be experiencing an event much like, it seems, one "sees stars" after having suffered a head trauma. We know that in certain controlled events where one is subject to various simulations of torque and the like, as in a fighter jet simulation, the individual subject reports experiences not dissimilar to this sight of light.

What differentiates, it appears, this fighter jet experience though from the NDE one is that the individual in the NDE describes this "light" as compassionate, "loving" "warm," and "comforting." This difference in the NDE from the experience in other situations of "seeing the light," has had others claim that certain endorphins released in the brain are responsible. At death they cause the perception of light to be felt as it is. It is not so much "light" that causes the serenity and the like but Nature preparing the individual for resignation and acceptance of what cannot be otherwise. Endorphins cling to molecules ("clip on" to them, as it were) that generate the defense mechanism reaction syndrome against death, and by that shut them down.

The explanation of the feeling of warmth and charm as a way Nature makes death more easeful and less to be defended against assumes that human actions are molecularly derived, that chemical synaptic neurotransmission is how "messages" to the limbs and body parts that set the body in motion are carried. We saw, however, that Libet's experiments seemed to put that thesis on difficult terrain as well as the work of Beauragard on obsessive-compulsive disorder. If the endorphin explanation, as well as the ketamine,[7] have this impediment to their explanatory power, what establishes the use of chemical compounds as the factor, to the exclusion of others, for the experience of the "being of light" and "easeful peace"?

The amount of debate on ketamine invites a bit more scrutiny. The assertion is that a 50-100mg dose of ketamine can reproduce the NDE via blockade of the N-methyl-D-aspartate, NMDA receptors in the brain for the neurotransmitter glutamate.[8] The evidence advanced is the discovery of the major neuronal binding site for ketamine, known as the phencyclidine (PCP) binding site of the NMDA receptor.[9]

The importance of NMDA receptors is well known. It has place in the cerebral cortex, particularly in the temporal and frontal lobes. The key role of these sites in cognitive processing, memory, and perception, their role in epilepsy, psychoses, hypoxic/ischaemic and epileptic cell damage (excitotoxicity) shows just how much. Ketamine provides prevention of cell damage. The discovery of substances in the brain called 'endopsychosins' which bind to the same site as ketamine, and understanding the role of ions such as magnesium and zinc in regulating the site, have furthered the understanding of ketamine.[10]

Ketamine produces an altered state of consciousness which is very different from that of the 'psychedelic' drugs such as LSD.[11] It can reproduce all features of the NDE, including travel through a dark tunnel into light, the conviction that one is dead, 'telepathic communion with God', hallucinations, out-of-body experiences and mystical states. If given intravenously, it has a short action with an abrupt end. Grinspoon and Bakalar[12] wrote of:

> 'becoming a disembodied mind or soul, dying and going to another world. Childhood events may also be re-lived. The loss of contact with ordinary reality and the sense of participation in another reality are more pronounced and less easily resisted than is usually the case with LSD. The dissociative experiences often seem so genuine that users are not sure that they have not actually left their bodies.

This can all be granted as factual. But does a pharmacological explanation suffice for the experience? No other account is needed or possible? Apparently not. There are other ways the experience comes about. We can cite Wilder Penfield's own work involving stimulation of the Sylvan fissure in the right temporal lobe of the patient. When it was stimulated, the patient would exclaim that he was leaving his body. On a number of other patients, they reported to be "half-in half-out" of their body; along with experiencing other features in the NDE that others have stated they had, such as hearing symphonic tones not heard on earth, seeing old acquaintances, and the like.[13]

Michael Persinger of Laurentian University, Ontario, has had similar outcomes in his work regarding right temporal stimulation.[14] The point is this: pharmacological excitation has nothing essentially or exclusively to do with the experience. If it did, no other approach would yield the results its advocates say. But, as we just saw, there are other such approaches that do.

If the stimulation accounts for this, how does one get a sense of a tunnel through which one passes to this "light" we mentioned? Is the "tunnel" experience actually the retina in the dying person losing its capacity such that the explanation is light through its photoreceptors gets narrower and narrower? Is this "narrowing" the "tunnel"? The electromagnetic radiation impulses that coursed through the retinal photoreceptors to the optic nerve during life, and which one experienced as light by which he saw his world, has "narrowed" capacity for that passage. Is this how or why we think of ourselves going through a tunnel?[15] It would perhaps be a possible explanation except when the retina cell dies, it does not come back. It cannot be revivified or renewed. Retinal thrombosis is an instance of retinal cell death. The retinal tissue scars. What occurs to sight is a cloud in the area scarred. Normally the cloud is not seen in everyday occurrence because the brain (more precisely, consciousness) "sees" the world and makes adjustments for the failed retinal capacity. In ophthalmologic testing, however, the blind field shows up in the patient's reporting of what he does and does not see. Those who have come back from the NDE and saw this "tunnel: have not reported this subsequent impairment of acuity, this absence of sight, or presence of cloud, that retinal death (the possible suspect in the "tunnel" experience) would cause. That would suggest the tunnel experience is not retinally related. And Carl Sagan's identification of the tunnel excursus experienced in the NDE with the birth canal exit by the infant has lost its sway now that we have evidence of how poor the eyesight of the newborn is.[16]

The suggestion the NDE is a defense mechanism against death, a sort of propaedeutic afforded by Nature in the temporal lobe to accept the inevitable, would have force were the NDE always what it was described above: a feeling of contentment in peace. But in some NDEs the individual has visions of punishment and hell, and has recounted that he sought desperately to be brought back to life so great was his fear.[17] This would not be a way to prepare one for easeful acceptance of the inevitable. The NDE emerges then as not a defense mechanism, an explanation some have advanced to show that it was not an event that was actually commensurate with an actual otherworldly dimension. Since the NDE presents both fearful and peaceful experiences of another world, we can only say that the NDE happens, and that the explanations for it being a defense mechanism do not hold.

The strength of the NDE report, as we noted, is the experience's widespread occurrence, in part or whole, among the living that have been declared clinically dead and been revived. Its breadth, according to the Gallup organization in percentage terms amounts to a 35% occurrence.[18] The possibilities here of prevarication, mass suggestion, and wish-fulfillment have been minutely examined and convincingly dismissed. Drug inducement of the NDE has been cogently ruled out with alert reasoning power by Kenneth Ring. Carol Zaleski, in analysis published after Ring, likewise concluded that the pharmacological explanation is not conclusive.[19] We also have stated similarly. given, as we saw, that electrode stimulation also generates the NDE. Accordingly, suggesting a pharmacologic provenance for the NDE requires explaining why no one has argued that electrode stimulation should also not be. Since it is, the pharmacological explanation does not sufficiently account for the NDE. To be scientifically conclusive, however, it must.

Neurophysiologic studies have yet to show that the near-death experience is, or might be, strictly a bodily defense mechanism, the brain's chemically fashioned weapon against the final test. Given the findings we just noted that experiences of horror come with some NDEs adds to what those neurophysiologic studies have yet to show. Kenneth Ring's *Life At Death* has enlighteningly addressed the difficulty: the current state of knowledge does not trace this reaction to the unknown to a programmed neurophysiologic response. Instead, those who have had an NDE have held it to be of at the least the same texture and presence (if not, in some cases, of higher acuity, definition, and clarity) as ordinary experience. That is what has compelled their insistence on the NDE as non-illusory, non-hallucinatory.

Psychiatric review of the NDE has shown it incompatible with mental disorder. Psychoses are cut from different cloth. A near-death experience is neither mental illness nor a symptom of it.

But those who have had an NDE that they reported did not die in it. Lazarus died. His story has been told elsewhere (*Jn.* 11:1–45), unaccompanied by an NDE narrative. He had been entombed. And in our day rigor mortis is still the sure sign that embalming may begin. No individual who has reported an NDE cited in the research has undergone rigor mortis in the NDE.[20] Kastenbaum has elaborated how it is that the NDE, on these grounds, does not move us one step closer to demonstrating the immortality thesis.[21]

He may have drawn this conclusion too quickly, given the frequently reported out-of-body experience (OBE) in the NDE. This particular facet of the near-death event his study does not treat. In contrast to the simple near-death experience, i.e., one unaccompanied by this OBE, might the OBE in the near-death trauma present tolerable evidence for an actual demarcation from the body by the one undergoing the near-death OBE? Is there in it ground for asserting a sure separation from matter, a positive delineation from corporeal limits, for the one who has had this OBE? If so, evidence of an incorporeal reality for man is suggested.[22]

In its most basic meaning, an out-of-body experience is a personal consciousness and activity accomplished without the body. The human person in the OBE realizes, in addition, that he is out of the body. He is certain that the body which he has always had in life, and through which he has been present in the world as a living being, is wholly separated from his out-of-body state. He is existing as self-continuous with his past, with the powerful exception that his selfhood, his existence, is not bodily. His identity is intact, and he knows this to be so. His material body, however, is not a constituent of that identity which he knows to be his, and which identity he knows in his OBE to be non-bodily. His human being is not bodily being. His existence as a self has "left the body behind." There has been a separation of consciousness from matter.

The description of the near-death OBE by those who have had it points to this separation:

> a real floating sensation....It seemed like I was up there in space and just my mind was active. No body feeling....Weightless, I had nothing....I was above. I don't know above what....like I didn't have a body....but it was not me. Not a body, but me....The real me was up there, not this here' (pointing to her physical body).[23]

"I was walking away from myself hanging there," is how a suicide attempt described his OBE. Another:

> I felt I had left my body and I had viewed it from the other side of the room....looking back at myself....I can remember seeing myself up there with a sheet and a hypothermia blanket on me. I was up in the left hand corner of the room, looking down at what was going on.[24]

From others:

I was just observing....It [the resuscitation procedure] 'didn't feel as though it was happening to me at all. I was just the observer'....'I was totally objective.... just an onlooker.'[25]

Kate also told of how she had traveled out-of-body to her home during her NDE. She socked her parents with the accuracy of her vivid account. She told them that she had observed her brother playing with a G. I. Joe in a jeep and her sister with he Barbie doll. She described the clothes her parents were wearing, that her dad sat in the living room, what her mother was cooking.[26]

In Ring's *Life At Death* sampling, 37% underwent a near-death OBE. But any value they would have as evidence for us of non-bodily awareness—of consciousness as immaterial—would require that the OBE reports of events prehended out of body be accurate. In the situation above of the hospital OBE patients, e.g., what they recounted would have to square with the events that those attending these patients could confirm as actually having happened.

In a comatose state—the near-death condition—the senses are inoperant. These are our channels of awareness to the world. Bodily embedded, they are our source of information about our environment and surroundings. In the absence of any one of them our awareness in some way becomes restricted. In the total absence of operating, working, sense-faculties we are shut off from the world. In the near-death state sensory capability has ceased. No one in this state is conscious externally, because sense-transmission has stopped. Physiologically, sensation has become incapacitated. Its integrity, which consists in the sense organ's vital interaction with various brain centers, has been impeded. In trauma, either part or all of the bodily sensory-neural-brain network has been injured or shut down. If sensation is our only avenue of awareness to the world, and is only bodily, awareness of the world in the absence of sensory powers would indicate non-bodily awareness.

The meaning from this: if human awareness is not only bodily, occurs independently of the body, being a conscious individual is not being only a bodily one. Human individuality and human body would not be the same, then. Corruption of the human body, accordingly, need not be corruption of the human individual.

To test the accuracy of the near-death OBE reports, reports held to be based on awareness of events in the absence of bodily sense transmission, Michael Sabom undertook a methodological inquiry into their veracity. If an unconscious near-death trauma victim claiming an OBE gave an account of his crisis treatment and surroundings seemingly derivable (which is what science teaches) only from bodily sense operations, his claim to being out of the body could not be lightly dismissed. To have an awareness of events in the absence of sensation is to have it without the body. The only routes for awareness are the sensory pathways. And they need a functioning body, one whose sense-faculties (sensory-neural receptors) are operant to carry out their work of data transmission.

Sabom's *Recollection of Death* is his scientific study of the phenomenon testing for inconsistencies in, and improbabilities of, the accuracy of patient resuscitation OBE reports. He pinpointed six representative OBE testimonials and corroborated them with the accounts of the medical team involved in the resuscitation with cross-reference to the patient's clinical records. Only trans-bodily capabilities, i.e., an actual OBE, could account, Sabom reasoned, for the accuracy of the patient's description of the clinical events surrounding revival. That is because an unconscious body cannot have the awareness indicated to be present in these OBE reports.

A patient declared clinically moribund would recount events, after medical restoration, in the resuscitation procedure inaccessible to one's awareness threshold in the comatose state. Verification of these events, e.g., the peculiarity of a medical procedure and its instruments, identification of individuals in that procedure, or the steps taken at the trauma center, would take place through testimony of the medical personnel involved. Actual hospital records and post-resuscitation/ operation data acted as a double-check on the reported OBE. For Sabom, the contention that there was an OBE was well-nigh authenticated, as his documentation argues.

What of Sabom's methodology? Is it exhaustive? Does it exclude all room for error? Are those certifying the accuracy of the OBE reports being less than candid? They have no reason to be. Nothing would be gained. And in light of the common skepticism in response to the unusual, the risk of those interviewed losing respectability would be great. While that is not indisputable confirmation of candor in the OBE verification by hospital personnel, it is perhaps the strongest that the cases allow. And that is all that can be asked in instances where evidence—absolute indisputability—is impossible of attainment. The level of indisputability the testimony of hospital personnel has here depends on how much strength we attribute to the motive against loss of respectability.

Was Sabom's method exhaustive? Is there some significant variable it failed to address? It does not appear so. In seeking to verify OBE accounts he has consulted all those who could verify them, and gone a step further through his cross-reference double-check. Does the methodology exclude all room for error? Error (as distinct from falsehood) could result from incompetence, lack of understanding, or faulty information.[27] None of the principals involved have suggested, after Sabom's interviews were published, that he was misinformed. And we have no evidence of incompetence. He has executed his research within the normal rigors of academic inquiry. That separates it from a merely anecdotal summary.

If there is, then, any incompetence in *Recollections* it would have to be in the very methodology of scientific inquiry itself. That would be a novel criticism, and not well-based. And nowhere in his deliberations has Sabom, a medical doctor, shown a failure to comprehend the data amassed, or their implications.

The Sabom data, accordingly, allow for a compelling case about non-bodily awareness. In terms used in law courts, might we have what is called "the preponderance of the evidence"? Witnesses certifying the accuracy of a near-death victim's OBE reports have come forth. Their testimony has been checked against other data for the sake of reverification. Lying has been ruled out, as far as circumstances allow. Further, no circumstances point to a compelling benefit to lie: motive has been eliminated.

Denying the validity of OBE reports is, then, to deny the preponderance of at least the data, if not the evidence. Assuring the veridicality of the OBE rests on the testimony of witnesses and objective records. For this reason, a strong case can be made for Sabom's results. Dr. Penny Sartori's[28] and Janice Holden's[29] separate research, both published after the turn of this century, confirm what Sabom found. If non-sensory awareness is a bodily impossibility, then those who claimed that their awareness of clinical events, whose accuracy was verified, was in fact out of the body have spoken factually.

The OBE in this situation transcends those arguments leveled against the near-death experience that does not contain it. While it could be argued that natural endorphins or drugs induced the feelings and visions reported in the NDE—even though there is no evidence for that claim—the veridicality of the OBE renders those arguments pointless. They have nothing to do with the circumstances of veridicality. In the OBE there is no "vision" for which to account. In the OBE it is the actual awareness of a comatose body that must be explained. We are faced with circumstances in which the bodily apparatus of sensory data-reception has ceased to function while the individual whose body has so ceased has nevertheless verified awareness of his surroundings.

There is some suspicion that the auditory apparatus may still have capability in the comatose body, a suspicion for which the neurophysiologic evidence is mixed, inconclusive. Even granting that capability, the visual accuracy exhibited in the veridicality of the OBE, in which the patient sees what is being done in the trauma setting, is inexplicable in bodily terms. The eyes are shut. If endorphins or drugs provide for trans-sensate awareness—out-of-body veridicality—how they provide sight in this instance becomes problematic.[30]

We have the similar difficulty in those who are blind from birth who, in an OBE, report accurately what those who can see know to be likewise accurate. Ring and Cooper report on this methodically.[31] "I am legally blind...I could see clearly what the doctors were doing." The vision, they note, however inexplicable, may be better termed "mindsight," rather than seen as an analogue of retinal vision. Kübler-Ross adds to the King-Cooper data in her account of a man born blind who in his OBE was able to describe the pattern of the operating physician's tie.[32]

In this way the point can be made: The materialist paradigm is inapplicable here. Awareness has become, apparently, non-bodily. How else does one account for seeing when the bodily faculty by which one sees is not in use? That is the issue, root and branch, in the out-of-body report at near-death. Until it is resolved the materialist doctrine that awareness can only be bodily appears, if not inconclusive, at least tenuous.

If the out-of-body experience does exist, the experience itself could not be bodily. This can be shown in both the order of thought and in that of actual existence. In the former, where it is just the notions involved, and thus without reference to an actual situation, the body cannot be conceived as separate from, outside of, itself, as that which, in the OBE separates from itself. Separated from body it would cease to be the body that separated. Body separate from itself would be body other than itself. Body separate from itself, as that which in the OBE was "out of" itself, involves necessarily the element of distinction. To conceive of the body as distinct from itself involves two mental objects: that of the body, and of the very same body separate from itself. In such a case we are thinking of two identical bodies as distinct from each other. Approached from the order of thought, then, analysis shows that the out-of-body experience cannot be the experience of a material, physical, mass, sc., the body.

In the order of *ens reale*, real being, (as opposed to the order of thought) a body actually distinct and separate from itself requires two existent bodies—the body and, in addition, the body from which it is distinct. But they are the same bodies: they must be to be the body of the person having the OBE. If not, we are left with two bodies different from each other, and inhabited by a consciousness that is (a) in the two bodies at once, (b) in the out-of-body body alone, or a situation in which (c) there are two minds in two bodies or (d) a mind in the comatose body and not the OBE body. One mind in two bodies for the same person seems inconceivable. How would it be present in them? Not by parts; the mind is not a magnitude.

A mind in the out-of-body body, instead of the comatose one, would mean the coming-to-be of a mind in that body, or a mind that left the comatose one to enter the out-of-body one. In the first, how did the mind come to be in it? In the second, how did it leave the comatose one? Two minds in two bodies involve difficulties similar to those just mentioned. And what happens to the second mind, which is necessary for awareness, in the out-of-body body, i.e., the body other than the comatose one, when the OBE ends? And a mind in the comatose body, but not the OBE one, would fail to explain awareness in the comatose one whose senses were not functioning, for it is senses that are the routes of awareness to and from the world. It is this comatose body, by hypothesis, which must account for the OBE awareness, since the mind, without which there is no awareness, is in our hypothesis now only in this body, and not the OBE one.

The assertion of two bodies in an OBE, consequently, appears without strength. The out-of-body experience, then, as addressed in terms of the order of being, has cause, in the same way we saw in the argument from the order of thought, for being viewed as non-bodily. The point is important, for we are seeking to ascertain if there is a non-bodily, a non-material, dimension in man. If the OBE excludes a body, which we have just argued it does, then we have the evidence of incorporeality that we need—if there are experiences out of the body. The grounds for excluding a second body, and thus the body altogether, in the

OBEs appear well-founded, if the reasoning process we just went through has the appropriate rigor.

In the OBEs the awareness must be non-bodily, non-corporeal. If there is an experience actually out of the body, consciousness is not bodily-constrained. The point in bringing up the out-of-body near-death experience should be plain, then. In the current state of science. it has no explanation. To label it hallucinatory, of course, is to misuse the adjective. Hallucinations have no veridicality. And it is that veridicality that requires a cause. How can one have awareness if it must be bodily-derived and the senses, bodily composed, are inoperant? All experience runs contrary to insensate awareness, an awareness not bodily derived: to the materialist, "insensate (not-bodily-sense derived) awareness" would be oxymoronic Unarguably, in a healthy state awareness is always sense-driven. We have argued that some immaterial capacity is requisite if sense transmission is to result in a percept, a conscious event. Here, however, in the OBE the necessity of embodied sense origination seems to be overridden.

Limiting ourselves, as we should, to what the data allow us to conclude, permits this reading of the OBE: either awareness can be bodily-originated in the absence of sense-faculties (something may account for awareness in what., therefore can only be an apparent comatose state of which we are not yet knowledgeable), or awareness does not, as a sine qua non, require the body, which it nevertheless does when one is functioning normally. There may be instances, i.e., in which communion with the body is suspended, breached, and consciousness takes on an existence of its own disjoined from the body. The alternative is equally problematic: awareness can require a body, but the sense powers are not what always generate it.

The only evidence we have of this is the OBE, which can be equally interpreted as evidence that consciousness can be non-bodily, that it does not require a body. This equality of interpretability of one and the same event becomes a difficulty for the materialist view of man. What it has asserted cannot be the case, that is, non-bodily or non-sensory originated awareness, appears, given the OBE's veridicality, equiprobable with what it has asserted must be the case, that is, the functioning of a healthy body in each case of awareness. Quite plainly this reduces the materialist tenet to the level of opinion, which requires, for its passage to that of truth, fact. This materialism cannot provide.

Given that, the OBE is not explicable in terms of bodily sensory powers. Accordingly, asserting a bodily, and therefore material, necessity, to awareness on the premise that human awareness requires man's physical sensory apparatus will leave unexplained an awareness capability that does not reduce to the materialist model. This is to say awareness has no determining materialistic explanation—which it needs if man is to be explained strictly (and completely) in terms of matter.

SENTIENT IMMORTALITY

We have noted in this work a number of reasons for the ascription of immortal personhood to the human being. (1) Concept formation, the ability to perceive a sameness in things otherwise different, argued for the capability of transcending singular existents, which matter designates. This means the ability to transcend matter, that component of the human being which it is that decomposes. Also, (2) the ability to form certain judgments, whose terms would be incomprehensible were the person simply a material creature. The judgment that two propositions cannot both be true if contradictory does not show a material derivation for its intelligibility. Into what material components the principle of non-contradiction can be broken seems an unintelligible question. It is because the components that go to make it up are not material constituents of any entity. (3) Consciousness, that "aboutness" by which that not possessed of it is differentiated from what possesses it, seems different than the property of matter. (4) The veridicality of the OBE offers us pause. How an OBE is veridical seems without explanation unless one is willing to consider a capacity of consciousness that is not bodily sense-bound.

We want now to consider whether immortality is strictly a feature of human personhood, or whether it goes beyond personhood Personhood is the capacity [and activity] to choose [to be unconstrained by an actual desire] and to reason abstractly. Reductionism, that inclination to speak and describe and attempt to account for all human activity in terms of material elements and causes, has sought to use neural and mathematical expressions to replace what has been called "folk psychology," i.e., the language of the masses, the unsophisticated (if not the unlearned, and unschooled). Because they do not speak "scientifically," they speak inaccurately. Insofar as neural activity is at best only a correlate, not a cause, of conscious acts, and percepts, folk psychology has emerged as the more plausible (even if not sophisticated) means of expressing what is actually occurring in human mentation. What neuroepistemology has termed "scientific" has resulted from identifying correlation with causation. We see no such misstep in the language of folk attitude.

Our question now has to pertain strictly to those entities that come to live, but are not members of the species *homo sapiens*. Immortality can only apply to an entity that once lived or is living. More specifically, to sentient life. Does sentience, consciousness, in living organisms outside of persons perish; or does it perdure in a way that gives the organism possessed of that sentience conscious continuity beyond death?

One difficulty that we have in addressing this question is our inability to look into, to know directly, what it is for an animal to have consciousness. If that is a difficulty, how can we know what it is for the animal to cease to have it, or to die? We cannot know directly, but surely we can know analogically, just as we know about other human selves. It is not by directly experiencing their selfhood that we know someone is a human self. It is by comparing their activities with ours and, upon seeing an identity (similitude) of capacities and activities, that we infer their selfhood. They act and operate the same way (or in similar mode as) we do, and we thus analogize those actions with our own.

With animals, we know of their possession of consciousness by the way they act. The same process of inference as we have with ascertaining human agency other than our own takes place in our awareness of animal sentience. In the same way we infer that an individual before us is human because of the way that individual acts, so also is the reasoning process in our inference that animals have consciousness. If we refer actions of a person to consciousness, by the same rule we need do it in the case of the animal engaged in the same or similar actions.

We have already argued that consciousness is an immaterial event. It is not a materially originated action of an organism whose decomposition indicates its total end. Consciousness is not an electrical phenomenon, we saw. It is not some magnetic field of resonant (or conflicting, for that matter) interactions among electrons and sub-atomic realities. Quite straightforwardly, we seem to know what it is not, rather than what it is. Reluctance to declare the nature of something in the absence of the evidence necessary to make the inference as to what it is is arguably of more value to science than hypothesizing what something in that case might be.

Critical to an objective attempt at approaching animal sentience is to realize that animals must not be measured against man: man, contrary to Protagoras, is not the measure of animals.[1] We certainly cannot consider animals automata, as Descartes, in a moment (perhaps among others) of misclarity, did. That is like equating their level of perception to that of a log which neither moves nor acts, nor feels a whip, or a savage kick, or the bullet or arrow of a gamesman out for the sport. Or of the bludgeoning that prepares it as material for a coat or shoe. The Cartesian view of existence is a penurious one, where economy and less seem preferable to abundance, difference, and variety.

To think of animals, as Descartes, as well Malebranche, did, as unfeeling and *sans connaisance*, fails to explain how animals clearly know that death is approaching them. They hide or seek shelter, seek to be alone, when death is nigh, as any cat owner knows. Dogs, we know, run into burning houses to save a family member: the stories like this about the canine breed are too number-less to suggest that these animals have no awareness of death. Dr. Adrian Kortlandt has pointed out the fear that chimpanzees show in how they draw back from a dead body.[2] George Beal Schaller's work on the gorillas of Kisoro shows similar reaction.[3] Biologist Lyall Watson's work, *The Romeo Error*, cautions us not to dismiss certain animal behaviors for they indeed seem to show a continuity with our own fear and dread of death.[4] Plants themselves, possessed of a growth principle for sure, have shown to Cleve Backster, an international polygraph expert for the United States Central Intelligence Agency, their definite relations/reactions to outside stimuli. In experiments with shrimp, his work has shown what he calls a subcellular level of commu-nication.[5] Zoologists Robert and Maurice Burton,[6] as well as the work of Jo-seph Banks Rhine,[7] seem to indicate a consonant principle of a perception ca-pability in various animals that may be outside the range of human capability.

Ethologists tells us the higher the level of intelligence (the ability to dis-criminate, associate, compare and then act) in an animal, the less it is guided by instinct. So we have examples of the dog, being forbidden cheese at his master's table, going to fetching a dog biscuit and returning to place it on his master's lap. Clearly, this is an example of the dog seeking to exchange what he is forbidden, the cheese, for what the dog apparently "feels" the master might appreciate just as the dog does—a biscuit. We have the instance of the cat tapping the surface of the stream to lure fish in imitation of a fly that like-wise "taps" the surface so only to be eaten by the fish.

Behaviorists have watched a dog push a stool over to a low gate in order that he may climb the stool and over the gate, elephants breaking off tree branches with their trunks and then using them to swat flies. If a squirrel stores nuts, are we to think that when he digs them up he has not done so for the pur-pose that we ourselves store things? Of the bird whose wing is damaged, what do we make of its plucking feathers from its own body and mixing them with mud or its coagulated blood to form, as it were, a splint, a cast? Has anyone watched a bird build a nest, or a beaver build a dam? All these are instances of process that calculate—not react, as is instinct's role. Calculation is to move through a process of ideas, or images, all relative to one end; instinct, just one.

Ornithologists report canaries at early stages making sounds that only af-ter a time come to sound like those of the mature canary, as the young canary itself matures. It is hard to state that simply a tone of chirped sound is chang-ing. The rhythm and cadence of the mature sounds is what strikes the student of birds, not the sound, and it is these that develop as the canary grows.

The behavior of ants is itself a wonder to observe in the animal kingdom. What level of intelligence do they possess such that they seemingly by a force of a unison that man cannot detect plan and fashion their hills and tunnels?

Japanese keep goldfish in their homes because of the earthquakes that Ja-pan has. When the goldfish start swimming wildly in their aquaria they are signaling what the human perception has not detected: an approaching quake.

The rain swallow, far ahead of an onrushing storm, will leave an area as a signal that what man cannot see is approaching. In the 1955-56 Bezymyanny volcanic eruption, Russian scientists report that hibernating bears, before the eruption, upped and left the area, while no seismologist had yet an indication of the approaching disturbance. Surely none of this is to be labeled "instinct." The adaptation of means to an end does not go by that name in man's activities. Why should it in the animal's?

In this regard, what does one make of the manifest feelings an animal has, as famed author Emile Zola reported of his dog upon Zola's being exiled? Zola tells us the dog, after searching a number of days for him, died in a grief that only humans are supposed to have.[8] There is the story told of Greyfriar's Bobby,[9] a dog (Skye Terrier breed) that was given a memorial for faithfulness by the famous Baroness Burdett Coutts. Every night the dog would go back to his dead master's grave site in the cemetery and sleep there, no matter where he had been during the day.

Remarkably, various religions have decried the notion of animal existence after earthly death, of sentient immortality to the being that either once flew in the air, walked the earth, swam the seas. It seems peculiar that such a stance would be taken in Christianity, for example, given what we have said about consciousness, that characteristic of "aboutness" which each material sentient being exhibits that differentiates it from simply material composition.

If we consider the sense-powers of some animals, consciousness takes on an even more pertinent hue for us. Consciousness as directionality for the avian flyer, the bird, has the question of sight posed before us: the bird is far, far superior in vision than man is. Some of that species have telescopic abilities unknown to us. What does this say about the directionality of that heightened power—vision—in the bird?

And what of the sense of smell? The feline species has a sense far superior to the olfactory capability of man. Without expatiating upon the exact physiology and histology of the sense-power, we can say here that the feline's sense is perhaps seventy times that of man. Smell is about odor: the power of that "aboutness" in the feline; the power of the "aboutness" of a bird's vision: both are quite manifestly directed at what is "other."

This directedness, we said, is a feature matter does not contain. Watch a bird's eye as it purveys and surveys its immediate world: they dart back and forth with an intensity and purpose that cannot be traced to the optical structure of the bird. The bird's eyes position towards an object with an interest and attentiveness that neural reverberations do not direct. An object catches the bird's attention as it rests on a tree limb: what reverberational mechanism in the ocular capacity of the bird positions the eyes so that it will focus, telescope, on that object which has caught its fancy? Do I say the object "out there" has caused the bird's ocular neurology to position it such that it telescopes the way it does? Or is the telescopic capacity of the bird an indication of something other than instinct? Of something more than neural reverberations in response to an object that the neuronal structure of the bird's eye can neither touch nor feel? Is the telescoping an automatic reaction, or is there something more than that automaticity, maybe even something "other" than complex matter? To claim the bird's reaction occurs automatically does not explain why at other times, in the same situation of tree limb, wind, breeze, light, the bird's eye positions elsewhere. The "automatic," or "instinctive," explanation seems not to provide the answer to our question. Easily, and simply, though, to say that the bird has a functionality of its own that does not succumb blindly to the forces around it, that it is "on its own" in certain ways, in other words, is an explanation that may in fact be closer to what goes in the speedwell's world, if not in the materialist's. Focusing, in other words, for the bird is not a "reaction," so much as possibly an "intention."

Thomas Aquinas held that since the mind thinks (reasons) without a sense-organ,[10] that is, is not dependent on the body for its thinking (as in the case of universals),[11] it is not united indissolubly to the body. Animals, he held, bereft of such a capacity, whose life principle is not self-subsistent, do not possess the capacity that makes man immortal.[12] Unlike the animals, man possesses an immortal soul in virtue of his reason. It is reason which differentiates man from the animals, and by which he has capacity for eternal being upon his coming to be.

The tradition in Christian (certainly Roman Catholic) thought seems to have been sealed with a certainty because it is philosophically based, that is, proceeds from the reasoning of the mind. With the appropriate principles that constitute the syllogism for the proof a necessary judgment as to man's immoral existence arrives.

Yet, the work that grounds Christianity, and gives it the basis for what it teaches, sc., the Scriptures, tells us this at *Romans* 8: 21: ὅτι καὶ αὐτὴ ἡ κτίσις ἐλευθερωθήσεται ἀπὸ τῆς δουλείας τῆς φθορᾶς εἰς τὴν ἐλευθερίαν τῆς δόξης τῶν τέκνων τοῦ θεοῦ. The great Apostle Paul, author of this missive to the community in Rome, under Divine and Godly inspiration is instructing the faithful that "the creation itself will be delivered from the bondage of corruption into the glorious liberty of the children of God." *Rev.* 4:11 tells us, Ἄξιος εἶ, ὁ κύριος καὶ ὁ θεὸς ἡμῶν, λαβεῖν τὴν δόξαν καὶ τὴν τιμὴν καὶ τὴν δύναμιν, ὅτι σὺ ἔκτισας τὰ πάντα, καὶ διὰ τὸ θέλημά σου ἦσαν καὶ ἐκτίσθησαν: Worthy You are, Oh Lord and God, the Holy One, to receive the glory and honor and power. You created all things. On account of Your will they were and they were created. *Gen.* 1:31, וַיַּרְא אֱלֹהִים אֶת-כָּל-אֲשֶׁר עָשָׂה, וְהִנֵּה-טוֹב מְאֹד: God saw all that He had done and unto Him it was good.

These are the three critical passages we can summon forth, passages declared true because they were possible only by Divine instruction which can never err, which can not lead us into falsehood. All that the Divine makes known is wholly true (*Is.* 8:20; *Jer.* 36:1-4; 1 *Cor.* 2:9-13; *Gal.* 1:11-12; 2 *Tim.* 3:16-17; *Heb.* 1:1-2; 2 *Peter* 1:19-21; *Rev.* 1:1-2).

We can, before we proceed, ask whether the Old Testament makes a distinction as to entitative reality between man and the animal. The question is, of course, the use of the word נֶפֶשׁ (*nephesh*). It appears first at *Gen.* 1:20, and in

its first four usages (1:20, 1:21, 1:24, 1:30) pertains to what we know as "animal." It next appears at *Gen.* 2:7, where we are told עָפָר מִן-הָאֲדָמָה, וַיִּפַּח בְּאַפָּיו ,
נִשְׁמַת חַיִּים; וַיְהִי הָאָדָם, לְנֶפֶשׁ חַיָּה וַיִּיצֶר יְהוָה אֱלֹהִים אֶת-הָאָדָם, the Divine brought man
to be by breathing into his nostrils that which He exhaled. It is by which he
came to his living.

What we have come to term "animal" has the same source of life as man
in Scriptural teaching. Right in the first book of the Old Testament we read
this. To this point we cite *Eccl.* 3:19, that man and animal all have one
"breath," (רוּחַ), and on this account, the Preacher seems to be instructing us,
neither has pre-eminence over the other.

Nephesh in the Old Testament occurs roughly seven hundred and fifty
times and in *Num.* 31:28 and *Prov.* 12:10 it is equally used of man and animal.
Lev. 17:10-11 tells us the *nephesh* of the flesh is in the blood; *Prov.* 6:30, that
a man steals food to satisfy his *nephesh*; *Is.* 29:8, that one's *nephesh* has an
appetite (desire). *Jer.* 38:17 appears to separate the body from the *nephesh*
when it writes, "your *nephesh* shall live." 1 *Sam.* 19:11, 1 *Kings* 19:10, and
Esther 7:7 seem to equate life with *nephesh*, while the Psalmist in *Ps.* 22:29
tells us no one can keep his *nephesh* living.

At the same time, it seems that what we say of *nephesh* for the human
person we can in many instances say of the animal, the organism that is said to
be without the reasoning capacity of man. To argue that *nephesh* does not apply to animals because nowhere does it say in the Mosaic account of creation
that *nephesh* came to breathed in them requires that we deny it of the first
woman, for nowhere does it say her life came to be through the imparting of
breath. *Gen.* 7:21-22 seems to account for this in its statements regarding the
flood: "all flesh dies that moved upon the earth….all in whose nostrils was the
breath of life." Additionally, when *Genesis* speaks of animal life coming to be
the word used to express the action, בָּרָא (*bará*),[13] is the same word used of the
causation of man's existence.

Gen. 1:20, 1:21 1:24; 1:28; 1:30 use *nephesh chayah* [or its cognates (נֶפֶשׁ
חַיָּה, וּבְכָל-חַיָּה, נֶפֶשׁ חַיָּה),] the meaning of which is a living *nephesh*, and in 2:7 it
is used for man (אָדָם). The point in this is that the Old Testament does not appear to make a distinction between the animal (the living fowl, the great sea
creature) and man, as the subsequent philosophic tradition in the West after
Plato did. Divinity brought to be the living *nephesh* of His creation, saw that it
was good, and nowhere are we told exists a distinction categorizing one as
mortal and the other as not. That the Old Testament appears to wait late in its
writings to speak of an afterlife does not invalidate our point. Scripture is not a
work one picks out piece by piece, but one that must be read in its entirety.
One does not read simply one book of it and assume all inspiration has come
to him. It must be read in all its statements together, and so read links animal
and human life under the Divine *nephesh*. Our *Gen.* 7:21-22 tells us all life has
"the breath of life," and makes no distinction as to the status of that breath
which is Divinely imparted, according to *Gen.* 2:7. The body exists, and upon
its dissolution, for Scripture as set forth in the New Testament, we would infer

that the being possessed of that body is subject to different laws than those in material existence.

In the prelapsarain state in Eden of comity, benevolence, and peace we find no mention of death. Man knew each living soul by its name. It appears that the Divine gave to the man and woman He created sufficient of non-animal bounty to survive. If we may understand the term "day,"[(יוֹם) yom] as translated to means other than a twenty-four hour cycle, perhaps even to the length of periods or epochs, then we can imagine a world, an Eden, of uninterrupted happiness settling over centuries. That would accord with the action and will of a God Who is good. For good, as Plato has told us, is what preserves one in being.[14]

Is it possible that we can speak of a world where harm was not known, was maybe even inconceivable? This, too, would accord with *Genesis* calling what was created "good." If God is all goodness, what He created then, in His seeing it as good, in someway must bear a resemblance to Him. In that resemblance can never be seen, one would proffer, any source for conflict, hatred, worry, anxiety, discord.

Quiet winds, warm breezes, a dove perched on a tree limb, a squirrel shoots across the verdant meadow, a lion's rich mane teased by a playful cub, a honey bee perhaps dancing on delicate flower petals, a lamb nearby watches her ewes gallop across the green sod, as the eagle alights on the sparkling rock by the stream that juts just past the banks of the river Gihon, a doe's large eyes cast a glance on the butterfly flight which rhapsodizes to the cadence of the whispering wings of the warbling, and the man and his helpmate watch them all. Was this the way it once was? A climate neither too hot nor cold to suit all land animals? Surely a providential Creator would provide for nothing less. Scripture tells us only that He commanded the man (the woman was told no such mandate, we are only told that the Divine told Adam not to take of the tree [*Gen.* 3:11]) not to eat of the tree whose fruit gave knowledge (רָע) of both good and evil (יֹדֵעַ טוֹב). The instruction is clear: knowledge (יֹדֵעַ) of evil would make man like unto his Creator in some way, and this the Divine did not want.

In what way man would be like unto God is a mystery to the student of the Writ inspired by Truth. Scripture, however, is not vague on the outcome. Woman, as a result of the transgression, was subjected to bearing children in pain; man would have to forage the earth for his sustenance. And his knowledge was enlarged to the understanding that he was simply dust, and to dust he would return (*Gen.* 3:19).

If we ask why the animals of the Garden where man first resided needed to undergo the same condition after Eden that came upon man, it can only be because of the similarity that man and the other "living souls" shares. Our *Romans* passage above tells us "the creature was made subject to vanity (ματαιότητι), not willingly, but by Him who has subjected the same in hope." The animal did not commit a transgression, unless one wants to state that the

Tempter, in taking on the form of the serpent, an animal, made it such that the animal kingdom would likewise suffer penalty.

Still, that does not tell us what we want to understand about the animal's plight, for an animal is incapable of the guilt that man can assume. An animal, that is, cannot sin. If the animal cannot sin, how is it that every animal has to suffer in the same way the one who named him must? Not only must the animal suffer. Like man, the animal after the Garden must likewise have to undergo death. Prior to man's violation of the ordinance forbidding seeking knowledge of good and evil man did not have the prospect of returning to dust. If he did, why he was told only after the Fall that he would return to dust appears senseless. It emerges as consequent to the Fall, and thus as a consequence of it.

The Apostle Paul (1 *Cor.* 15:22) tells us that inasmuch "as in Adam all creation (πάντες) died, so in Christ it is made alive"; the Evangelist (*Rev.* 21:4), "the former things are passed away." Is there any significance, then, to our inquiry into animal immortality here that at His birth surrounding Him were animals (*Lk.* 2:7; cf. *Is.* 1:3)? Over the centuries after the expulsion from Paradise these creatures would be preyed upon and warred against, one species against the other, in the horror of blood and ripped flesh, teeth-sliced bone, gouged out eyes, lacerated entrails. In their own hell did not these creatures over the aeons suffer the most savage diseases? Species became extinct at the caprice of merciless winds, frigid temperatures, speeding comets and asteroids. Drought and a punishing sun dried them to agonizing death, and unforeseen climactic vicissitudes brought their starvation. All this does not include what man, who had once been summoned as their custodian (*Gen.* 1:28), in febrile sadism and unrelenting desire for profit, would do to numberless animals repeatedly and seemingly without surcease over days and years and centuries that too cannot be numbered.

So one has to look at these creatures, these *chayahim nepheshim*, called by the Divine to be man's companion, to be his company while he would till the paradisiacal ground (*Gen.* 2:5; 15). We have already noted that Scripture does not appear to subordinate their being, their nature, to man; only their role in the economy of Paradise. Serving as a real expression of the Divine's love for life and the possibilities of its many ways, they were important enough to each merit a name (שֵׁם) by which first man would call them (*Gen.* 1:19). The seas are not even given a name; nor is any rock. We read in *Genesis* that the rivers flowing through the Garden have a name; and there is the rock that does—but not that their name came from man. The names of the animals, the living souls, do.

Christ tells us of the lamb and how important it is to the shepherd. He himself is the good shepherd, "I know mine, and mine know Me" (*Jn.* 10: 11-18). He instructs us how the birds of the air are each known by His Father, and not one dies without His knowledge (*Mt.* 6:25-34). He tells us in all things be kind (*Lk.* 6:36). For what purpose do we extend kindness to His *chayhahim nepheshim*, His "living creatures, living souls," unless to the Godhead they mean something?

In dying for man, Christ eliminated once and for all the sacrifice of animals to His Father. We do not know why the chosen people felt it requisite to offer blood to the Divine, as they did. The angel told father Abraham not to offer up his boy in sacrifice, and there appeared for him a ram which he took as the sacrifice to his God instead of dear Isaac in the region of Moriah which he named afterwards *Adonai-jireh* ({יְהוָה יִרְאֶה} or the place where the Lord (Yahweh) is seen [*Gen.* 22:14 cf. 1-24; *Heb* 11:17]).[15]

In this *akedah*, taken in conjunction with *Jer.* 32:35, we learn of the Divine's abhorrence of child sacrifice, but not of a command to take a ram. Abel, we know, offered a sacrifice pleasing to the Lord (*Heb.* 11:4) before Cain killed him (*Gen.* 4). The sacrifice of blood (*Heb.* 9:22) takes on the reality that to clothe the first parents, shamed in their nakedness (*Gen.* 3:10), the Divine had to take the skins of animals, presumably requiring their death. But we do not read that the animal skins came by way of God specifically taking the lives of the animals for that purpose. Indeed, *Hosea*, speaking the word of the Lord, declares Him not to want sacrifice, or burnt offerings, but mercy (6:6).[16] What element in animal existence could then supersede mercy as acceptable to the Divine does not appear biblically.

Meditation on goodness and Divinity inclines one to argue that because animals committed no transgression—indeed, without the power of choice, cannot—justice would require that the suffering to which they have been subject as a result of the Fall requires that what the Divine intended for them in Paradise be restored. To go further, if the purpose of God was their well-being in the Garden, the Fall frustrated that purpose, a frustration that cannot hold, given Divine omnipotence. The fulfillment of His purposes is always in order, and that would make animal freedom from death as a final end in need of actuation too. What sort of Deity, we need ask, in any event would allow the termination completely (annihilation [total nothingness without any remains of matter]) of animals that have shown traits of faithfulness, friendliness, and care and in point of fact have done nothing to deserve an end that complete individual extinction in each case of death would bring? The student of Scripture cannot conclude to such a Deity. It would be one that cannot be found in its verses.

Why, further, does the Divine tell Noah, after the Flood (*Gen.* 9:9-11), that He will provide a new covenant (בְּרִית), one that He shall hold between Noah and all life, if animals were of subordinate import to Him? Indeed, God names animals in this passage, and in the Hebrew tradition to name something was to acknowledge to it an import. Does not the Psalmist's exhortation (*Ps.* 150:6), "Let all that has breath (נְשָׁמָה) praise the Lord," comport with this? To what end is the exhortation given if the praise has no value? And if there is not a greater value than praising the Lord (which includes doing His work, and acting "according to the kind after which" He has made you), then the import of the being who does the praising takes on a significance that denying it immortal existence clearly contradicts.

Postulating a Divine that would provide man in this existence with living gifts of His creation only in an afterlife to have those gifts withdrawn would puzzle one as to their purpose in one existence (here) and not the other. Would not the immortality of the human person be in one way markedly different in that the companions he had in animals on earth would be completely gone in the eternity the Savior's redemption brought him? What purpose does the affection an animal shows for his master serve if we are to say of the animal it does not, in some way, possess that endlessness that is in his master's soul?

The stories of the Saint Bernard breed of dog rescuing the lost in the Alps does not comport with our notion of instinct. Instinct is something spontaneous, on the spur of the moment. It is immediate and without forethought. Does the Saint Bernard go out into the freezing blizzard and look for the lost by instinct?

What of the dear affection the dog shows his master, a sentiment that is without guile or deceit? There is no calculation in his way. The dog does not seek anything more than to have his master, by way of petting or a nod, acknowledge that the master is him for whom his affection exists, as well, in instances of the family, of the children and the wife. Is this instinct? Or is it something other? And where does one in the dog's body find this source of the love that the canine has for the family, for his master? Is it in the bones? Is it in the paws? Or does this expression have a cause other than these? If the canine, or any animal, shows what we recognize as affection and attentiveness, why would we ascribe that behavior in the lower animal to something other than that to which we would ascribe it in ourselves?

Indeed, we know that the neuronal matter of all sentient beings have comparative histological and physiological structures that link them along the chain from lowest to higher intelligence. Consciousness is afforded all up and down this ladder of complexity and physiology. What makes it immortal in one and not the other? If man's memory is included in his post-mortem existence as a person, if post-mortem memory includes that of his pets, and of animals that he has seen and with which he became acquainted here in his Master's world, what of the content of that memory in post-mortem being? Is it gone? Is it wiped away? The continuity that we see in Nature ("nature abhors a vacuum"), suddenly becomes undone. Nature on earth does not follow that Nature we wonder about in the post-mortem world, absent that continuity. For animals are not there, if animals do not possess immortal being, as man, we are suggesting here, should believe he does.

How does man say that the animal has no desire for or comprehension of what man almost from the moment he can understand seems to seek, namely, unending life? Surely if man seeks it, and does so through desire, what is it about an animal's desire that man can say does not seek to ever end? There has also been the doctrine, offered by Kant[17] among others, that justice requires an afterlife because it is not meted out fully in this. If we look at the animal tested for all sorts of medicines, misdirected and cruel interests, foul pleasures and strange amusements, do we limit the mercy of the Divine only to man, to whom much injustice is done in this life? Or do we acknowledge that the mercy of which Scripture speaks pours forth to all that have come to be in this existence called sentient life, conscious being? Even more so to the sinless it would seem this mercy must come, as well as those who seek to avoid sin.

The Apostle's inspired writing which we cited above, that all creation will be made anew and rescued from the groans and travails of this temporality, would have us reason to an afterlife where Nature is restored to its primeval perfection of harmony and concord ("where He looked upon everything and saw that it was good"), and where indeed the child shall have no fear in being in the presence of the lion.

"The wolf shall dwell with the lamb, the leopard lie with the kid; the calf and the lion and the fatling together; and a child shall lead them," *Is.* 11:6 tells us, while further on "and dust shall be the serpent's food" (65:25). If it is the serpent that tempted the first parents and by whose beguilement man's Fall came, that Isaiah in the view of what shall eventuate for all mankind in a God-ordered existence tells us at the same time a child shall lead these animals, the exegete is hard pressed not to see in this prophesy that the child is Immanuel of 7:14, the Redeemer that shall be the cause of the universe's restoration, even as Peter speaks of it in *Acts* 3:21 (ἀποκαταστάσεως πάντων). The Greek tells us of all things being put back together, and that must refer to a time before now. It is difficult to think of what that time can be if it is what God had spoken by the words of His prophets of long ago except that time when nothing had been dirempted, fractured, broken; but when all was seamless and entire in a unity that had simply the differentiation of excellences fitting what was fruitfully possible, and not subjected to what interfered with that possibility.

What adds to the difficulty of arguing against animal immortality is the Evangelist's own claim in *Revelation* 5:11 that around the throne of the Divine not only did he see angels and the elders, but also living animals (ζῴων). The passage could not be clearer:

Καὶ εἶδον καὶ ἤκουσα φωνὴν ἀγγέλων πολλῶν κύκλῳτοῦ θρόνου καὶ τῶν ζῴων καὶ τῶν πρεσβυτέρωνκαὶ ἦν ὁ ἀριθμὸς αὐτῶν μυριάδες μυριάδων καὶ χιλιάδες χιλιάδων λέγοντες φωνῇ μεγάλῃἌξιόν ἐστιν τὸ ἀρνίον τὸ ἐσφαγμένον λαβεῖν τὴν δύναμιν καὶ πλοῦτον καὶ σοφίαν καὶ ἰσχὺν καὶ τιμὴν καὶ δόξαν καὶ εὐλογίαν.

St. John is telling us, under Divine inspiration, that a vision of the eternal was given to him, a vision of where the Divine is enthroned. And in that vision did he see tens of thousands upon thousands of angels, and elders, and living animals[18] in unison voicing the praise "Worthy is the Lamb." This, a vision of heaven after Christ's redemption has restored all things.

If Divine revelation is without error, one patently must go back to Thomas Aquinas then, as the *Revelation passus* just quotes makes plain, and ask him, as well as his adherents, how he came to his assertion in the *Summa*, "animae brutorum corrumpuntur, corruptis corporibus, anima autem humana non posset corrumpi (the souls of animals and their body are both corruptible, but the soul of man is incorruptible.)" What perhaps makes the reading grievous to a Christian reader is that Scripture has primacy over a philosophic treatise for the Christian, and philosophy cannot conclude or assert what Scripture contrarily affirms. In this case, we do not have simply a contrary but a proposition in one that contradicts what is in the other.

In fact, this seems to make clear our passage in the Preacher where he writes (*Eccl.* 3:19) that man and animal are of one breath. It had been opined that Solomon, in telling us that what befalls man befalls the creature that perhaps there was a note of mortal end in Solomon's declaration. Quite the contrary appears the case. The belief that Solomon was committed to such appears in his plaint that to dust man and animal both return. Indeed, this is true; that, however, does not rule out a return to existence in a perfected state, which we saw implicit in the Divine's declaration that He would bring forth the woman that would crush the head of the serpent who had deceived Eve—and, as Scripture unfolds, instructs us that "all will be made new in Christ."

ANOTHER WORLD

It appears quite reasonable, then, that consciousness is immortal, that we do not wholly perish. This is not to say that we survive only to come back again. That is the theory of reincarnation.[1] In reincarnation, however, there is no first birth; thus, how can there be a second or subsequent? That, however, is what reincarnation argues: birth upon subsequent birth till moral perfection is reached. The number goes back endlessly, thus not allowing for the necessary "first" that is required of there is to be a second.

The Apostle Paul tells the Christian community in first century Corinth that over five hundred are still living at the time of his letter to them (1 *Cor.* 15:6) who saw Christ after He had risen from the dead. Since they were alive at the time they surely could have come forward and challenged Paul's statement about them, even denying what he said. There is no history or record of such a challenge. What does one do in the face of this claim? One can deny it, pass it off as propaganda, and return to the everyday life of the here and now.

Miracles are cited in the Christian process of canonization as evidence that someone to whom the miracle has been ascribed is therefore in heaven. He or she is indeed immortal, as the evidence of the miracle suggests. Miracles are certainly not out of the question as to their possibility, as we have argued in a prior work, along with many other right seeing students of Nature and its operations.[2] However, that a miracle occurs does not necessitate someone is in heaven to whom it has been ascribed by a believing hierarchy. That is, miracles are not necessarily evidence of immortality.

The problem with the question of immortal life is quite straightforward: we have no direct evidence of it. Evidence that is, of an individual who died and has returned to tell us about his death, his subsequent entry into an existence living differently than in this. It seems, also, that we have no indisputable evidence of communication with the dead who are in an existence where they can receive the communication and thus would not have experienced the annihilation of their consciousness. Much has been written on the paranormal, necromancy, spirit communications and the like. Nothing that has been convincing appears to have come forth. Claims about ghosts and poltergeists also fall on deaf ears: ears twitching to hear of any confirmation that this life is not all that there is.

The effort in our undertaking requires us to ask whether the evidence we want is only possible from a single line of inquiry. Or, must we look at the question from a number of avenues to see if they on their own contribute to our reaching an answer that is satisfactory? For the one who starts with the order of a benevolent Deity, it seems clear that understanding what that Deity means would advance us to a commitment to a belief in an afterlife that was also aided by what we have done here. Namely, an analysis of the nature of consciousness, the study of partibility of matter, and the study of whether purpose in the universe exists and the question whether desires represent something structural in the intelligence of creative purpose and design. Is the desire for immortal life, or the fear of annihilation, any indication that conscious existence was made not to end, but to eternally perdure? Evidence of the drive for life arises in every instance of our seeking to survive whatever the costs in the face of greatest dangers to our life. We seem to almost blindly struggle, as when caught in the ferocious waves of an unyielding sea as we gasp uncontrollably for air, of fleeing a murderer intent on ending our life whatever the strength of our limbs and muscles, of fighting with every ounce of effort the pernicious drive of bacteriological poisons. The drive for life and survival seems almost identical with who each person is.

To say that energy is neither created nor destroyed by ordinary means does not advance our inquiry. Energy is quantitative, but we have argued that consciousness is without size or dimension or divisibility. We have seen, however, that various pathologies in behavior, such as obsessive-compulsive disorder can be controlled when there are new neural pathways created in the brain. The brain does not make such pathways: the coincidence doctrine here, that the neural pathway was coincident upon the subject engaging in a new behavior, a new way of processing the data from its world, does not have the "feel" of truth to it. Something more is attendant here, sc., causality. The subject has caused the change in the cortical map of the brain. The subject is other than the brain. It is what others call "mind" or "self." Suggesting that one has hurried to this conclusion is indicative of that criticism that offers itself as science while presuming as true what it sets out to prove through the presumption of the proof's truth, which is precisely the issue in debate.

That activated neurons consume more oxygen and sugar in thought process, that metabolism differs with different thought operations and thus chemical reactions are instrumental to them, are examples of assuming what has to be proven if one goes the next step and says these metabolic processes show that mentation, consciousness, is chemically based and driven after all. Since the metabolic processes are so unlike the thoughts in which they are said to be instrumental a serious problem for the proponent of the chemical hypothesis arises. Proving that no other process can be instrumental to the thoughts we have seems a necessity in order to show that chemical-neural processes, though difficult to observe and so unlike the thoughts in which they are said to issue, are what bring about the thoughts (or percepts) we have. The presumption is most blatant in the commentaries that read "the brain reads this," "the brain calibrates these numbers," "the brain works through these conundrums," and the like. No one has demonstrated any reality close to this for cerebral activity. The "brain" does not read; it does not "hear"; It does not "love." It is a mass of complex neuronal lattices, and networks, themselves made of cell tissue. The neuronal cell set apart reaches no percept. How many must be in "synchrony" for the percept to occur? We have detected nothing that inheres through their complex network that accounts, or can account, for any power these cells as a mass aggregate unit can accomplish. Yet, frequently in explanations disseminated in the culture, the only agency one hears about is the "brain," and never the "mind."

One cannot go to asserting that NDEs and OBEs are indicative of the postmortem existence of consciousness. While in the case of NDEs more than a few flatline minutes seems necessary to make such a pronouncement, in the case of OBEs it is difficult to advance these as categorical evidence of an afterlife. That the embodied senses may indeed not be the only conduits for our awareness does not necessitate that we conclude that awareness that is not sensibly grounded, sensibly originated, is evidence of eternal life. We know only that "the mind does not think without a phantasm," as Aristotle wrote. It does not have experience or cognition in the absence of sense-content.[3] That it cannot have cognition except through a living contact through the body with the sense world would have to be proven to show that OBE accounts are simply imagined. That cognition in the form of a direct acquaintance with, or apprehension of, comes only through the embodied senses has never been proven, however. Only that we don't know of any other way it comes about. To the materialist, the OBE could never be proof given its paradigm for the "production" of consciousness.

What the OBE and NDE phenomena seem to suggest is that assertions that human existence is extinguished whole and entire at death, that animal existence is likewise, may not have any probity to them at all. If the physical senses are not the only conduits for awareness, how an OBE has awareness leans heavily towards the proposition that consciousness is not sense-constrained. Any movement away from sense-constriction is a movement towards what is not sense-bound, physically constricted.

The very nature of awareness, however, as being so totally other than that of which one is aware, indicates that existence is bifurcated along lines that difference and dissimilarity from that of which one is aware are at their greatest. Nothing in our awareness has any of the characteristics of resistance, solidity, temperature, color, odor, taste. Yet our awareness is of these features which have no possibility of showing up in cortical form, in the material substrate that is known as the brain. The neuroelectric events of the brain which sometimes correlate with a sensation and other times do not, show nothing of the qualities that we have just named. These qualities, however, are publicly observable. This (public observability) is what science wants, as we saw. But while these things are publicly observable, consciousness, where these features are experienced, is not. Nor is the reality that I know whatever thoughts I have as mine with the thoughts I am having. The thought does not come first, and then the awareness that it is my thought. The two are together, inseparable. Self-consciousness occurs simultaneously with the thought of anything I have. It and the thought I have are neither of them publicly observable.

Consciousness, however, and pain are not inseparable; nor are taste and consciousness. Pain is not "about" anything; nor is taste. Thus again, that which consciousness feels and what consciousness is show a difference in that only consciousness possesses this "aboutness" that makes it other than everything, but most importantly other than matter.

Our consciousness, unlike the electron, does not move; nor locate from place to place: nor does it move quickly or slowly, in a straight line or curved. An electron, further, is never "confused," or "uncertain." Surely, though, consciousness is.[4]

Consciousness, the more one examines it, appears beyond the bounds of scientific study, of what science studies. This should not be surprising given science's own dictum that only what is publicly observable can come into the laboratory. Anything else is not within the confines of the empirical, the palpable.

Science, that is, is not privy to introspection, the private awareness that I have. Simply because something is not public does not mean it does not exist. The person has a private capacity established by his ability to observe what no one else can, sc., what is in his consciousness. All that goes on it, his awareness of yesterday's bicycle ride, his awareness of the store to the right of him as he walks—no scientist will find that in his cortex. The synaptic connections, the agonists, the dendrites that constitute the neuroelectric world of the brain, do not show the scientist any of this "inner" content.

This would point to another difference of consciousness from matter: privacy. It is something, we may add, that you cannot cut into two, quantify, put under the microscope. It apparently has features that the other feature of consciousness, "aboutness," has: for "aboutness" has no divisibility, partibility, or numerability either.

Descartes was thinking along these lines when he wrote that while the existence of the world can be doubted, my existence cannot be. That would, that is, point to the world, matter, or extension, as being inherently different than consciousness. I do not end in self-contradiction when I doubt matter. I do, however, when I doubt my own existence: to doubt it I must exist.

Descartes, then, has given the most puissant reasoning possible to establishing the difference of one thing ("mind") from the other ("world," "matter"), sc., the support of the principle of non-contradiction. In the case of doubting matter, it is not violated; in the case of doubting consciousness, my awareness of my existence, it is.[5] And while the principle[6] does not assure us of the absolute truth of what is involved, it makes that which is contradictory unintelligible in that no language, no thought, no statement, can take place, or in the least be intelligible, unless the principle of non-contradiction undergirds it.

If, though, brain and awareness are so totally different, how does one come to suggest that the brain produces consciousness? How can the brain which is clearly something in place, of a certain depth and extension, as well as texture, produce that which is absolutely without any of those features? Water cannot produce what is dry; heat cannot produce what is frigid. Both are material. So is the brain. Run an electric current through water; run one through a heated surface. Nothing conscious occurs. Take from a living human neuronal fluid, perhaps one that quickens synaptic interchange, and with the water run an electric current once more, as well as through the heated surface. Still, no consciousness.

Let us go far further, and assemble a motherboard with thousands upon thousands of circuit connectabilities through the chips and electromagnetic fields that provide for storage and the placement of those colors we see and the sounds we hear on a computer screen and from the computer's audio files. I know how these colors and sounds came about because of software programs fashioned for the production of these occurrences. The software, however, is not aware of these colors or sounds. The motherboard is not. The electromagnetic fields acting as the power transfer medium for those colors and sounds is without the awareness of them also. However long the power lasts, however the software application by its binary ordinances effectuates the color and sound schemes, what has been assembled to generate these colors and sounds has not one whit of awareness as to what it is producing.

It is known the cortical neuronal cells are similar in histology and chemical properties to that of the cells of the spine. It might even be argued that there are no differences, depending on how close to the skull one gets. Yet, the spine is without awareness. No stimulation of it generates a percept. What is of greater import, though, is that the neuronal cell, that found in the cortex, is known to be similar in chemical structure and composition to other bodily cells. However, we do not give those other cells the vaunted position of responsibility for our awareness, or for producing our awareness.

Long-term memory, as we saw, also shows up as something other than the material world we encounter in that we have no ability to locate it in the cortex, or anywhere else. If it is indeed not a spatial event anywhere in the brain, how do we come to think of all human awareness as spatio-temporally bound?

Our path of evidence is leading to the recognition that one may reasonably postulate, argue, that awareness does not come within the confines of three-dimensional rigors. Matter and space do not contain, do not hold, the capacity of sentience and reasoning that reductionism has wanted to argue it must—even in the absence of its own evidence for the claim.

That hydrocephalic patients have been able to function, as we earlier mentioned, in the manner of those whose brain matter has not been compromised is a most serious obstacle to the reductionist. Brain mapping seems a suspect endeavor when neither hydrocephalous nor brain tissue redundancy as a solution explaining how hydrocephalous is overcome have any consistency with a search for evidence. To argue dogmatically against a status of consciousness not materially originated in the light of the fact that almost nothing is known about the brain at all makes the philosopher wonder what procedure is being followed that leads to such dogmatism.

Let us allow that the materialist case has been disproven, or at least greatly weakened, by the evidence presented here. There is still a large question in front of us. It could even render inoperable our solutions to the problem of consciousness, leaving materialism and our solution as both unable to give an account of consciousness. The issue is this: can we speak with any intelligence on the content of another world, one where we exist post mortem? A grave difficulty, it appears, to the claim of possible post-mortem survival is the issue of how content comes to the consciousness that is no longer in need of physical sense faculties. The body has perished. Its sense faculties would, therefore appear to be gone also.

The NDE hinted at the possible severance from sense organs as the conduit for awareness, but the awareness in question was the awareness of what was occurring in this three-dimensional world. How does content of consciousness occur in a world to which no one has ever been previously? And a world it surely must be. We carry our memories with us in the new existence, if it is a reality, and what memory can be carried in an existence where the original situs of the memory is still in some way intact in our new existing realm? How are memories sensibly achieved in this world carried into the next, if our sense-faculties embodied here are no longer there? Our memories constitute part of who we are and carry with them this world in every way. For the continuity of self to be experienced (which, is a tautologous expression in a way since self-hood implies continuity)[7] in a following existence, the memories from the prior world would be carried into the new existence. This entails that the world we left would be with us in the new existence.

Sensory content similar to what we encounter in this world is not a contradiction in a world other than the one–this one–where we now live and exist. The question is how do we maintain continuity with this world if our sense powers are shut down? What world would be present to our awareness faculties?

First, we can suggest that the images present to each individual in his post mortem consciousness would be private, just as they are in this world. While I can have a sensory experience of chair, or emerald, or lilac, in the next world, my experience of emerald, for instance, would differ from anyone else in that the way the experience would occur to me would surely be conditioned by memories from this earth and other attitudes I bring to the experience of an emerald. These attitudes make who I am in a way, and in so far as they are good surely would not be absent in the next existence.

Though I am in this post mortem existence "disembodied," this does not mean that I would be lacking sense powers. It is conceivable to imagine an existence where sense powers are not conditioned by the limits of space-time. Working in conjunction with the mind, my experiences in the next world could be of a far more refined and precise capacity. "Chairness," "whiteness," sweetness," would present themselves to me in a richer and more vibrant way than the way the sense-powers working through the body in this existence would afford.

There is no reason to believe that the existence in a new world would be so radically other than this that all content would be totally unintelligible to us in the next world. It is not necessary to think of a world where all experience would be so other that the world we knew would be unintelligible to us in comparison with the new world we now inhabit in the next life, or vice-versa. It is that post mortem experience is of a world that is not encumbered by the sloth of senses enmattered and embodied. The senses, instead, have the perfection original to their form, perhaps, as taught in Scripture.

If matter here is an encumbrance, and it is aligned to motion in space-time, perhaps freed of this encumbrance the individual takes on a matter that is not condensed to three dimensions, Instead, it is one that is transparent and fine. It reflects more of the individual's own spirit that guided the sluggish matter of the pre- post mortem existence (i.e., the existence on earth), a matter now more like the spirit that guides it now for eternity. It is to such a spirit status that all our talk on consciousness here has been hinting.

Matter in the post mortem existence becomes more of the spirit than it was here, where it rather fought the spirit, instead of conformed to the spirit. Matter, that is, becomes more perfect as it throws off the limitations of movement and speed that encumber it in this existence. Physical matter and spirit become more "interactable," and not at a conflict that characterized much of earthly being.

It is not, then, an incongruity or impossibility to have this world carried into the next as we have described is possible. The content of our new world would be in line with this world, only without the limitations of time and space that have encumbered us here. Time ages in this existence; in the next, the post mortem, it is without span, but simply a measure of permanence. In this way, it becomes a measure of eternity. Eternity is not an extent of time, but instead time freed of extent.

Spatial constrictions in this existence are freed in the next. Thinking oneself into a new location becomes the means of change in space rather than the expenditure of effort bodily existence here necessitates. Thinking has become, among other perfections, the new means of change of space. Where in this existence one can imagine being on another sphere, or in another orbit, in an existence freed from spatial restrictions thought and reality converge. In the next existence thought makes it be to the extent that thought's created capacity for human personhood affords.

We brought up in our study earlier, even isolating it for a brief chapter, the question whether man, since he dies, was born to die. Here we link that question to the nature of the Creating cause of life. The illogic of being born only so that one may die strikes forcefully enough the note that what has been brought to life was not meant to die. Being born only to die, after all, leaves the question: why have any occurrence of life in the first place? If life is meant only so that death may occur, and death is non-existence after life, and thus the non-existence of life, it would be more rational not to bring life into existence at all. More rational because it would be more in line with what existence was supposed to exemplify according to this model, sc., death, or the non-existence ultimately of life.

In a study of immortality for any existent, more than just the structure of the existent's operations must come into play. The thinker cannot consider just the existent itself, as something atomistic, totally unrelated to any other existent. If we know an existent is caused, looking to the cause of the existent plays into the consideration of what has gone into the existent in question. And that would bring us to consider the nature of what has brought the existent to be. Is it malevolent or benign? Is it good or demonic?

If the nature of the existent that brings something to be is malevolent, why it would allow for existence in the first place is odd in that existence is a good. A malevolent agency would seek to bring to an end as swiftly as possible—if not outright block—the existence of anything that has come to be. Malevolence seeks no good. It seeks only what is without good, i.e., without being, to the extent that that is possible. It would seek, in the end, its own total annihilation in fact except for the fact that as an existent it has in some way an aspect of good which it has not lost (to its continuing disgust). That aspect is a feature of being something that exists. For to have existence is in some way to have what is good.

We thus have to look at the character of what has brought things to be. Since it has allotted a span of existence to these things, we can be confident it is not the malevolence of the demonic entity we just postulated above. Bringing things into being and allowing their existence, conserving it, would indicate that since being is a good, the entity that brings these things to be in some way is good—as well as of unimagined power.

Does it seek the perdurance of what it has brought into being, or their end? For what purpose would a benign Power bring things to be that have an aspect of themselves that does not possess matter if only to put to an end totally that which It has brought to be? If so obviously beings that have life have a conatus to continue, a drive towards enduring, what purpose does the conatus, the drive towards existence, preservation, serve if in the end annihilation is the state of anything that has ever lived, has ever had consciousness?

To the extent that consciousness is a good, and this Agency has brought it to be, it would not make sense to bring what it has brought to be into nothingness. Why bring it out of nothingness in the first place? The simple fact that all being, insofar as it exists, evinces this Agency's power and glory, which evincing itself is a good, would make us lean towards arguing that It, what some refer to as the Divine, would not annihilate that which It has brought to be. It would be annihilating a good—a good that It has deemed apt and fitting to bring into existence.

Looked at from this perspective, from more than just the structure of the individual existent whose immortality is in question, we come to a larger understanding of both the existent and the nature of the Existent that brought it to be. And in coming to that understanding, immortality seems to become an essential ingredient to that understanding, an essential feature of what we come to realize in existents that have had a conscious sojourn before passing on to decomposition of their body.

The decomposition does not indicate the end of the consciousness. Their bodily form has changed in power and capacity, it has not brought about an end to their conscious being. And the atoms that have taken up the new form of the matter that has decomposed also do not pass away. The matter has itself changed into those atoms that one can argue spirit more perfectly energizes. But more importantly, is that the consciousness, that provided the individual the ability to work his or her way through this world, in its existence has not ended. It has the mark of immortality.

NOTES

Preface

1. Jeffrey Long with Paul Perry, *Evidence of the After Life. The Science of Near-Death Experiences* (New York: Harper, 2010). His work, over a decade in duration, catalogues and systematizes the evidence from thirteen hundred near-death-experiences [(NDEs), see 44–45], the largest body of published evidence in English (so far as I am aware) on this subject.

2. Aristotle, *De Anima*, 402a 10–12: πάντῃ δὲ πάντως ἐστὶ τῶν χαλεπωτάτων λαβεῖν τινα πίστιν περὶ αὐτῆς.

The *De Anima* is of unquestioned import in the study of mind. See the W.S. Hett translation in the Loeb Classical Library edition (Cambridge: Harvard University, 1957). For the Greek of any of Aristotle's work cited herein see the Loeb Classical Library editions.

Valuable commentaries on the *De Anima* are by H. G. Apostle, *Aristotle's On the Soul*, translated with Commentaries and Glossary (Grinnell: The Peripatetic Press, 1981); R. D. Hicks, *Aristotle De Anima* (Cambridge: University Press, 1907); Ronald Polanski, *Aristotle's De Anima* (Cambridge: University Press, 2007); W. D. Ross, *Aristotle De Anima*. Edited with introduction and commentary (Oxford: Clarendon Press, 1961). Cf. I. Block, "Aristotle and the Physical Object," *Philosophy and Phenomenological Research* 21 (1960): 93–101; R. Bolton, "Aristotle's Definition of the Soul: *De Anima* II, 1–3," *Phronesis* 23 (1978): 258–278; David Bradshaw, "Aristotle on Perception: the Dual-Logos Theory," *Apeiron* 30 (1997): 143–161; Sarah Broadie, "Aristotle's Perceptual Realism," *Southern Journal of Philosophy* supplement 31 (1993): 137–159; Miles Burnyeat, "How Much Happens When Aristotle Sees Red and Hears Middle C?" in Martha C. Nussbaum and Amélie O. Rorty, *Essays On Aristotle's De Anima* (Oxford: Clarendon Press, 1995); Victor Caston, "Aristotle and the Problem of Intentionality," *Philosophy and Phenomenological Research* 58 (1998): 249–298; "Aristotle on Consciousness," *Mind* 111 (2002): 751–815; Stephen Everson, *Aristotle on Perception* (Oxford: Clarendon Press, 1997); T. K. Johansen, *Aristotle on the Sense Organs* (Cambridge: University Press, 1997); Deborah Modrak, *Aristotle: the Power of Perception* (Chicago: University of Chicago Press, 1997); Joseph Owens, "Form and Cognition in Aristotle," *Ancient Philosophy* 1 (1980): 17–27; Allan Silverman, "Color and Color-Perception in Aristotle's *De anima*," *Ancient Philosophy* 9 (1989): 271–292; John E. Sisko, "Material Alteration and Cognitive Activity in Aristotle's *De Anima*," *Phronesis* 41 (1996): 138–157; Richard

Sorabji, "Aristotle on Sensory Processes and Intentionality: a Reply to Myles Burnyeat" in D. Perler, ed., *Ancient and Medieval Theories of Intentionality* (Leiden: Brill, 2001); Julie K. Ward, "Perception and Λόγος in *De anima* ii 12," *Ancient Philosophy* 8 (1988): 217–234.

3. Robert Geis, *Personal Existence After Death: Reductionist Circularities and the Evidence* (LaSalle, IL: Open Court, 1995).

Quantum Theory and the Realities of Distincton

1. Hume argues the idea of the self (substance, mind), since not derivable from any impression(s), is fictitious, and simply without basis in fact. *Treatise of Human Nature*, I, iv, v-vi. His explanation of how the idea arises requires, as is well known, that whose existence he denies (or claims is without evidence for the assertion of such an existent), sc., an agent that remembers and imagines.

2. Quantum theory has many means of expression, seemingly little of which take clarity as one of its valued forms. In any event, for an approach to it see R. P. Feynman, *The Character of Physical Law* (Cambridge: MIT Press, 2001); *QED: The Strange Theory of Light and Matter* (Princeton: Princeton University Press, 1985); J. Gribbin, *Q is for Quantum: Particle Physics from A to Z* (London: Weidenfeld & Nicolson, 1998); C. Itzykson, J-B. Zuber, *Quantum Field Theory* (New York: McGraw-Hill, 1980); G. L. Kane, *Modern Elementary Particle Physics* (New York: Perseus Books, 1987); R. Loudon, *The Quantum Theory of Light* (New York: Oxford University Press,1983; F. Mandl, G. Shaw, *Quantum Field Theory* (New York: John Wiley & Sons, 1993),
3. וַיַּרְא אֱלֹהִים אֶת-כָּל-אֲשֶׁר עָשָׂה, וְהִנֵּה-טוֹב מְאֹד.
4. See Thomas Aquinas, *Summa Theologiae*, I^a q. 104 a. 4 arg. 1 – 4 ad 3:

Ad quartum sic proceditur. Videtur quod aliquid in nihilum redigatur. Finis enim respondet principio. Sed a principio nihil erat nisi Deus. Ergo ad hunc finem res perducentur, ut nihil sit nisi Deus. Et ita creaturae in nihilum redigentur.

I^a q. 104 a. 4 arg. 2 Praeterea, omnis creatura habet potentiam finitam. Sed nulla potentia finita se extendit ad infinitum, unde in VIII Physic. probatur quod potentia finita non potest movere tempore infinito. Ergo nulla creatura potest durare in infinitum. Et ita quandoque in nihilum redigetur.

I^a q. 104 a. 4 arg. 3 Praeterea, forma et accidentia non habent materiam partem sui. Sed quandoque desinunt esse. Ergo in nihilum rediguntur.

I^a q. 104 a. 4 s. c. Sed contra est quod dicitur Eccle. III. *Didici quod omnia opera quae fecit Deus, perseverant in aeternum.*

I^a q. 104 a. 4 co. Respondeo dicendum quod eorum quae a Deo fiunt circa creaturam, quaedam proveniunt secundum naturalem cursum rerum; quaedam vero miraculose operatur praeter ordinem naturalem creaturis inditum, ut infra dicetur. Quae autem facturus est Deus secundum ordinem naturalem rebus inditum, considerari possunt ex ipsis rerum naturis, quae vero miraculose fiunt, ordinantur ad gratiae manifestationem, secundum illud apostoli I ad Cor. XII, *unicuique datur manifestatio spiritus ad utilitatem*; et postmodum, inter cetera, subdit de miraculorum operatione. Creaturarum autem naturae hoc demonstrant, ut nulla earum in nihilum redigatur, quia vel sunt immateriales, et sic in eis non est potentia ad non esse; vel sunt materiales, et sic saltem remanent semper secundum materiam, quae incorruptibilis est, utpote subiectum existens generationis et corruptionis. Redigere etiam aliquid in nihilum, non pertinet ad gratiae manifestationem, cum magis per hoc divina potentia et bonitas ostendatur, quod res in esse conservat. Unde simpliciter dicendum est quod nihil omnino in nihilum redigetur.

Iᵃ q. 104 a. 4 ad 1 Ad primum ergo dicendum quod hoc quod res in esse productae sunt, postquam non fuerunt, declarat potentiam producentis. Sed quod in nihilum redigerentur, huiusmodi manifestationem impediret, cum Dei potentia in hoc maxime ostendatur, quod res in esse conservat, secundum illud apostoli Heb. I, *portans omnia verbo virtutis suae.*

Iᵃ q. 104 a. 4 ad 2 Ad secundum dicendum quod potentia creaturae ad essendum est receptiva tantum; sed potentia activa est ipsius Dei, a quo est influxus essendi. Unde quod res in infinitum durent, sequitur infinitatem divinae virtutis. Determinatur tamen quibusdam rebus virtus ad manendum tempore determinato, inquantum impediri possunt ne percipiant influxum essendi qui est ab eo, ex aliquo contrario agente, cui finita virtus non potest resistere tempore infinito, sed solum tempore determinato. Et ideo ea quae non habent contrarium, quamvis habeant finitam virtutem, perseverant in aeternum.

Iᵃ q. 104 a. 4 ad 3 Ad tertium dicendum quod formae et accidentia non sunt entia completa, cum non subsistant, sed quodlibet eorum est aliquid entis, sic enim ens dicitur, quia eo aliquid est. Et tamen eo modo quo sunt, non omnino in nihilum rediguntur; non quia aliqua pars eorum remaneat, sed remanent in potentia materiae vel subiecti.

Annihilation appears to mean a sudden termination, instantaneous reduction to non-being, to nothingness—the very opposite of creation, the bringing to be out of nothing. We have no experience of annihilation for which reason I am not certain of the force a discussion on it has to could suggest. While we also have no experience of creation, one can reason to its arguability, while arguing for annihilation would appear to argue against a Being whose very essence constitutes goodness. Once such a being is accepted, as in Aquinas, arguing annihilation seems clearly out of the question by that Being.

We may note here, additionally, that Aquinas is probably the most lucid expositor of the doctrine of being as self-diffusive "bonum diffusivum sui." See Aquinas, *Summa Theologiae*, Iᵃ q. 19, a. 2:

Unde, si res naturales, inquantum perfectae sunt, suum bonum aliis communicant, multo magis pertinet ad voluntatem divinam, ut bonum suum aliis per similitudinem communicet, secundum quod possibile estif (Natural things, in so far as they are perfect, communicate their good to others, much more does it appertain to the divine will to communicate by likeness its own good to others as much as possible.)

Cf. Thomas Aquinas, *De Veritate,* q. 21, a. 1, ad 4. Here Aquinas speaks of the notion more in terms of final causality, rather than efficient:

licet secundum proprietatem vocabuli videatur importare operationem causae efficientis, tamen largo modo potest importare habitudinem cuiuscumque causae sicut influere et facere, et alia huiusmodi. Cum autem dicitur quod bonum sit diffusivum secundum sui rationem, non est intelligenda diffusio secundum quod importat operationem causae efficientis, sed secundum quod importat habitudinem causae finalis; et talis diffusio non est mediante aliqua virtute superaddita. Dicit autem bonum diffusionem causae finalis, et non causae agentis: tum quia efficiens, in quantum huiusmodi, non est rei mensura et perfectio, sed magis initium; tum etiam quia effectus participat causam efficientem secundum assimilationem formae tantum, sed finem consequitur res secundum totum esse suum, et in hoc consistebat ratio boni (Though, according to the word's proper meaning, to 'pour out' seems to imply the operation of an efficient cause, taken broadly it can imply the status of any cause, as to influence, to make, etc. When 'good' is stated to be of its very notion diffusive, however, one should not understand 'diffusion' as implying the operation of an efficient cause. Instead, he should be thinking in terms of 'final cause.' Nor does such diffusion eventuate through the mediation of any added power. 'Good' expresses the diffusion of a final cause and not that of an agent, both because the latter, as efficient, is not the measure and perfection of the thing caused but rather its beginning. Also, because the effect participates in the efficient cause only in an assimilation of its form, whereas a thing is dependent upon its end in its total existence. It is in this that the character of good was held to consist.)

Also, *Summa Contra Gentes*, I, 37, (§307):

Agendo autem esse et bonitatem in alia diffundit. Unde et signum perfectionis est alicuius quod 'simile possit producere,' ut patet per Philosophum in IV *Meteororum*. Ratio vero boni est ex hoc quod est appetibile. Quod est finis. Qui etiam movet agentem ad agendum. Propter quod dicitur bonum esse 'diffusivum sui et esse.' (Now a thing acts through being in act: and by acting it bestows being and goodness on other things. Wherefore, it is a sign of a thing's perfection that it is able to produce its like, as the Philosopher declares (4 *Meteor.*) Again, the very core of the 'good' is that it is something desired: and this is an end. And the end moves the agent to act. Hence, 'good' is said to be diffusive of self and being.)

And *Summa Theologiae*, I[a] q. 5, a. 4, ad 2 ("Ad secundum dicendum quod bonum dicitur diffusivum sui esse, eo modo quo finis dicitur movere."); cf. Thomas Aquinas, *De Potentia Dei*, Qu. 3, art. 15, ad 12. There is an intimation of this in Augustine, *Confessions*, XII, 1, "if things are deprived of all good, they will cease to exist," [Albert C. Outler, tr., *Augustine: Confessions and Enchiridion* (Philadelphia: Westminster, 1955].) Cf. VII, 12, "si omni bono privabuntur, omino non erunt." Cf. J. A. Aertsen, "The Convertibility of Being and Good in St. Thomas Aquinas," *The New Scholasticism* 59 (1985): 449–70.

By far the most important recent treatment of this notion of the self-diffusive character of the good in Aquinas is Father Blankenhorn's, "The Good as Self-Diffusive in Thomas Aquinas," *Angelicum* 79 (2002): 803–837. Cf. Klaus Kremer, „Das 'Warum der Schöpfung': 'quia bonus' vel/et 'quia voluit'? Ein Beitrag zum Verhältnis von Neuplatonimus und Christentum an Hand des Prinzips 'bonum est diffusivum sui'" in K.

Flasch, ed., *Parusia: Studien zur Philosophie Platons und zur Problemgeschichte des Platonismus* (Frankfurt am Main: Minerva, 1965).

(For the Latin text of Thomas Aquinas I have used, unless otherwise cited, the text as prepared under the enviable supervision of Professor Alarcón, Universidad de Navarra [*Optimae editiones operum Thomae de Aquino* conscriptus ab Enrique Alarcón atque instructus ad Universitatis Studiorum Navarrensis aedes Pampilonae ab MMII A.D.], as well as the Leonine edition [Editio Leonina (*Sancti Thomae de Aquino Opera omnia iussu Leonis XIII P. M. edita*)] and that of Pierre Mandonnet, *S. Thomae Aquinitatis Opuscula Omnia* (Parisiis: Sumptibus P. Lethiellieux, 1927). Translations of Aquinas for the most part are mine.

Methodology

1. Method as a separate, deliberative epistemic approach appears in Plato's (for the Greek text see the Loeb Classical Library editions of his works, [publication various years]) *Phaedrus* (265d 3–266c 1; 273d 7– 4; 277 b 5–8), *Republic* (511 b 7–c2; 532d–535a), *Sophistes* (224c 9; 230b 6; 251 8; 267b 1; 219a 4–7; 221c 5–d 6; 253d 1–4; 253 d 9–e 6;, 261 d 7–9; 262 a 5–c 1), and *Statesmen* (267 b 6; 278 c 5; 308 c 6; 311 a 1) under the various guises of "hypothesis," "collection" and "division" and the calibrations Plato applies to them in the search for the Forms. Aristotle takes up an arguably different method in the aporematic approach, especially in the *Metaphysics* (see, e.g., Alan Code, "The aporematic approach to primary being in Metaphysics Z," in F. J. Pelletier and John-King Farlow, ed., *New Essays in Aristotle* [Guelph, Ontario: Canadian Association for Publishing in Philosophy, University of Calgary Press 1984], 1–20; Joseph Owens, *The Doctrine of Being in the Aristotelian Metaphysics* [Toronto: Pontifical Institute, 1978], Chapter Six: "The Aporemaic Treatment of the Causes {Book B}"; Ronald M. Polansky, *Aristotle's De Anima*, 41 ["Aristotle's aporematic method, beginning from the *aporiai* to point the way to the issues that must be resolved....". Cf. Michael Woods, "Form, Species, and Predication in Aristotle," *Synthese* 96 {3} 1993: 399–415).

Descartes' *Discourse on Method* probably is the first to focus philosophic inquiry on what it considers the necessity of taking into account the mind in a programmatic step-by-step procedure in inquiry (Descartes works are available in Rene Descartes, *Oeuvres De Descartes*, Charles Adam and Paul Tannery, eds., [Paris: Librairie Philosophique J. Vrin, 1983] Eleven Volumes (hereafter *AT*); *Descartes Oeuvres et Lettres. Introducions, Chronlogie, Bibliographie, Notes* par André Bridoux (Saint Catherine: Editions Gallimard, 1953) and *The Philosophical Writings of Descartes*, John Cottingham, Robert Stoothoff, and Dugald Murdoch, eds., [Cambridge: Cambridge University Press, 1985]. Translations here are mine). Kant's first *Critique* (all references to it here are from the edition of Paul Guyer and Allen Wood, tr., ed., [Cambridge: Cambridge University Press, 1998]) introduced an approach to metaphysics that sought to discern what was necessary for knowledge to occur, what was that without which knowledge could not occur, in his "transcendental method." In Hegel's Preface to the *Phenomenology* one sees comments on self-validating method, and in Husserl comes a new approach to the science of thought in eidetic insight achieved by method purgative of all, to the extent possible, societal beliefs and philosophic prejudices. Whether one can reach a state of *tabula rasa* in the mind where it can commence from a presuppositionless beginning seems an ideal at best. This, especially given the argument that even grammar, however its rules are set forth, itself has presuppositions (as e.g., the order of words in different languages). Nevertheless, to the extent that one can proceed without preconceptions one, it seems, should, and in our look at consciousness this is what we have sought to approximate to the extent possible.

2. Reductionists such as Dennet and Churchland refer to common speech about the cognitive functions as simply examples of "folk psychology." This manner of speech, they hold, is unscientific. We address their outlook with the criticism it invites in subsequent chapters.

3. We bring up this term again in the chapter "Indivisble Senation and Zombie Theory." See its note one below.

Consciousness

1. See Rene Descartes, *Meditations*, I, 12; III, 4; *AT* 7:257-258; *Principles* I, 5 (*AT*8a: 6). While the reading is not unanimous, the Evil Demon, lacking omnipotence [Descartes nowhere ascribes it to him], is not (cannot be) God (Whom Descartes also posits as a hypotetical *deceptor* in his Augean project of hyperbolic doubt). I believe *Meditations* I, 12, makes clear God is not the evil deceiver ("Supponam igitur non optimum Deum, fontem veritatis, sed genium aliquem malignum, eundemque summe potentem & callidum"). The Evil Daemon is capable of simulating an external world and bodily sensations, but incapable of rendering dubious things that are independent of trust in the senses, such as pure mathematics, eternal truths, and the principle of contradiction. See O. K. Bouwsma, "Descartes' Evil Genius," *Philosophical Review* 58 (1949): 141-151; Alex Gillespie, "Descartes' demon: A dialogical analysis of 'Meditations on First Philosophy,'" *Theory & Psychology* 16 (2006): 761-781; David Frederick Haight and Marjorie A. Haight, "Dialogue between Descartes and the Evil Genius," in David Frederick Haight and Marjorie A. Haigt, *Scandal of Reason: Or Shadow of God* (Lanham: University Press of America, 2004) 49–70; Richard M. Kennington. "The Finitude of Descartes' Evil Genius," in Richard M. Kennington, *On Modern Origins: Essays in Early Modern Philosophy* (Lanham: Lexington Books, 2004), 146.

2. In its realist setting, the act of existence synthesizes an entity's content, its richness, of form (what makes it knowable and what it is) and attributes (those features not essential to the particular entity for what it is but which it possesses in its individuality [e.g., color, weight, location, breadth, depth, softness, hardness]) into the actual individual unity that it is in existence, in our world. In knowledge, that very synthesis occurs in the mind in an immaterial way such that the mind becomes that synthesis immaterially. This is how knowledge of any thing that exists occurs in the human setting. The account of knowledge through synthesis by existence traces its way through the realism of the Schools, and is in direct contrast to the Cartesian approach which locates error in the senses without noting that error may be the result of the mind, in a judgment of what is before it, having added to the percept present in the mind what is not in the synthesis occurring in the world. All knowledge is a judgment, and the existential synthesis occurring in the world is a judgment formed in the mind when the mind becomes that existential synthesis in the immaterial way that it must in order for knowledge to occur at all in it. (The clearest, and most precise, exposition of this extensive tradition appears in Joseph Owens [in their entirety], *An Interpretation of Existence* [Milwaukee: Bruce Publishing Company, 1968] and his work *Cognition: An Epistemological Inquiry* [Notre Dame: University of Notre Dame Press, 1992]).

For our purposes here we need not address the issue of whether Descartes located error in the will. Error does come about, and it seems that correction of error does not come by withdrawal of the will but by additional evidence coming forth that brings the mind to no longer add to the synthesis what was not in the existential synthesis in the first place.

We note that this approach, which is the "common sense" approach to the world, the approach that the everyday individual takes, appears to comport well with Occam's principle that explanations need to be kept to a minimum. That principle lines up with the belief that Nature uses as few instruments as possible in its bringing something to be, This "realist" approach to the world will immediately bring us to acknowledge that not every entity in existence has the capacity for awareness, which we identify as "directionality towards," or "intentionality."

3. Husserl is an important thinker in the philosophic study of human consciousness, more of which we will detail through other endnotes as we proceed. While the method he enunciates has high merits as a tool to reach the things of the world as they manifest themselves, it has difficulties which we will present here as we discuss his doctrines.

On the expression of awareness as being "minded in a determinative descriptive fashion" see Edmund Husserl, *Logical Investigations*, tr. J. N. Findlay (New York: Humanities Press, 1970), VI, §2, 559. "Minded" here does not mean simply cognitive activity, but any "obectivating act" (an act correlative with which is an object), as in emotional, aesthetic, or any experience whatsoever. Husserl recognizes an almost seemingly endless number of species of such acts, which became the subject of "pure" description to this founding thinker of phenomenological exposition.

4. In our era, this term appears first used by Franz Brentano (cf. his *Psychologie vom empirischen Standpunkt* [Hamburg: Meiner, 1973]. {Translated into English by A. C. Rancurello, D. B. Terrell, and L. L. McAllister, *Psychology From an Empirical Standpoint*, Second Edition [London: Routledge, 1995]}. It can arguably be traced to Aristotle, *Metaphysics*, 1021a 29. In his 1889 lecture, *The Origin of Our Knowledge of Right and Wrong*, 14, tr. Roderick M. Chisholm and E. H. Schneewind [London: Routledge & Kegan Paul], Brentano writes "intentional «refers to» a relation to something which may not be actual but is presented as an object." In the Schoolmen, following on Aristotle, the term has a rich tradition in commentaries since the time of Aquinas. (For a background on this doctrine, see Dominik Perler, ed., *Ancient and Medieval Theories of Intentionality*. Leiden: Brill, 2001.)

While our presentation of consciousness in this chapter is not in any way a survey of prior treatments, it is probably useful to give a little history of the problem as it began to percolate in nineteenth-century Germany. So, we may be traversing ground already walked by Meinong, Höler, Husserl, Heidegger, Merleau-Ponty, but only as a recognition that some of their insights have value for us in this treatment of immortality, not as an exegesis of their texts which goes far beyond the scope of our inquiry.

Brentano, we may begin, was once a priest who left orders when his rejection of the dogma of papal infallibility resulted in the usual pressures that disagreement with any authority brings down upon the individual. While, subsequently, on the faculty of the University of Vienna he married, and again had pressures brought against him on account of the Austrian Concordat with Rome by which Austria refused to recognize the marriage of former clerics. He continued in Philosophy, nevertheless, and wrote, e.g., against the correspondence theory of truth claiming that there were two judgments involved, one the correspondence, and then the judgment of whether there was a correspondence. This claim is incorrect (one does not find it in Aristotle or the Schools), but that notwithstanding he came to his doctrine of *Evidenz*: the correspondence (*adequatio*) in truth is between the thing given and its self-givenness. If what is judged carries with it evidence, its own evidence, the one judging through that evidence is in possession of truth.

While he would come to discard this approach to truth, he did assert, in line with Aristotle, that the mind can know itself directly in its acts of awareness (whatever the object in its awareness with it is), an immediacy that gives the grounds for absolute certainty regarding a science of consciousness. For a full explanation, see his *Wahrheit und Evidenz*, red. Oskar Kraus (Leipzig: Meiner, 1930). {Translated into English by R. M. Chisholm, et al., *The True and the Evident* (London: Routledge & Kegan Paul, 1966)}. For the Aristotelian passus, see *De Anima*, 429b 9–10, καὶ αὐτὸς δι' αὑτοῦ τότε δύναται νοεῖν ("the mind too is then able to think itself" [Oxford translation, J. A. Smith], "moreover the mind is then capable of thinking itself" [Loeb translation, W. S. Hett]). An exegesis of the text appears in Joseph Owens, "A Note on Aristotle, *De Anima* 3.4, 429b 9," *Phoenix* 30 (1976), 2, 107–118. Cf. *De Anima* 425b 12ff which raises the issues of whether sight can have itself as an object, to which the reply is color is the object of sight, not sight. Sight knows that it is seeing only *per accidens*.

This doctrine of direct awareness, that inner perception is (in the Cartesian sense) infallible, has important ramifications for a possible science of consciousness itself, for a transcendental investigation (one that looks into what the structures of consciousness [the *a priori* connections between meaning-intention and meaning-fulfillment {cf. Edmund Husserl, *Logical Investigations*, Introduction, §2, and 252–3} are] so that awareness comes about. Part of this science, of course, will involve laying down the right order and establishing the correct classification of the parts of awareness and how those parts interrelate and relate.

Brentano does not allow outer perception any such veracity, stating in fact that outer perception (*äußere Wahrnehmung*) "presents us with nothing that appears as it really is. The sensible qualities do not correspond in their structure to external objects, and we are subject to the most serious illusions with respect to rest and motion and to figure and size." (See Appendix ["On the Lorenz-Einstein Question," 30 January 1915] to Franz Brentano, *The Theory of the Categories*, tr. Roderick M. Chisholm and N. Guterman (The Hague: Martinus Nijhoff, 1981), 208.

This is the classic Descartes-Lockean attitude, but whether only primary qualities (shape, size, etc.) are the only features available to awareness that give us anything of the world, or whether secondary qualities (color, taste, sound, etc.) are part of the mix is a question to which we shall turn later. The answer does not invalidate the central insight that consciousness is, at its core, other-directed.

There was, of course, some debate as to what "existence" might mean in a doctrine where it was sometimes posited that the intentional object as "immanently objective" in consciousness must exit. Part of the difficulty stems from the question "but in what way?" Meinong took up the issue with some respectable vigor. That seems to have invited Russell's rejoinders whose purpose was to bring about an attitude of bafflement towards what Meinong wanted to hold (e.g., that a square circle does exist, but not in the way we normally think of "exist." (This, apparently, was Twardowski's view, also [cf. Kasimierz Twardowski, *On the Content and Object of Presentation: A Psychological Investigation*, tr. R. Grossman {The Hague: Martinus Nijhoff, 1977}, 35]).

In this setting one comes to appreciate Bernard Bolzano's discussion (*Wissenschaftslehre. Gesamtausgabe* Reihe 1, Band 11–13 {Stuttgart: Jan Berg, 1985–1992}, Book 1, §67) on "objectless presentation," (like that of a centaur or a unicorn). If these do not "exist," in what way can they be an "object" to the mind setting them forth?

In the end Brentano did not want to limit existence at all to some *ens rationis*, [("When I ask a woman to marry me it is the woman as actually existing, and not an *ens rationis* that I am asking," {14 September 1909 Letter to Oscar Kraus, quoted in *Psychology from an Empirical Standpoint*, 285}; for this citation, see Dermot Moran, *Introduction to Phenomenology* (London: Routledge, 2000), 50]. He, in fact, wanted the act of consciousness to be understood not strictly in terms of immanent objectification. This he held has the status, true, of a relation to a world not of its making. He argued for more, however, sc., a world which is its correlative. In line with this thinking, he will be able to give inner perception (e.g., the *act* of hearing) a status of absolute evidence because as an act it has *eine wirkliche Existenz*, even though that to which the act (something in outer perception) refers in fact might not. Brentano eventually will posit a doctrine of *pararergo*, which addresses the intended act and its content, but is not necessary, for our treatment of immortality, to review.

As his thinking on these matters continued, we should note, Brentano's notion of object asserted a doctrine of *reism*—only a real thing is an object of thinking (only concrete individuals [*realia*], in the end, exist.) Only objects with existence independent of consciousness can be said to be "real."

5. See Franz Brentano, *Psychology From an Empirical Standpoint*, 88 (cf. his *Psycholoigie von empirischen Standpunkt*, Band 1, Buch Zwei, Kapitel 1, §5, 124–125).

6. Franz Brentano, *The Origin of our Knowledge of Right and Wrong*, 14.

7. Illustrative of this tenet is Wittgenstein's well-known statement, "Ich sehe nihct, daß die Farben der Körper Licht in mein Auge reflektieren." (*Bemerkungen über die Farben*, hrsg. G.E.M. Anscombe [Berkeley: University of California, 2007) II, ʃ20.

8. That concepts, the mental recognition of sameness in things otherwise different, actually occur in human thought, i.e., are not simply words or conventions, we take up later on. That ratiocination, the process of step-by-step reasoning, as in a syllogism, is a work of mind, and not binary systems in the neural matter of the brain, we take up in our discussion of Gödel's theorem.

9. See my *On the Existence of God* (Lanham, University Press of America, 2010), 1–5, 165.

10. This will be the rough form of the argument Husserl will advance in his defense of the world as something objective, as that which is transcendent to the "ego," and not that about which we can be the skeptic, the dilettante doubter, as it were. Questions, in fact, on how the skepticism could have arisen in the first place are the genuine point at issue given that our experience of the world is one of direct contact, immediacy, with an "other." The questions arise from failure to report the world as in fact it is experienced.

11. Probably best stated in Husserl's principle of principles, i.e., "every originary presentive intuition is a legitimizing source of cognition" (see his *Ideas Pertaining to a Pure Phenomenology and to a Phenomenological Philosophy* [*Ideen zu einer reinen Phänomenologie und phänomenologischen Philosophie*], tr. F. Kersten (Dordrecht: Kluwer, 1983) First Book, 1, and 1, §19). Cf. Edmund Husserl, *Experience and Judgment: Investigations in a Genealogy of Logic*, tr. J. S. Churchill and K. Ameriks, revised and edited, L. Landgrebe (Evanston: Northwestern Unversity Press, 1973), §10, 45, 44. "Intuition" (*Anschauung*), of course, means sensuous content, in the Kantian sense.

12. I follow Brentano on this. See his *Die Psychologie des Aristoteles insbesondere seine Lehre vom Nous Poietikos* (Darmstadt: Wisenschaftliche Buchgesellschaft, 1967).

13. The term "content," as some have argued, is ambiguous ("synsemantic" [the term is Brentano's, cf. his *Psychology from an Empirical Standpoint*, 294; also 284]). Cannot "content" mean "object," also? It can, but that is not necessarily to give "objectivity" to what consciousness has in its field. (Kasimierz Twardowski, *On the Content and Object of Presentation: A Psychological Investigation*, tr. R. Grossman [The Hague: Martinus Nijhoff, 1977], 16) seems to have given us the "content" as a means to the "object," but this does not clarify the objectivity aspect.

Suffice it to say the ambiguity does not hold back our inquiry into the nature of consciousness as evidence for immortality. We need establish that there is a difference between consciousness and its correlate, and that distinction will lead us to address whether the difference suffices to give conscious activity something impossible to unconscious existence.

14. The content can be anything, and need not be an object of which affirmation or denial is made, nor any other judgment (as in William James) with respect to it cast. It is simply a presence to consciousness that is not consciousness itself. Brentano will state this succinctly enough in *Psychology From an Empirical Standpoint*, 198, "it is impossible for conscious activity to refer in any way to something which is not presented." (Whether "judgment" at this level is involved appears to have received different opinions from Brentano over his lifetime.)

The level to which attention is paid to this presence will dictate, it appears, the difference between "perceiving" and "noticing." E.g., a trained ear will detect in a chord what an untrained ear will not, or a trained eye a shade not noticed by the passerby.

15. Insofar as, and to the extent that, anything is "meant," has a "meaning," it is objective to consciousness. "Objective" here does not mean a ground of validity, or "valid" for all beings, but strictly, in its etymological root, that which is "thrown up against."

16. Husserl, one of whose principle concerns appears to have been to find out how consciousness "constitutes" its world ("object") and, reflexively, how the world becomes constituted for consciousness, does not accept the School doctrine of judgment of existence as an existential synthesis as we have described here (see my *On the Existence of God*, Chapter Five, "From Idea to Idea," for elaboration of this, and note one above in the chapter "Consciousness"). Instead, Husserl maintains (Edmund Husserl, *Husserl. Shorter Works*, tr. and ed. Frederick Elliston and Peter McCormick [Notre Dame: University of Notre Dame Press, 1981]), 10–11:

> To every object there corresponds an ideally closed system of truths that are true of it and, on the other hand, an ideal system of possible cognitive processes by virtue of which the object and the truths about it would be given to any cognitive subject.

Difficult for the reader of such a teaching is the declaration about evidence (*Evidenz*), cognition given with insight [(*Einsicht*), knowledge self-validatingly given, knowledge validated "right now," "at once." "Inward evidence" is the criterion for correctness. This "*Evidenz*" ("a mental seeing of something itself," [Edmund Husserl, *Cartesian Meditations*, tr. Dorion Cairns {The Hague: Martinus Nijhoff, 1967} §5, 2) reaches us when no further verification about what is before us is called for. *Evidenz* is the experience of truth (Edmund Husserl, *Logical Investigations*, Prolegomena, §51). The object "gives itself" such that there is nothing that can add to what is knowable about it. (Thus, e.g., whatever we know about it cannot be contravened by something new for there is nothing new with respect to the object's essence). It is the fullness of intuition (*anschaüliche Fülle*) that consciousness possesses. *Evidenz* is originary presentive intuition, originary self-givenness (Edmund Husserl, *Ideas Pertaining to a Pure Phenomenology and to a Phenomenological Philosophy* [*Ideen zu einer reinen Phänomenologie und phänomenologischen Philosophie*], R. Rojcewicz and A. Schuwer (Dordrecht: Kluwer, 1989) Second Book, §24, 44. (Cf. Edmund Husserl, *Logical Investigations*, Prolegomena, §6, 61–62).

Consciousness, though, and here is our first problem, cannot provide this fullness, this *Einsicht*, because then it would already have the awareness. But is this not what one would take from that term "constitution," that the one that constitutes is the one that fashions, makes, what is constituted? Whence the awareness of the world that consciousness, as we just saw, cannot produce? How does it "constitute" the object since, as we just saw, that requires that it already have constituted the object? Or does constitution mean consciousness synthesizes in accord with necessary structures? In this respect, consciousness would not be in possession of what it is constituting, for it would take materials from which it constitutes through its *a priori* necessary structures the object of which it becomes aware (and which it constitutes). Thus, it does not have the problem of being already in possession of what it is supposed to constitute.

But if consciousness' role in constitution is to employ necessary ideal structures by which the object comes into its field, how does consciousness know when to stop the fashioning? Does the data that consciousness synthesize have an automatic "cut off" switch by which consciousness realizes it is "time" to stop the synthesizing, that synthesis if compete?

This "constitution" notion surely is a problem for the reader of Husserl. Husserl acknowledges that the referent for meaning can be the same while the expressions for that meaning can be different. "The vanquished at Waterloo," and "the victor at Jena," both refer to Napoleon (see *Logical Investigations*, 1, §12). The meaning refers to the Emperor, yet how do we know that the expressions for the meaning can (and do) [(both)] refer to Napoleon if Napoleon is in any way part of how consciousness "constitutes" its world? The more important question is, would consciousness ever constitute such a world in the first place and, if the answer is affirmative, then towards what end would it? What rationale would ground its constructing a world where a character such as Napoleon has such fluidity of referentiality? Why would consciousness constitute an object which can be referenced in more than one way such that it is referred to as both a victor and a loser in the same sentence?

Or, we can consider this problem: if consciousness constitutes its world and object, what is the purpose of objects so constituted that bear equivocation (Napoleon is the vanquished; is the victor [one term, two meanings])? Why would consciousness "constitute" a world where objects can have such imprecision?

Questions such as these could go on and on in the dispute over how consciousness can take on the role of that which constitutes the objects of its experiences and world. They seem to be without a response that can explain why constitution would take the turns we have just identified. To the realist, Husserl's penetrating insights into consciousness notwithstanding, these questions of "constitution" are questions as to how meaning, at its origin, can be the work of consciousness, of awareness.

Husserl's doctrine of "categorial intuition" [(*kategoriale Anschauung*), for which see *Logical Investigations*, VI] also adds to the quandary for the realist. Husserl acknowledges a gradation of intuitions in consciousness, and that beyond (significantly above) sensuous intuition is categorial intuition, the awareness that "something is the case," not simply that before one is "the case." E.g., a categorial intuition is expressed by the statement, "This pen is blue." In the intuition is grasped the "property" of the pen as being not just blue but "this is blue." One imagines that mental synthesis occurs in accord with the essential structure of the categorical judgment. Yet, again, Husserl seems to want to avoid any possibility that the synthesis actually occurs in the object itself and, immaterially, in the mind, and this is actually how something comes to be known as "being that which is X."

Disregarding his sentiment that existence is a property (which it is not), Husserl's doctrine of "constitution" seems to originate from a distrust of taking things as, in fact, they are given to us. His method, though admirable in objective, is not as "open" to reality as he wants it to be. He has accepted the senses as a faulty conduit and thus has to adjust how appearances come to consciousness without the errors that Descartes' sense criticism held. We need, accordingly, the rigorous work of a consciousness that acts in accord with structures that precede any grasp or awareness of content, object, meaning to guard us from any simple realism. That realism, in its putative naïveté, is passive before a world that cannot in any wise give us any evidence of its legitimacy. Descartes, as Husserl accepts, showed us this. *A priori* structures of consciousness are the noetic guardians against any deception in what comes to us. Their universality makes for a world where science is possible, but only if one accepts Descartes' claims against certainty through sense-apprehension. If error is a result of the mind introducing what is not in the object, as was held in the Schoolmen, Descartes' epistemology, not simple realism, is what is at issue.

The Husserlian doctrine of eidetic reduction, of *epoché* ([ἐποχή] suspension), also arises as a concern. It poses the issue whether the philosopher, Husserl, in some way, has approached the object of consciousness, or of study, in a manner that is not in line with the nature of consciousness itself, or of the conscious agent. Husserl denies intuition (*Anschauung*) can be of the rawness that Kant clearly gave it. The sensuous content already has some articulation, it has some *Sinn* (sense) to it, when it is being taken up by consciousness or sensation. There is not, as I take it, some whirl of totally chaotic sense content thrown to the synthesizing activity of the conscious being. Without arguing the point (and I think Husserl is far more correct on this aspect of consciousness than Kant), *epoché*, in seeking to get to the pure structures of meaning, consciousness, intention, and the like clearly is a stance that backs off from this immediacy of sense data to which Husserl denies a blind chaos.

Epoché (in its broadest sense—Husserl has a number of nuances for this activity [*Enthaltung, Einklammerung, Ausschaltung*]), steps back from any outward influences, prejudices, or preconceptions, conventions, and opinions of the day, and absolutely from the question of the existence of what is before the philosopher. This stepping back, Husserl wants to suggest, gives us access to the ability to identify and prehend the structures by which meaning and consciousness are possible and constituted. (*Logical Investigations*, V, §14). This, as we just saw above, is because he accepts he Cartesian explanation for error (as partially sense-caused). While the attitude of looking at the world without prejudices is thus admirable, one has to suggest that the attitude towards the senses (preventing the untrammeled openness of realism) Husserl has accepted and against which he has cautioned is an impediment to his hope for pure inquiry.

In a way Husserl is telling us that through *epoché* we can look at the intentional world in the very depths of its possibilities and lawfulness without needing to have a world that actually exists (see Edmund Husserl, "Phenomenology and Anthropology," in Thomas Sheehan and Richard Palmer, (eds.)., *Psychological and Transcendental Phenomenology and the Confrontation with Heidegger* (1927–1931), Collected Works VI, [Kluwer: Dordrecht, 1997] 165.) We can move in the realm of unmixed (pure) possibility, in the sphere of essences upon which all science ultimately rests. More than that, in the *epoché* we come to see in its purity that which is before us in a way that we prehend its otherness from consciousness, an otherness we can take up only if the object is itself immanent to our consciousness in the first place.

Husserl tells us in this "eidetic" seeing is a likeness to the way the Divine sees (Edmund Husserl, *The Idea of Phenomenology*, tr. W. P. Alston and G. Nakhnikian [The Hague: Martinus Nijhoff, 1964] 44–45), reminiscent, one may want to opine, of Spinoza's doctrine of viewing things "*sub species aeternitatis.*" In the same way Husserl speaks of apodictic (versus adequate) evidence, this suggestion in *The Idea of Phenomenology* may be an exaggeration, or a recommendation of an ideal that the phenomenologist seeks to secure, and not an actual equivalence to Divine "sight." Kant rightly notes that the Divine's knowledge of something makes it be, while surely Husserl is not trying here to say that the phenomenologist's "seeing" (*Wesenserchauung* [*Ideas*, First Book, §1, 3, 8) brings the essential structures in question "to be."

This doctrine of "intuitive seeing," however, does not show itself to be a method by which "pure" structures come into view. Husserl does not advance any evidence that "bracketing" out the question of *Wirklichkeit*, actual existence (*Dasein*), in any way gets us to simple "possibility." Plato, of course, speaks of "seeing the Forms," in the final ascent to reality. He occasionally will speak of this in terms of the method of division, other times he seems to give it a more ethical tone. "Seeing," i.e., is the reward, result of having abided the norms, the measure, of the Good. One does get to the indivisible for Plato through division, and the indivisible is the Form.

But Husserl does not advance such a method for reaching "pure possibility." One is to focus exclusively on what is before one, and this for Husserl excludes automatically the question "Does what is before me exist?" Nowhere have I seen Husserl argue for how or why this is so. As such, it makes his theory of reduction strictly one more in a number that have offered how it is that one comes to essences. It does not, however, advance, so far as I can see, how we are to understand what exactly consciousness is, which is the purpose of our undertaking here. Consciousness "exists." To "bracket off" the question of its existence in reduction at whatever stage of phenomenological (scientific, philosophic) inquiry does not appear to take consciousness in its absolute fullness.

In his *Prolegomena* [to *Logical Investigations* (published separately to the *LI* in 1900, and which precedes Volume Two, where the Six Investigations unfold)], Husserl states we must distinguish instantiations of ideal meaning from their ideality. A red ball is an instantiation of *eine ideale Einheit*, a transcendental meaning (here, Röte [red]) that neither comes to be nor passes may. The science of Philosophy (i.e., "pure phenomenology") is concerned with the *a priori* manner in which these transcendental meanings (these eternal unities) are related and interrelated, as well as that by which they are.

In this important manner Philosophy differs from psychology in that psychology generalizes from instances (*Prolegomena* §21), while Philosophy seeks what is ideally prior to any such basis of generalization. Psychology sees these meanings, these "self-identical unities" as images (e.g., the color "red"), but these "meanings," as the philosopher, the phenomenologist, understands them, are in no way images of any sort. Philosophy seeks to clarify, [bring to pure expression (*zu reinem Ausdruck* {*Logical Investigations*, I, Introduction, 249}] the manner in which experiences are constituted in the lived, concrete, everyday world. It seeks, i.e., to pinpoint the possibilities by which consciousness constitutes meanings (either a unity apart from others, or a web of unities) and by which meanings are constituted. Meaning-intention and meaning-fulfillment are correlatives wherein whatever occurs in consciousness occurs according to laws, and thus must occur as they do without exception when they do occur.

Husserl, in this regard, will not allow for an Aristotelian theory of abstraction of form (εἶδος, [the cognitional content of the individual reality, as well as that which makes it be what it is) from the particular object as a means of reaching these "idealities," these "essences," because nothing in Philosophy for Husserl can first be experience-dependent, or contingent upon findings in everyday experience. Necessity can never be reached that way, but can only appear before us as what precedes, makes possible, whatever it is that we experience. The lived world (*Lebenswelt*) is contingent, while philosophy (eidetic discipline [the focus on the purely necessary and structural in all experience]) must overcome all contingency (see *Ideas*, First Book, §1, 2). Husserl's denial of necessity *in* experience is a denial of causal interaction, which brings us to absolutely necessity of a being that causes something to come to be. That he accepted the Kantian causal approach, that he has dismissed causal necessity as derived *from* experience, argues further against his claim of looking at experience without preconceptions or pre-judgments.

In any event, Husserl's assertion, which we may term more of an "idealism," than the "realism" that characterizes the pre-Cartesian Schoolmen and Aristotle, does not affect the study of what embodied consciousness is. Husserlian "constitution" (*Konstitution*) does have a non-realist ring to it (see Husserl's use of the terms "productions" or "products" of consciousness in [*Cartesian Meditations*, §38, 77]. While in Heidegger's interpretation of his teacher it means "letting the entity be seen in its objectivity" (Martin Heidegger, *History of the Concept of Time*. Prolegomena. tr. Theodore Kisiel [Bloomington: Indiana University Press, 1985] §6, 71; 97), I am more inclined to see an activist role of consciousness in Husserl's doctrine of constitution, Sokolowski's view notwithstanding (Robert Sokolowski, *The Formation of Husserl's Concept of Constitution* [The Hague: Martinus Nijhoff, 1964], 196. I say this especially given what Husserl writes in *Ideas Pertaining to a Pure Phenomenology and to a Phenomenological Philosophy*, Second Book, §10, 23). Whether he is an idealist or not (a question I think is not able to be resolved. He says, e.g., in *Ideas Pertaining to a Pure Phenomenology and to a Phenomenological Philosophy*, First Book, §23, e.g., that essences are not produced in our thinking, but grasped, framed, in our acts of thinking. This is clearly akin to the realism evident in *Logical Investigations*. Yet this very *Ideas* work is where the well-known 'transcendental turn,' the founding of objectivity in subjectivity, takes place, a turn that is clearly not sympathetic to a realism of experience taught in the Schools.

So, Husserl's statement in the *Nachlass* (as translated in Rudolph Bernet, Iso Kern, and Eduoard Marbach, *An Introduction to Husserlian Phenomenology* [Evanson: Northwestern University, 1993], 59: "Subjectivity, and this universally and exclusively, is my theme" clearly expresses an attitude that Father Sokolowski's point of view does not pick up. Again, however, the failings in Husserl which we have noted here of "openness to," or "pure looking" as a goal by which to approach consciousness does not affect the immortality aspect of our study here on the actuality, the reality, of consciousness. We have argued for phenomenology as our method because phenomenology is self-correcting and the most dedicated to description of the lived world.

We have taken some of his insights, along with others of the school of Phenomenology, to enhance or explanation of what consciousness is. It is that which is "other-directed" to its core, and this suffices for our purposes to examine the possibility this holds for disembodied existence. The exact nature of the "object" in consciousness' field, i.e., what role in its constitution consciousness may or may not play, leaves unaffected our claims about how the nature of consciousness differs so radically from the object in its field. It is important to our inquiry to identify this object as being intrinsically "other" than consciousness, however. It cannot be a product or creation of the ego. It must be substantively different in its very being from what consciousness is. We will address that as we move further along in the study.

17. Edmund Husserl, *Ideen zu einer reinen Phänomenologie*, 1 (cf. note 10, "Consciousness" above), (written during his "middle period" in 1913, during which [1905–1928] he would moved towards his founding of the method of reduction {*epoché* } and the *a priori* analysis of transcendental subjectivity) §129; cf. *Logical Investigations*, V, §11.

As an indication of Husserl's genius, the reader should note that the remarkable *Ideen* 1 was written in about three months. While he does appear to have had an interest in Berkeley in his University of Leipzig attendance, Husserl clearly began his studies in Philosophy in earnest with Brentano from 1884–6. (Cf. Martin Heidegger, a student of Husserl's, *History of the Concept of Time. Prologomena*, tr. Theodore Kisiel

[Bloomington: Indiana University Press, 1985], 23). Their relationship ultimately ceased to have the smoothness, cohesion, one looks for between Professor and student, (surely not anything unusual in academic settings [at least as reported by Husserl in a 1937 correspondence with Marvin Farber {see Kah Kyung Cho, "Phenomenology as Cooperative Task: Husserl-Farber Correspondence during 1936–7," *Philosophy and Phenomenological Research* 50 [Supplement] Fall, 1990, 36–43}]). Gottlob Frege and Husserl were at differences over just how close Husserl was to a purity of science, as evinced in Frege's criticism of Husserl's failure to draw a precise enough distinction between an actual presentation (*Vorstellung*) and the *object* in the presentation. Husserl was too close to a psychologism, a criticism his *Logical Investigations* either accepted as valid or had already anticipated (commentators disagree) in its movement towards the necessity of a transcendental ground if there was to be the clarity that Philosophy deserved.

Apropos the interest in Berkeley, one should note Husserl's admiration for Hume's work, which he shared with teacher Brentano. It seems to me that Huserl attributes to Hume the important establishment to phenomenological science of "constitution" (of which Husserl's *Ideen* 2 [Zweites Buch]) is perhaps the most thoughtful exposition {cf. Louis Sandowski, "Hume and Husserl: The Problem of the Continuity or Temporalization of Consciousness," *International Philosophical Quarterly*, Pt 1 (181):59–74}) as a philosophical moment of transcendental import, especialy as given Husserl's interpetation of Hume's approach to the issue of causality. (See Edmund Husserl, *Formal and Transcendental Logic*, tr. Dorion Cairns, [The Hague: Martinus Nijhoff, 1969], §100; cf. his *The Crisis of European Sciences:and Transcendental Phenomenology. An Introduction to Phenomenological Philosophy*, tr. David Carr [Evanston: Northwstern University Press, 1970], §24). The agreement with Hume is a matter of historical arcana, for one does not need agree with Hume to reach an understanding of consciousnes that is free of subjectivist-imposed constraints. For a treatment of Hume and causality see, among others, my work *On the Existence of God* (Lanham: University Press of Amerca, 2009), Chapter 1 and endnotes or Chapter 1. The best critique of Hume's causation doctrine is D. J. B. Hawkins, *Causalty and Implication* (London: Sheed and Ward, 1937). We may quickly note here that not all of Hume received praise from Husserl, as his work, *Logical Investigations* (Second Investigation), 190, 212, makes plain. Cf. Ram Adhar Mall, *Experience and Reason: The Phenomenology of Husserl and its Relation to Hume's Philosophy* (The Hague: Martinus Nijhoff, 1973); Richard Timothy Murphy, *Hume and Husserl: Towards Radical Subjectivism* (The Hague: Martinus Nijhoff, 1980); Saranindranath Tagore, "Husserl's Conception of Hume's Problem: towards a Transcendental Hermeneutic of Hume's Treatise," *Man and World* 27 (1994) 257–269; Theodorus de Boer, *The Development of Husserl's Thought*, tr. T. Plantinga (New York: Springer, 1978), 215, "the British empiricists (e.g., Hume)....explanation lacks a descriptive foundation and thus can make no claim to being scientific."

18. In our era it is probably Hume that is most quoted as the opponent of any possible philosophical rationale for asserting the "self" exists. A permanence to the individual is requisite for him to be able to say or write anything that lasts longer than a second, and such permanence is the beginning of selfhood. Which apparently Hume possessed, since he both wrote and spoke. What Hume's point was to the denial of a philosophical proof for the self, what it was supposed to resolve, emerges as fanciful speculation. That not everything, or proposition, is provable does not mean neither is true. Not all truth or evidence comes by way of demonstration, as Aristotle's *Posterior Analytics* has argued (rather successfully), while his *Ethics* councils (wisely) that an intelligent man does not always look for a proof (or, contrarily, it is only a foolish individual that seeks a proof for

everything.) Arguably, these comments apply to arguments regarding the realty of self-hood.

19. Levinas has written two important works on our topic, *The Theory of Intuition in Husserl's Phenomenology*, tr. A. Orianne (Evanston: Northwestern University, 1973) and *Totality and Infinity*, tr. A. Lingis (Pittsburgh: Duquesne University, 1973).

20. So Merleau-Ponty speaks of "the natural and antepredicative unity of the world and of our life," (Maurice Merleau-Ponty, *Phenomenology of Perception*, tr. C. Smith [London: Routledge and Kegan Paul, 1962], xviii). I experience the world as "real in one blow," a world that is *un tissue solide*, (ibid., x), wherein, in fact, the relations between body and world constitute the true synthesis, the true reality, the interworld (*l'intermonde*). "Our own body is in the world as the heart is in the organism....and with it forms a system," (ibid., 203, 235). Merleau-Ponty's *The Structure of Behavior*, tr. A. L. Fisher (Boston: Beacon Press, 1963) is a useful, if not extraordinary, critique of mechanistic stimulus/response interpretations of human behavior.

Other

1. As a matter of historical interest, it is Aristotle who appears to have first held the mind knows itself in knowing the object (*De Anima* 429b 6–10, especially 10 [αὐτὸς δι' αὐτοῦ τότε δύναται νοεῖν]). This has received varied and voluminous interpretations over the millennia, but none which have ever rejected the notion that the mind is aware of itself when it is aware, and of whatever it is aware. Specifically, the *De Anima* tenet is "the mind is capable of thinking itself in thinking the object." Cf. the *Ethics*, which identifies the self with mind [διανοητικοῦ (1166a 16–17; 1168b28–1169a 3)].

Recent secondary literature on this subject appears, e.g., in I. Block, "Three German commentators on the individual senses and the common sense in Aristotle's psychology," *Phronesis* 9 (1964): 58–63; Charles Kahn, "Sensation and consciousness in Aristotle's psychology', *Archiv für Geschichte der Philosophie* 48 (1966): 43–81; L. A. Kosman, "Perceiving that we perceive: On the Soul, III.2," *Philosophical Review* 84 (1975): 499–519; C. Osborne, C. (1983), "Aristotle, De Anima 3.2: How do we perceive that we see and hear?", *Classical Quarterly* 33 (1983): 401–411; J. Schiller, "Aristotle and the concept of awareness in sense perception," *Journal of the History of Philosophy* 13 (1975): 283–296. Of exceptional merit, from a formalist perspective, is Gert-Jan C. Lockhorst, "Aristotle on Reflective Awareness (De Anima III.2 and De Somno 2)," *Logique & analyse*, Nouvelle Série, 37e année, No 146 (Juin 1994):,129–143.

2. Is not, i.e., a totally passive existent, something simply "awaiting" an object for its presence, but is what is by its very structure that which "tends towards," moves into, the ambit of, the "other."

3. See Bertrand Russell, "Knowledge by Acquaintance and Knowledge by Description," *Proceedings of the Aristotelian Society*, 11 (1910): 108-128.

Color and Objectification

1. See R. Menzel, "Color Pathways and Color Vision in the Honeybee" in D. Ottoson and S. Zeki, (eds.), *Central and Peripheral Mechanism of Color Vision* (London: Macmillan, 1985), 211–234.

2. For this characterization V. S. Ramachandran tells us to think of "color" and the neurophysiologic process as essentially two different ways of addressing the same thing. The neurophysiologic process, however, as we will discuss, is not color at all.

See his Reith Lectures, Lecture 5 (2003) @http://www.bbc.co.ukradio4/reith2003/

3. For a manageable presentation on this difficult subject see J. J. McCann and J. L. Benton, "Interaction of the Long-wave cones and the Rods to Produce Color Sensations," *Journal of the Optical Society of America* 59, 103–107.

4. See Frank Jackson, "What Mary Didn't Know," *Journal of Philosophy*, 83, 5, 291–295.

5. Color is a subject of a most difficult sort to even begin to understand, what with all of the preconceptions and "visions" of the electromagnetic field that we bring to the subject. The most accomplished works on it, and on which my discussion is heavily dependent, are G. Brindley, *Physiology of the Retina and Visual Pathways* (Baltimore: Williams and Wilkins, 1970); R. L. Gregory, *Eye and Brain* (New York: McGraw-Hill, 1973), Second Edition; C. L. Hardin, *Color for Philosophers* ((Indianapolis: Hackett, 1988), Rolf Kuehni, *Color: Essence and Logic* (New York: Van Nostrand Rhinehold, 1983); and Kurt Nassau, *The Physics and Chemistry of Color: the Fifteen Causes of Color* (New York: John Wiley, 1983).

6. A full discussion on this is A. L. Yarbus, *Eye Movements and Vision*, tr. B. Haigh (New York: Plenum, 1967).

7. See E. L. Holman, "Is the Physical World Colourless?," *Australasian Journal of Philosophy* 59, 295–304 and "Intention, Identity and the Colourless World: a Revision and Further Discussion," *Australasian Journal of Philosophy* 59, 203–205.

8. James Cornman, *Perception, Common Sense and Science* (New Haven: Yale, 1975).

9. Aristotle, *De Anima*, 426a 27 – 42b 7. Insofar as the sense organ and sense quality are the same in sensation, though immaterially, color, as a sense-quality, and the sense-organ (which is a λόγος for Aristotle) are the same and hence color (which is also a form [εἶδος]) is a λόγος too.

10. See Aristotle, *De Anima*, II. 7; 419a 11–15; 424a 17–24; *De Sensu*, 439b 9–10.

11. *De Anima*, 418b 17–20. I know of no argument that has successfully answered Aristotle's objection to the theory of light being in any way a "body" of any sort.

12. See Michael Tye, "The Adverbial Approach to Visual Experience," *The Philosophical Review* 2 (1984): 196–197.

The Extralinguistic Object

1. A. J. Ayer, *The Problem of Knowledge* (New York: Macmillan)1956, 94–95

2. See my discussion on this in Robert Geis, *Personal Existence After Death: Reductionist Circularities and the Evidence*, 21–37. The doctrine of universals has a long history, but finds its clearest exposition in Aquinas (especially *De Veritate*, X, 8; the *Summa*, I^a, Q. 75, article 5; and chapter four of his *De ente et essentia*, 4.) The universal is not a "thing," but is the form or essence in each thing known by the mind as being in other than just one thing. It is present in the mind because the form or essence which the mind prehends as in different things is present in the mind. As such, the mind is not limited to a singular thing in its knowledge of things or its acquaintance with them. In knowing them as being the same, but numerically different, it has transcended the limits of each thing's singular status. In this way, it has transcended likewise their material status. Aquinas also in the *Summa Contra Gentes*, II, 49–51, gives an extensive argument on why the mind is immaterial, and in this regard is indestructible.) My discussion in *Personal Existence After Death*, 21–37, comments on the self-refutational character of the Berkely-Hume rejection of universals.

3. Richard Rorty, "In Defense of Eliminative Materialism," in D. M. Rosenthal, ed., *Materialism and the Mind-Body Problem* (Englewood Cliffs: Prentice Hall, 1971), 228–229.

4. Aristotle, *On the Gait of Animals* (tr. A. S. L. Farquharson), Part 11.

Disintegration and Partibility

1. Some have claimed in the transference from one orbit to another in this "disbonding," the electron, e.g., ceases at one point to exist only to re-exist at the point it is in the new orbit. This would appear to break the first law of thermodynamics (energy can be neither created nor destroyed), and if in fact such a dis-existence, and then re-existence, occurred the charge involved in the electron would no longer exist either—raising the issue, it seems, of what it is that determines the subsequent orbital.

This metaphysical difficulty makes it difficult to fathom quantum mechanics' doctrine that how electrons, in this respect, are simply possibilities, and not actually occurring existents in space and time. Their existence is only a potential at any given moment; when they "jump" from one orbit to the other they actually only "reappear," as we saw, at the different level, not travel through space and time. Actually, for the quantum physicist, there is nothing *in between* the orbits. It is only when we attempt to "measure" them that we make them "real." We have no way of possessing certainty about where they may be at any given instant [(Heisenberg's uncertainty {indeterminacy} principle.) See Timothy Ferris, *The Whole Shebang: A State of the Universe's Report* {New York: Simon and Schuster, 1997}, 97].

The issue has no bearing on the constitution of any physical entity. On the gross level of interaction, of where all components of the physical entity composed of the subatomic quantum particles effect and affect against one another and themselves in their valence and co-valence existence, a lawfulness takes place. Uncertainty has given way to predictability and order. The transformation from a quantum world to the world we know seems to indicate perhaps that there may be something deeper than quantum mechanics that is a substrate to its activities. As such the lawlessness on that level is not at all on this substrate level. Discussions on that, however, take us far afield from where we are now.

Importantly, however, on the quantum level, if the particles of the neuronal "matter" act in such an indeterminate way, determinism (the doctrine that a given condition or cause makes a subsequent condition or cause ineluctable, such that its non-occurrence is contradictory) as a hindrance to human action appears non-existent. Behavior is not driven to a set of predetermined ends. If the uncertainty we cited above has to do not with the electron "de-existing" and then "re-existing," but rather at where we determine it to be (or must accept statistically where it might be at any of its moments), then our metaphysical difficulty fades. What we have is a situation of the person capable of indeterminism at his or her very root, very center, sc., at the locus whence all action originates, sc., the mind. (See J. M. Schwarz, H. Stapp, and M. Beauregard, "Quantum Theory in Neuroscience and Psychology: A Neurophysical Model of Mind/Brain Interaction," *Philosophical Transactions of the Royal Society B: Biological Sciences* 360 (2005): 1309–1327.

2. See H. Diels and W. Kranz, *Die Fragmente der Vorsokratiker* (Berlin: Weidmann, 1952), B 116, on Democritus' assertion about absolute "uncuttables" (a-toma [ἄτομα], atoms). His process of reasoning to it has received voluminous commentary over the centuries. What is important to us here is the ascription to him as the originator of this theory. It is quite clear that he did not perceive "atoma" as we do today. He saw the necessity of some such reality, however different in conception his approach and conclusion is from current science. Cf. Francis M. Cornford's judicious essay "The In-

vention of Space," *Essays in Honor of Gilbert Murray* (London: Allen & Unwin, 1936), 215–235.

Justice to the Abderite's doctrine cannot occur in any summary of it. Perhaps the reader's interest can move towards further study of Democritus through some comments. The clearest statement of Democritus comes in a fragment from Aristotle's (no longer extant) *On Democritus* preserved in Simplicius' commentary on the *De Caelo* (DK 68A 37). Aristotle (who actually cites Leucippus as apparently the originator of the "smallness of bits" (σμίκρότητα τῶν ὄγκων) notion, but not their uncuttable status [see *De Generatione et Corruptione*, 325a 23–28] tells us that for Democritus coming to be and passing away are accomplished by way of the void and atoms. Atoms, he tells us, are (as the word indicates) indivisible, homogenous in make-up (made of the same "stuff"), infinite (it is not clear if this is actually infinite or potentially) in number, possessed of different sizes, shapes, and (it appears) weights. There are no other characteristics he lists.

Atoms, in Parmenidean language, have the appellation "the what-is" or the full; the void, "what-is-not." Whatever exists, Aristotle tells us, for Democritus is a result of the interaction of the void and atoms. It is not clear whether everything to us is named or experienced by convention, or only what we call, after Locke, secondary qualities [{(flavors, color, hot, cold, and the like)}; cf. DK 68B9 = BA25; DK68A 49)]. This is not to say Democritus anticipated the seventeenth-century distinction between primary and secondary qualities. Robert Pasnau, e.g.,"Democritus and Secondary Qualities," *Archiv für Geschichte der Philosophie.* 89 [2] July 2007: 99–121, has argued that for Democritus all sensible qualities are conventional.

Atoms are constantly in motion and their density of arrangement in the void dictates what structures constitutes our world and the cosmos (according to Theophrastus' *De Sensibus*, [DK 68A 135.62, 65–67]). Whether the atomist void itself is or is not has two interpretations, one that it is (in accord with the Parmenidean doctrine that one cannot possibly assert of what is not that it is [DK 28B7. 1], the other that it is not {see C. C. W. Taylor, *The Atomists: Leucippus and Democritus: Fragments* (Toronto: University of Toronto Press, 1999)}]. For Democritus atoms are not perceptible. However whatever they arrange may be or may not be. (The issue of their weight appears in Alan Chalmers, "Did Democritus Ascribe Weight to Atoms?" *Australasian Journal of Philosophy* 75 (3) 1997: 279–287. We come to postulate the existence of atoms through a process of connecting cognitively with what is real, which sense-perception does not enable, but only (it appears) through a mental process of moving to what is finer and finer till we reach the truth that all is composed of indivisibles without, however, ever actually perceiving them (See Sextus Empiricus' account in DK 68B 11) .

Plato will, apparently, attempt to make triangular shape the indivisible constituent of physical body, for which Aristotle will provide no agreement (On Aristotle's disagreement, see Keimpe Algra, *Concepts of Space in Greek Thought* [Leiden: Brill, 1995], 110–117). Plato's basic building blocks, to be specific, are two different types of triangles. One is half of the equilateral triangles that make up the faces of the pyramid, octahedron, and icosahedron. This is a right triangle with angles of 30 degrees, 60 degrees, and 90 degrees. The other is half of the square that is a face of the cube. This triangle is a right isosceles triangle.

Plato argues that these triangles are also the best and most perfect. If, though, transformation of all the basic elements into one another is Plato's main goal, he does not achieve it with these triangles. One can interchange the half equilateral triangles to make the faces of pyramids, octahedra, and icosahedra, but the half squares obviously cannot be used to construct anything but cubes. A further problem is that the dodecahedron requires pentagons for its construction.

Later ancient mathematicians demonstrated that the pentagon faces could indeed be divided into thirty congruent scalene triangles, but of course different from those comprising the three polyhedra with triangular faces. See Francis MacDonald Cornford, *Plato's Cosmology, The Timaeus* (Humanities Press, 1952) for a detailed explanation of Plato's approach, 210–239;. 298. Cf. Dougal Blyth,"Platonic Number in the Parmenides and Metaphysics XIII," *International Journal of Philosophical Studies* 8 (1) 2000: 23–45;.and Paul Friedländer, *Plato* (Princeton: Princeton University Press, 1969), vol. 1, chap. 14. Apropos this, *Meno* 76a tells us that shape is in fact a kind of limit, "the limit of a solid" (ὅπερ ἂν συλλαβὼν εἴποιμι στερεοῦ πέρας σχῆμα εἶναι).

3. Aristotle's *Metaphysics*, Book 5, chapter xxv, will set forth meanings of "part" (μέρος) also, and is probably the first time one has a lexicon of its philosophical designations.

4. A "property" is that which can be in more than one thing at the same time, e.g, redness in a ball and in a hat. This is in contrast to an individual substance, which can never be in anything, nor ever predicated of anything. The individual substance is the most basic metaphysical entity in realty; a property is not as basic, accordingly, since it is what is in a substance and cannot exist without the substance. A substance, however, can exit without being, having the property of, "red."

5. Space and extension have a reality, and one finds perhaps the most helpful reasoning on this in Plato (*Timaeus* 50b–c [(εκμαγεῖον) *ekmageion* here appears to indicate space is that which is like a lump in which impressions are caused or fixed.]) Cf. Keimpe Algra, *Concepts of Space in Greek Thought* (Leiden: Brill, 1995), 38–52; Francis MacDonald Cornford, *Plato's Cosmology, The Timaeus* (New York: Liberal Arts Press, 1957), "The Receptacle is that in which qualities appear"), 187; Jacques Derrida, "*Chōra*," (in *Poikilia: Festschrift pour J.-P. Vernant* {Paris: Ecole des Hautes Etudes, 1987} "the Receptacle is nothing other than the totality of the process of what comes to be inscribed 'onto' it, regarding its subject precisely its subject, but itself is not the subject or present support of all [this], 273) (translation mine); Pierre Duhem in M. J. Cakep, *The Concepts of Space and Time: Their Structure and Development* (Dordrecht: Reidel, 1976), 22–23; Aristotle, *Categories*, 5a 9–14; *Physics*, 211a 23–28; 210b 34–35; 209a 4–5.

Cf. Pierre Duhem's commentary that for Aristotle place is the fixed term by which we judge a body as in rest or in motion (*Le système du Monde* [Paris: Hermann, 1913)] I: 200). One finds concurrence on the actuality of place in as contemporary a thinker as Whitehead ("everything is positively somewhere in actuality," in *Process and Reality*, ed. D. R. Griffin and D. W. Sherburne [New York: Free Press, 1978], 40, cf. 46, 59, 231.)

On this theory of place as that wherein something rests the debate over wherein rests the heavenly spheres has been protracted. Cf. W.D Ross' *Commentary on Aristotle's Physics* (Oxford: Clarendon Press, 1936), 57. Note that the condition that the place of a thing must be no larger than the thing itself [on the notion of place as that which contains] proves incompatible with the requirement that the place of a thing must be at rest. Duhem (chapters five and six, *Le système du Monde*) and Aquinas' *Commentary* on Aristotle's *Physics* passus 214–216 have written incisively on this issue of celestial spheres rotating in "space," as has Bergson (a body possesses a place [*lieu*] on the condition of being at a remove (*éloigné*). ("L'Idée de Lieu chez Aristote," *L'Études Bergsoniennes* (1949) 2: 84–87. Aristotle's doctrine of place, nevertheless, when we do not look to the galaxies and its possible movements, seems to have found acceptance as a substantially valid notion of place in the history of philosophy.

Interestingly, cf. *Physics* 212b24–28 where Aristotle notes that a point is without place (cf. 208b 24–25). On this see Hussey's (*Aristotle's Physics, Books III and IV* [Oxford: Clarendon Press 1983], 102; also 121) comment on *Physics* 209a 71–13 that the place of a point would have to be without extension, like the point itself, and therefore itself a point; but two distinct points cannot coincide. H. A. Wolfson notes an objection in *Crescas' Critique of Aristotle: Problems of Physics in Jewish and Arabic Philosophy* [Cambridge: Harvard University Press, 1929], 44. Aristotle speaks in terms of a point as a unit with position (*De Anima* 409a 5 [cf. *Posterior Analytics* 87a 36–37; *Metaphysics* 1016b 31 ["That which has not position is a unit, that which has a position a point."]) Cf. *Categories* 5a 1–5; *Physics* 215b 19). Cf. Stefan Körner, *The Philosophy of Mathematics* (London: Hutchinson, 1960), 18–21; Proclus, *A Commentary on the First Book of Euclid's Elements*, ed. and tr. Glen R. Morrow (Princeton: Princeton University Press, 1970), 73–74; 79ff.

G. E. L. Owen (in his *Logic, Science, and Dialectic: Collected Papers in Greek Philosophy*, "Aristotle, Method, Physics and Cosmology" [Ithaca: Cornell University Press, 1986], 155) has maintained that at *Physics* 219b 16–22 Aristotle goes against the notion that a point has no place. Aristotle here, however, even as Owen admits, is merely correlating moving objects with place. That "the 'now' corresponds to the body that is carried along" does not equate the now ("point") with place—anymore than the body does.

Edward S. Casey's unsurpassed *Getting Back into Place* (Bloomington: University of Indiana Press, 2009), Second Edition,(ix–xvii), suggests a way to understand the importance of place is to consider "placelessness." Can one possibly imagine what it would entail, or mean? Contrast the reality that a tree, e.g., stays and thrives in its own "place," while mobile man must move continuously from place to place in his development and living. Or the fact that for a person to stay in one place without possibility of being elsewhere is almost a "hell," and yet to be placeless is sheer fright, sheer dread.

It is not surprising that man has such a drive for territoriality, for having a "place," if not even more so have a nostalgia for the original place whence he came, perhaps as a child, or perhaps as a person who cherishes the memory of the place where his first child was born. Place itself can have an effect on us as that which alienates, or that to which we do damage and destruction.

Place's importance has a significance perhaps for Aristotle in how he characterizes the soul as "a place for forms" (those realities in Aristotelian knowledge and ἐπιστήμη that bring an entity to be and constitute its knowable content. See *De Anima*, 429a 25–26 [καὶ εὖ δὴ οἱ λέγοντες τὴν ψυχὴν εἶναι τόπον εἰδῶν, πλὴν ὅτι οὔτε ὅλη ἀλλ' ἡ νοητική, οὔτε ἐντελεχείᾳ ἀλλὰ δυνάμει τὰ εἴδη {Those who speak of the soul as a place for forms speak well; we can only add that this 'place' is the forms potentially, not in actuality /this place is potentially all the forms it contains/}], translation mine).

A systematic study of consciousness as an intentionality towards place, while it itself is in place, harbingers many new understandings. It, however, is beyond the ken of this study.

Meaningful enquiries into place in the human setting are, in addition to Casey's Henri Lefebvre, *The Production of Space*, D. Nicholson-Smith, tr. [Oxford: Blackwell, 1991 (a vigorous neo-Marxist exposition of space that brings to the fore attitudes and perceptions worthy of analysis, whatever one's disagreements or agreements with neo-Marxism might be)]; J. E. Malpas, *Place and Experience* (Cambridge: Cambridge University Press, 1999); Doreen Massey, *For Space* (London: Sage, 2005).

6. While citing Augustine, Aquinas uses the term, it appears, approvingly at his *Super Sent.*, lib. 1 d. 3 q. 4 a. 5 co.:

Respondeo dicendum, quod, secundum Augustinum differunt cogitare, discernere et intelligere. Discernere est cognoscere rem per differentiam sui ab aliis. Cogitare autem est considerare rem secundum partes et proprietates suas: unde cogitare dicitur quasi coagitare. Intelligere autem dicit nihil aliud quam simplicem intuitum intellectus in id quod sibi est praesens intelligibile. Dico ergo, quod anima non semper cogitat et discernit de Deo, nec de se, quia sic quilibet sciret naturaliter totam naturam animae suae, ad quod vix magno studio pervenitur: ad talem enim cognitionem non sufficit praesentia rei quolibet modo; sed oportet ut sit ibi in ratione objecti, et exigitur intentio cognoscentis. Sed secundum quod intelligere nihil aliud dicit quam intuitum, qui nihil aliud est quam praesentia intelligibilis ad intellectum quocumque modo, sic anima semper intelligit se et Deum indeterminate, et consequitur quidam amor inde-terminatus. Alio tamen modo, secundum philosophos, intelligitur quod anima semper se intelligit, eo quod omne quod intelligitur, non intelligitur nisi illus-tratum lumine intellectus agentis, et receptum in intellectu possibili. Unde sicut in omni colore videtur lumen corporale, ita in omni intelligibili videtur lumen intellectus agentis; non tamen in ratione objecti sed in ratione medii cogno-scendi.

Death and Purpose

1. Nihilism is the motif of ascribing nothingness or absence of meaning to any as-pect or all aspects of existence. Camus, Derrida, and Sartre are among its most prolific proponents, with Ionesco and Celan perhaps its most artful.

Indivisible Sensation and "Zombie" Theory

1. For familiarity with "zombie" theory, see David Chalmers, "Facing Up to the Problem of Consciousness," *Journal of Consciousness Studies*, 2, no. 3 (1995): 200–219; *The Conscious Mind: In Search of a Fundamental Theory* (New York (Oxford University Press, 1996); "Consciousness and its Place in Nature", in S. Stich and F. Warfield, *The Blackwell Guide to the Philosophy of Mind* (London: Blackwell, 2003); "Imagination, Indexicality, and Intensions," *Philosophy and Phenomenological Research*, 68, no. 1 (2004): 182–190; Daniel Dennett, "The Unimagined Preposterousness of Zombies," *Journal of Consciousness Studies*, 2, no. 4 (1995): 322–326; "The Zombic Hunch: Ex-tinction of an Intuition?" Royal Institute of Philosophy Millennial Lecture, 1999; Robert Kirk, "Sentience and Behaviour", *Mind*, 83 (1974): 43–60; Saul Kripke, "Naming and Necessity" in D. Davidson and G. Harman, (eds.), *Semantics of Natural Language* (Dordrecht, Holland: Reidel 1972), 253–355; Thomas Nagel, "Armstrong on the Mind," *Philosophical Review*, 79 (1970): 394–403; "What is it Like to Be a Bat?" *Philosophical Review*, 83 (1974): 435–450; N. J. T. Thomas, "Zombie Killer," in S. R. Hameroff, A.W. Kaszniak, & A.C. Scott (eds.), *Toward a Science of Consciousness II: The Second Tuc-son Discussions and Debates* (Cambridge, MA: MIT Press, 1998), 171–177; Stephen Yablo, "Textbook Kripkeanism and the Open Texture of Concepts," *Pacific Philosophi-cal Quarterly*, 81 (2000): 98–122.

Coherence, Percept, *Qualia*

1. See S. P. Vecera and K. Gilds, "What Is It Like To Be a Patient with Appercep-tive Agnosia?" *Consciousness and Cognition* 6 (1997), 237–266.
2. Thomas Metzinger, *The Science of the Mind and the Myth of the Self* (New York: Basic Books, 2009), 29.

3. Thomas Nagel, "What is it like to be a bat," in Thomas Nagel, *Mortal Questions* (Cambridge: Cambridge University Press, 1979), 165–180; cf. "Brain Bisection and the Unity of Consciousness" in Thomas Nagel, *Mortal Questions*, 147–164.

4. This is not to deny access to "objectivity." Inasmuch as the object is not subjectively constituted, the experience in qustion is "objective."

5. Arguably first proffered by Hume, a modern day presentation occurs in David G. Meyers, *The Human Puzzle* (New York: Harper and Row, 1978), 77–88. Kant's own unity of apperception argument in the *Critique* seemingly would make one hesitant to take this Humean position seriously, yet as in many other quarrelsome circles much ink has been spilt on this denial of the seemingly obvious. After all, if I walk down the street and get run over, is this someone different than the one who walked down the steps first to get to that street where the being run over occurred? Cf. Geoffrey Madell, *The Identity of the Self* (Edinburgh: Edinburgh University, 1981).

6. See Roderick Chisolm, *The First Person* (Minneapolis: University of Minnesota, 1981) for elaboration.

7. Bernard Williams, *Problems of the Self* (Cambridge: Cambridge University, 1973), 46–63.

8. On Kant here see his *Critique of Pure Reason* B413–415. Regarding his distinction between intensive and extensive quantity (magnitude), see B208–210. That Kant equates intensive magnitude with quality I take as following from his claim that sensation has intensive, as opposed to extensive, magnitude. And what is sensation (e.g., taste, sense) if not a presence of quality to awareness?

9. Roderick Chisolm, *On Metaphysics* (Minneapolis: University of Minnesota, 1989), 56.

10. Eliminative materialism refers to such terms as the parlance of a "folk psychology." Eventually all such terms will be reducible to the neural. See Daniel C. Dennet, *Breaking the Spell: Religion as a Natural Phenomenon* (New York: Viking), 207.

11. See B. Alan Wallace, *The Taboo of Subjectivity: Toward a New Science of Consciousness* (Oxford: Oxford University Press, 2000), 139.

12. See Robert Geis, "Descartes' Res: An Interactionist Difficulty" in Brendan Sweetman, ed., *The Failure of Modernism* (Washington, D.C.: CUA Press, 1997).

13. The doctrine of creation is not only that at an instant was all the cosmos brought into being *ex nihilo*. It is also the doctrine that the Creator must conserve and sustain in being at every instant that which He has brought into being. This is the gloss Ockham in his doctrine of the "unconserved Conserver" places on creation *ex nihilo*. See William of Occam, *Philosophical Writings*, tr. with an introduction by Philotheus Boehner (New York: Bobbs-Merrill, 1964), 136-137: "Whatever is really produced by something is also really conserved by something, as long as it remains in actual being."

14. Daniel C. Dennet, *Brainchildren: Essays on Designing Minds* (Cambridge: MIT Press, 1998), 346.

15. Patricia Smith Churchland, *Neurophilosophy: Toward a Unified Science of the Mind/Brain* (Cambridge: MIT Press, 1969), 288–33.

16. In this regard Paula Churchland herself seems unable to avoid the "folk psychology speak" that she criticizes to explain her own positions. E.g., in her *Neurophilosophy* she uses the adjective "cognitive," but such usage admits of a difference from the neurobiological, a difference she denies (see 309–310).

17. Peter Watson, "Not Written in Stone," *New Scientist*, 29 August 2005.

18. Patricia Smith Churchland, *Neurophilosophy: Toward a Unified Science of Consciousness*, 277–347.

19. No comment is needed on the sentiment that in the same way a computer's disc drive is replaced when faulty, but the computer undergoes no punishment, so also with the individual human agent. Punishment, the sentiment holds, is not the answer to legal redress, simply replacement of motive (software) is. This is the assertion that arises when identities of human and computer behavior are taken to their extremes.

20. See Sir John Carew Eccles and David Robinson, *The Wonder of Being Human: Our Brain and Our Mind* (New York: Free Press, 1984), 36.

21. Roger Sperry in his Nobel address (8 December 1981) asserted "the whole world of inner experience….becomes included within the domain of science," a view Nobel winner Eccles rejects in his statement "materialist solutions fail to account for our experienced uniqueness." John Eccles and David Robinson, *The Wonder of Being Human: Our Brain and Our Mind* (New York: Free Press, 1984), 43.

22. Gerald M. Edelman and Giulio Tononi, *A Universe of Consciousness: How Matter Becomes Imagination* (New York: Basic Boos, 2001) xi.

23. Daniel Dennet, *Kinds of Minds: Towards and Understanding of Consciousness* (New York: Basic Books, 1996), 55.

24. John Eccles and David Robinson, *The Wonder of Being Human: Our Brain and Our Mind,* 47.

25. Eric Harth, *The Creative Loop: How the Brain Makes a Mind* (Reading, MA: Addison-Wesley, 1993), 102.

26. The belief ("promissory materialism") that, given enough time, eliminative materialism will have the final say Sir John Eccles calls a "superstition" (Sir John Eccles, *The Evolution of the Brain: Creation of the Self* [London: Routledge,1989], 241.

Other Difficulties for Neurophilosophy

1. Matthew Botvinick and Jonathan D Cohen, "Rubber Hand 'Feels' Touch that Eyes See,'" *Nature*: 391 756 (1998).

2. Certainly not a new idea, and one that even precedes Hume, See, e.g., T. Stcherbaatsky, "The Soul Theory of the Buddhists," *Bull. Acad. Sci. Russ.* 845 1919, quoted in Appendix to the Eighth Chapter of Vasabandhu's Abhidarmakoça, §9,100.b.7, "There exists no individual), it is only a conventional name given to a set of elements."

3. For this see Thomas Metzinger, ed., *Neural Correlates of Consciousness: Empirical and Conceptual Questions* (Cambridge: MIT Press, 2000).

4. The literature on this contention (and its many nuances) is vast. E.g., Robert Becker and Gary Selden, *The Body Electric: Electromagnetsm and the Foundation of Life* (New York: William Morrow, 1985); F. Calvin, *The Cerebral Symphony* (New York: Bantam Books, 1989); J.-P. Changeaux, *Neuronal Man:The Biology of Mind* (New York: Oxford University Press, 1985); Jon Franklin, *Molecules of the Mind: The Brave New Science of Molecular Psycholgy* (New York: Laurel, 1987); R. Gerber, *Vibrational Medicine* (Santa Fe: Bear and Co., 1988); Stansilav Grof, *The Holotropic Mind* (San Francisco: HarperSanFrancisco, 1990); F. David Peat, *Synchronicity: The Bridge Between Matter and Mind* (New York: Bantam, 1987); John Searle, *Minds, Brains, and Science* (Cambridge: Harvard University Press, 1984); S. R. Hameroff, "Fundamentality: Is the Conscious Mind Subtly Linked to a Basic Level of the Universe?" *Trends in Cognitive Science* 2, Number 4 (1998): 119–127; Robert Jahn, and Brenda Dunne, *Margins of Reality: The Role of Consciousness in the Physical World* (San Diego: Harcourt, 1987); Stephen M. Kosslyn and Olivier Koenig, *Wet Mind: The New Cognitive Neuroscience*

(New York: The Free Press, 1982). For the "quantum" flavor of this hypothesis see David Bohm and Basil Hiley, "The Causal Interpretation of Quantum Theory" in David Bohm and F. David Peat, *Science, Order, and Creativity* (New York: Bantam Books, 1987); S. R. Hameroff, "Quantum Computing in Microtubules: An Intraneural Correlate of Consciousness?" *Cognitive Studies* (Bulletin of the Japanese Cognitive Science Society) 4, Number 3 (1998):67–92; Henry Stapp, *Mind, Matter, and Quantum Mechanics* (New York: Springer–Verlag, 1993).

5. Among others, see, e.g., Daniel Dennett and Marcel Kinsbourne, "Time and the observer: the where and when of consciousness in the brain," *Behavioral Brain Sciences* 15 (1992) 183–247.

6. See Benjamin Libet, *Neurophysiology of Consciousness* (Basel: Birkhäuser, 1993). Cf. G. Gomes, "The timing of conscious experience: a critical review and reinterpretation of Libet's research," *Consciousness and Cognition* 7 (1998), 559–595.

7. Daniel Dennet, *Consciousness Explained* (Boston: Little, Brown, 1991), 141 ff.

8. A view of a general outlook on the phenomenon of backwards referral appears in Patrica S. Churchland, "On the alleged backwards referral of experiences and its relevance to the mind-body problem," *Philosophy of Science* 48 (1981): 165–181.

9. Karl R. Popper and John Eccles, *The Self and its Brain: An Argument for Interaction* (New York: Springer Verlag, 1977), Part II, 314.

10. Ibid., II, 476.

11. John Zachary Young, *Philosophy and the Brain* (New York: Oxford University Press, 1988), 73, has asserted that Libet's findings show simply that "the brain is at work before a subject's conscious intent to act." The experiment to which he refers in his book, however, is not the one we have cited in our work, which means Young has not addressed the experiment that has been set forth as datum (e.g., by Eccles [see note nine]) that neural events are not wholly explanatory of awareness. In any event, while he did not, his comment that the brain may show neurophysiologic changes prior to a conscious decision to act is not laboratory evidence that such changes result in conscious decisions. It is not clear that Young intends one to draw such a conclusion. It is also not clear why he would make the comment if that was not the conclusion he wished one to draw.

12. Daniel Dennet, *Consciousness Explained*, 154–67; Patricia S. Churchland, "The Timing of Sensation: Reply to Libet, *Philosophy of Science* 48 (1981): 492–497; Benjamin Libet, "The Experimental Evidence for Subjective Referral of a Sensory Experience Backwards in Time: Reply to P.S. Churchland," *Philosophy of Science* 48 (1981): 182–97; "Subjective Antedating of the Sensory Experience and Mind-Brain Theories," *Journal of Theoretical Biology* 114 (1985): 563–70; and "The Timing of a Subjective Experience," *Behavioural and Brain Science* 12 (1989): 183–85.

13. Gilbert Ryle's less than admiring description of René Descartes' mind-body dualism as found in Ryle's *The Concept of Mind* (Chicago: University of Chicago, 1949), along with his "category mistake" nomenclature; Ryle's work had made opportune many doctoral dissertations, but has in no wise discredited or invalidated the central Cartesian tenet that the mind and body do differ and accomplish two different things.

14. Professor DeMarse received his M. S. (1992) and Ph. D. (1997) in Learning and Memory at Purdue University. From 1997 to 1999 he worked as a postdoctoral researcher in the Behavioral/Cognitive Systems Group at Arizona State University. From 1999 to 2003 he worked as research fellow in the Biology Department at the California Institute of Technology and the Biomedical Engineering Department at Georgia Tech interfacing cortical neurons to computer systems. He is currently an assistant professor in the Department of Biomedical Engineering at the University of Florida in neural engineering

and is head of the Neural Computation and Robotics lab (NCR) conducting investigations on neural interface technology, learning in living neural systems, and epilepsy.

15. See Professor O'Reilly's general overview of this in H. E. Atallah, M. J. Frank, and R. C. O'Reilly, "Hippocampus, cortex and basal ganglia: Insights from computational models of complementary learning systems," *Neurobiology of Learning and Memory, 82/3* (2004): 253–67; J. D. Cohen, T. S. Braver, R. C. & O'Reilly, "A Computational Approach to Prefrontal Cortex, Cognitive Control, and Schizophrenia: Recent Developments and Current Challenges," *Philosophical Transactions of the Royal Society (London) {B}, 351* (1996): 1515–1527; M. J. Frank, B. Loughry, B. and R. C. O'Reilly, "Interactions between the frontal cortex and basal ganglia in working memory: A computational model," *Cognitive, Affective, and Behavioral Neuroscience, 1* (2001): 137–160; T. E. Hazy, M. J. Frank, and R. C. O'Reilly, "Towards an executive without a homunculus: computational models of the prefrontal cortex/basal ganglia system," *Philosophical Transactions of the Royal Society B, 362* (2007): 1601–1613; Y. Munakata, & R. C. O'Reilly, "Developmental and Computational Neuroscience Approaches to Cognition: The Case of Generalization," *Cognitive Studies, 10* (2003): 76–92; R. C. O'Reilly, T. S. Braver, and J. D. Cohen, "A Biologically Based Computational Model of Working Memory" in A. Miyake & P. Shah (eds.), *Models of Working Memory: Mechanisms of Active Maintenance and Executive Control* (New York: Cambridge University Press, 1999), 375–411); R. C. O'Reilly and Y. Munakata, "Computational Neuroscience and Cognitive Modeling" in L. Nadel, ed., *Encyclopedia of Cognitive Sciences* (London: Macmillan, 2003); R. C. O'Reilly, and M. J. Frank, "Making Working Memory Work: A Computational Model of Learning in the Frontal Cortex and Basal Ganglia. *Neural Computation, 18* (2006): 283–328; R. C. O'Reilly, "Six Principles for Biologically-Based Computational Models of Cortical Cognition," *Trends in Cognitive Sciences, 2,* 455–462.

16. See "Brain circuitry findings could shape computer design," *MIT News* 24 March 2004.

17. *Newsfactor@http://www.newsfactor.com/story.xhtml?story_id=30799&page=1#swfp=0*, Pam Baker, "The Bleeding Edge of Computing."

18. The theorem can be set forth as follows: Within an axiomatic system, an equation can be constructed such that X=Y, where X states Y cannot be proven. If Y could be proven, what X states is false. But no formal system is such that it permits false propositions to be proven (one cannot prove a false proposition). Therefore, there can be no proof of Y. But this is what Y is asserting, that is cannot be proven. Therefore, Y must be true and true without proof

Some have reduced the debate in this discussion about Gödel's theorem to this issue: Could a computer program be written by a computer that is true, but could not be proven by us to be true? If such a program could be written, is this not the same as saying it has proceeded algorithmically?

Only if programming can occur without an algorithm at all could this be entertained as a possibility. A computer, though, cannot begin any program without instruction. The instruction, however, cannot be self-given by the computer, since then the program would never have had a beginning: as self-given there is no point where the computer could not already have been programming. Since it needs instruction, an algorithm, to begin programming, it cannot reach a non-algorithmic assertion. To do so would be like reaching what cannot be proven through what can be.

19. Aristotle, *Posterior Analytics*. Introduction and commentary by Sir David Ross, tr. (Oxford: Clarendon Press, 1949). In II. 19 the Stagirite argues how not all knowledge is demonstrable or, therefore, demonstrative. Demonstration requires ultimately principles not in need of demonstration if demonstrative conclusions (conclusions prehended as

necessary in virtue of the premises conjoined in thought to yield them) are to ever be possible. To deny the claim is itself in need of demonstration, thus confirming Aristotle's thesis.

20. GNCC, or "global neural correlate of consciousness" (as the term "global" implies), is meant to indicate the entirety of neuronal apparatuses that one can call upon to explain that your world (the entirety of all your experiences from the first to the last) is actually capable of being experienced if those correlates can be electrically stimulated. This makes an appeal to a world independent of you unnecessary, for all that is needed is the electrode(s) that can stimulate the sum aggregate of the countless neurons-synaspses that go to make up the neuronal apparatus that can, according to the Botvinick-Cohen theorists, just as easily create the consciousness that you ascribe to "the world out there." NCC would be the apparatus correlate of just one experience (at any given moment), not your entire world (the sum total of all of your consciousness from the womb to the grave.)

21. See David Hume, *Enquiries Concerning the Human Understanding and Concerning the Principles of Morals,* L. A. Selby-Bigge, ed., (Oxford: Oxford University Press, 1972), Second edition, 20–21:

> There is, however, one contradictory phaenomenon, which may prove, that it is not absolutely impossible for ideas to arise, independent of their correspondent impressions. I believe it will readily be allowed, that the several distinct ideas of colour, which enter by the eye, or those of sound, which are conveyed by the ear, are really different from each other; though, at the same time, resembling. Now if this be true of different colours, it must be no less so of the different shades of the same colour; and each shade produces a distinct idea, independent of the rest. For if this should be denied, it is possible, by the continual gradation of shades, to run a colour insensibly into what is most remote from it; and if you will not allow any of the means to be different, you cannot, without absurdity, deny the extremes to be the same. Suppose, therefore, a person to have enjoyed his sight for thirty years, and to have become perfectly acquainted with colours of all kinds, except one particular shade of blue, for instance, which it never has been his fortune to meet with. Let all the different shades of that colour, except that single one, be placed before him, descending gradually from the deepest to the lightest; it is plain, that he will perceive a blank, where that shade is wanting, and will be sensible, that there is a greater distance in that place between the contiguous colours than in any other. Now I ask, whether it be possible for him, from his own imagination, to supply this deficiency, and raise up to himself the idea of that particular shade, though it had never been conveyed to him by his senses? I believe there are few but will be of opinion that he can: And this may serve as a proof, that the simple ideas are not always, in every instance, derived from the correspondent impressions; though this instance is so singular, that it is scarcely worth our observing, and does not merit, that for it alone we should alter our general maxim.

While Hume did not believe it worth much exercise of concern, much has been written about this problem. Recently, e.g., Robert E. Cummins, "*Philosophical Review* 87 (October 1978): 548–565; Robert J. Fogelin, "*Philosophy and Phenomenological Research*," 45 (December 1984): 263–272; D. M. Johnson, "Hume's Missing Shade of Blue, Interpreted as Involving Habitual Spectra" in Stanley Tweyman, ed., *David Hume: Critical Assessments* (New York: Routledge, 1994) Volume 1, 207–217; Thomas M. Lennon,

"Hume's Ontological Ambivalence and the Missing Shade of Blue" in Stanley Tweyman, *David Hume: Critical Assessments*, 198–206; Bernard E. Rollin, "Hume's Blue Patch and the Mind's Creativity" in Stanley Tweyman, *David Hume: Critical Assessments* ,Volume III, 145–57); Timm Triplett, "Tye's Missing Shade of Blue," *Analysis* 67 (294) 2007: 166–170; William H. Williams, "Is Hume's Shade of Blue a Red Herring?" *Synthese* 92 , 1, 1992: 83-99.

We should note, as a scientific aside, that a human eye can only differentiate 110 colors, a microspectrophotmeter 2,000 and more.

22. See J. A. Hobson, R. Stickgold, and E. F. Place-Schott, 1998, "The Neuropsychology of REM Sleep Dreaming," *Neuroreport* 9 (1998) R1–R14; cf. A. R. Braun, et al. "Dissociated Pattern of Activity in Visual Cortices and Their Projections During Human Rapid Eye Movement Sleep," *Science* 279 (1998): 91–95; P. Maquet et al., "Functional neuroanatomy of human rapid-eye-movement sleep and dreaming," *Nature* 383 (1996): 163–166; Mark Solms, *The Neuropsychology of Dreams: A Clinico-Anatomical Study* (Mahwah, NJ: Lawrence Erlbaum Associates. 1997); and Rüdiger Vaas, "Blick ins Reich der Träume," *Bild der Wissenschaft* 5 (1998): 108–109. Vaas ("Why Neural Correlates are Fine, but Not Enough," *Anthropology and Philosophy* Volume 3, Number 2, 121 – 141), presents these correlates:

Phenomenal features of REM sleep dreaming	Neurophysiological correlates
vivid visual hallucinosis	extrastriate cortices
	primary visual cortex
spatial imagery construction	right parietal operculum
motoric hallucinosis	basal ganglia
bizarreness (incongruity, discontinuity, uncertainty)	frontal cortex (dorsal, orbital)
delusion (being duped into believing to be awake)	aminergic demodulation
	(noradrenergic and serotonergic
	neurotransmitter)
deficits of self-reflective awareness, directed thought, insight in illogical and impossible experience, and memory ("dream amnesia")	
strong emotions (especially anxiety, fear, anger,	(paralimbic system
elation	amygdala
	anterior cingulate
	temporal pole)

23. Singer is widely known in neurosynchrony and neurocausality circles. His work is extensive, and three most representative of his general approach are (all published by Suhrkamp Verlag, Frankfurt am Main): *Der Beobachter im Gehirn. Essays zur Hirnforschung* (2002); *Ein neues Menschenbild? Gespräche über Hirnforschung* (2003); and *Vom Gehirn zum Bewußtsein* (2006).

24. Robert Lewin, "Is Your Brain Really Necessary?" *Science* 210 (12 December 980): 1232–34.

25. D. H. Wilson, A. G. Gazzaniga, and C. Culver, "Cerebral Commisneurotomy for the Control of Intractable Seizures," *Neurology* 27, 708–715.

26. A sampling of the difficulties here appears in Roger W. Sperry, "Mind-Brain Interaction: Mentalism, Yes; Dualism, No," *Neuroscience* Volume 5 (1980): 195–201.

27. In reporting on this, Stuart Hameroff writes:

The authors compared EEG in two subject groups before and during meditation—not of an object or activity, but of a pure feeling of unreferenced compassion. Dare I say this pure feeling might be deemed a *quale*?

One subject group was composed of young students trained for a week in meditative technique; the second group consisted of Tibetan Buddhist practitioners with 15 to 40 years of meditation training and practice. The EEG methodology was rigorous, and the results were clear. Compared to novice meditators, the highly trained Tibetan Buddhist meditators had markedly higher amplitude, long-range global gamma synchrony in bilateral frontal and parietal/temporal regions. An increase in gamma synchrony was also observed in baseline measurement (before meditation) which became enhanced and more global during meditation in the trained Tibetan meditators.

For technical reasons (possible muscle artifact and 60 Hz AC interference) the absolute frequency spectrum was not determined, though the experimenters hinted of a significant rise in synchrony and amplitude in the 80 to 120 Hz range during the Tibetans' meditation. The coherence and power in the range of 25 to 42 Hz was significantly increased statistically. Amplitude of the synchronized gamma activity was greater than any previously reported nonpathological (i.e. non seizure-based) gamma synchrony.

So, what does this tell us about consciousness? Well first, there is an increase in gamma synchrony amplitude and coherence during what I think is fair to call an enhanced state of consciousness—pure intense experience unfettered by cognitive contents. This supports the notion of gamma synchrony as an electrophysiological correlate of consciousness.

Second, the trained Tibetan meditators had baseline increases in gamma synchrony and amplitude, suggesting long-term changes in their brains from years of meditation. One might say they are more highly conscious in a baseline state, achieving even greater intensity of consciousness during meditation.

In a book titled *The Quantum and the Lotus* by Mathieu Ricard and Trinh Xuan Thuan (Crown Publishers, 2001), Ricard (a molecular biologist turned Buddhist meditator and co-author of the Lutz study) describes the Buddhist concept of three levels of consciousness, including the most important "fundamental luminosity of the mind." This is a "state of pure awareness that transcends the perception of a subject/object duality and breaks free from the constraints and traps of discursive thought." Moreover this form of consciousness, according to Mathieu Ricard, can exist independently of the brain, and in fact pervades the universe. Presumably, the meditative state marked by enhanced gamma synchrony represents an immersion of the subjects in this fundamental luminosity. (Such a connection may possibly be explained through the quantum approach to consciousness. For example the Penrose-Hameroff model suggests a connection between brain processes and a fundamental Platonic realm embedded in the space-time continuum.

28. Jeffrey Schwartz and Sharon Begley's *The Mind and the Brain: Neuralplasticity and the Power of Mental Force* (New York: HarperCollins, 2003), 17–90.

29. Mario Beauregard and Denyse O'Leary *The Spiritual Brain: A Neuroscientist's Case for the Existence of the Soul* (New York: Harper One, 2007), 126–130.

30. See Mario Beauragard, J. Lévesque, and P. Bourgoín, "Neural correlates of Conscious Self-Regulation of Emotion," *Journal of Neuroscience* 21 (2001): RC165 (1–6).

31. M. Brass and P. Haggard, "To Do or Not To Do: the Neural Signature of Self-Control," *Journal of Neuroscience* 27 (2007): 9141–9145.

32. For the details see F. Benedetti, L. Colloa, E. Torre, et al., "Placebo-Responsive Parkinson Patients show Decreased Activity in Single Neurons of Subthalmic Nucleus," *Nature Neuroscience* 7 (2004): 587–588; Raül de la Fuente-Fernández, et al., "Expectation and Dopamine Release: Mechanism of the Placebo Effect in Parkinson's Disease," *Science* 293 (10 August 2003): 1164–1166.

33. Tor D. Wager, James K. Rilling, Edward E. Smith Alex Sokolik, Kenneth L. Casey, Richard J.Davidson, Stephen M. Kosslyn, Robert M. Rose, Jonathan D. Cohen, "Placebo-Induced Changes infMRI in the Anticpation and Expectation of Pain," *Science* 2003, no. 5661 (20 February 2004): 1162–67. Cf. also on this issue of placebo, R. Kanigel, "Placebo: Magic Medicine?" *Johns Hopkins Magazine* (August 1983): 12–16; B. O'Regan and T. Hurley, "Placebo: The Hidden Asset in Healing," *Investigations* (Research Bulletin of the Institute of Noetic Sciences) 2, Number 1 (1985): 5; L. White, B. Tursky, and G. Schwartz, *Placebo: Theory, Research and Mechanics* (New York: Guilford Press, 1985). Of further interest in this area are A Mandell, "Toward a Psychobiology of Transcendence: God in the Brain" in R. S. Davidson, ed., *The Psychobiology of Consciousness* (New York: Plenum, 1981); T. J. Mansen, "The Spiritual Dimension of Individuals: Conceptual Development," *Nursing Diagnosis* 4, Number 4 (October-December 1993): 140–47.

34. Michael Storm, *The Anatomy of Evil* (New York: Prometheus Books, 2009), 326. Neurotransmitters (dopamine, serotonin, norepinephrine) aid in conveyance of nerve (neuroelectric) impulses from one neuron through the synaptic cleft to another (the second) neuron. In certain key brain pathways the neurotransmitter may build up in the synpatic cleft "overloading the circuits" as it were. This higher level can lead to overexcitation of the enzyme MAOA, whose job is to inactivate (metabolize) the neurotransmitters.

Conceptualization, Memory, Immateriality

1. Nominalists consider only individual things (physical particulars in space and time) to be real, while universals are "vocal utterances" (*flatus vocis*), strictly sounds that we make, as apparently in Abelard's teacher Roscelin's explanation (1050–1123), with no derivation from individual things (or their natures) themselves. To the true nominalists, there are no such realities as natures, essences, or forms. They take them more to be occult significations or terms or words that actually have no referent outside of what convention awards them.

"Universal" is an English translation of Aristotle's technical term *katholou* (καθόλου) [*Metaphysics*, 1038b 11–12; cf. *De Partibus Anmalium*, 644a 24–25]) a contraction of the phrase *kata holou* (κατά ὅλου), meaning "on the whole" which he coined specially for the purpose of discussing the problem of universals. They do not exist in a special realm apart from things; nor are they in things. Universals are the mind's recognition that things share a sameness while otherwise different ("unde intellectus est qui facit universalitatem in rebus" (Thomas Aquinas, *De ente et essentia*, iv) and by that sameness can be classified and placed in classes (abstrahit ab utroque esse, secundum quam considerationem considerattur natura lapidis vel cujus cumque alterius, quantum ad ea tantum quæ per se competunt illi naturæ (*Quaestiones Quodlibetales*, Q. I, a. 1 [Roma: Marietti, 1956 {for background on the QQ see Sandra Edwards, *Quodlibetal Questions 1 and 2 by St. Thomas* [Toronto Pontifical Institute, 1983)}.

    2 Aristotle, *De Anima*, 431b 21.

    3. See Thomas Aquinas, *Summa Contra Gentes*, II, 49–51; *Summa Theologiae*, 1.75.2 and 5; *Quaestiones Disputatae De Anima*, 111.7.680, and 14; *Quaestiones Disputatae De Veritate*, X. 8; *De Ente et Essentia*, 4.

    4. See Rene Descartes, *Meditations on First Philosophy*, L. J. Lafleur (Indianaopolis: Bobbs-Merrill, 1960), 23.

    5. This notion of image as essentially a domain of memory appears in Thomas Hobbes' Leviathan, C. B. McPherson, ed. (London: Pelican, 1968), 89: "Imagination and memory are but one thing, which for divers considerations hath divers names."

    6. So Aristotle, *De Memoria et Reminiscentia* 499a 15, "memory is of the past."

    7. Surely something Nietzche has in mind when in his theory of eternal return he speaks of the heavy burden (*das schwerste Gewicht*) of remembering, of bringing back to mind over and again endlessly, and bringing that too over and again, almost *usque ad nauseam*. (See Milan Kundera, *The Unbearable Lightness of Being*, tr., M. H. Heim (New York: Harper and Row, 1985), 5.

    8. See Plato, *Meno* 81a ("searching and learning are, as a whole, recollection) and Aristotle, *De Memoria et Reminiscentia* 453a 15–16, "recollection is a search in something bodily for an image."

    9. Harry Wolfson in his *Philosophy of Spinoza* (New York: Meridian, 1950), 2:82, points out this classification has roots in medieval Hebrew and Arabic texts

    10. Reverie as an activity of memory receives unparalleled insight in Gaston Bachelard, *The Poetics of Reverie: Childhood, Language and the Cosmos*, tr. Daniel Russell (Boston: Beacon Press, 1969) and Colette Gaudin, tr., *On Poetic Imagination and Reverie: Selections from Gaston Bachelard* (Dallas: Spring Publications, 1971). Memory in general as a phenomenn of mentation has no equal in Edward Casey's *Remembering* (Bloomington: Indian niversity Press, 2000), some of whose categories I have used here.

    11. Benedict Spinoza, *The Ethics*, R. H. M. Elwes, tr. (New York: Dover, 1951), Book 2, proposition 18.

    12. David Hume, *A Treatise of Human Nature*, L. A. Selby-Bigge, ed., (Oxford: Oxford University Press, 1967), 9. Hume, though, does seem to relent a bit on the insistence on ordering as part of memory's duties (see 85).

    13. Immanuel Kant, *Critique of Pure Reason*, Norman Kemp Smith, tr. (New York: St. Martin's Press, 1965), 132–133, 143–144, 146, 165, 183). It appears only "productive imagination" for Kant has "transcendental status," for which see *Critique*, 142–143.

    14. William James, *Principles of Psychology* (New York: Dover, 1950) I: 643–652.

    15. Penfield's map for cerebral localization is still in use today. On the procedure see Wilder Penfield, "Epilepsy and surgical therapy," *Archives of Neurology and Psychiatry* 36 (1936): 449–484; and E. Boldrey, "Somatic motor and sensory representation in the cerebral cortex of man as studied by electrical stimulation," *Brain* 60 (1937): 389–443. (With Boldrey, Penfield established cortical maps for motor and sensory responses, now depicted by the sensory and motor homunculus). Cf. also Wilder Penfield and Theodore C. Erickson, *Epilepsy and Cerebral Localization: A Study of the Mechanism, Treatment, and Prevention of Epileptic Seizures* (Springfield, IL: Charles C. Thomas,1941);

and H. Flanigin, "Surgical therapy of temporal lobe seizures," *Archives of Neurology and Psychiatry* 64 (1950): 490–500; and Herbert J. Jasper, *Epilepsy and the Functional Anatomy of the Human Brain* (Boston: Little, Brown, 1954).

16. Wilder Penfield, *The Mystery of the Mind* (Princeton: Princeton University Press, 1975), 21.

17. Ibid., 21–22.

18. Ibid., 24–27.

19. Wilder Penfield and Phaner Parot, "The Bain's Record of Auditory and Visual experience: A Final Summary and Discussion," *Brain* (December, 1963) Volume 86, Part 4. Cf. Wilder Penfield, "Functional Localizaton in Temporal and Deep Sylvan Areas" in H. C. Solomon, S. Cobb, and W. Penfield (eds.), *Research Publications* (New York: Association for Research in Nervous and Mental Disease, 1954); Wilder Penfield, "The Role of the Temporal Cortex in Certain Psychical Phenomena," *Journal of Mental Science* 101 (1955): 451–65. Cf. T. L. Babb, C. L. Wilson, and I. Isokawa—Akesson, "Firing Patterns of Human Limbic Neurons During Stereoencephalography and Clinical Temporal Lobe Seizures," *Electroencephalography and Clinical Neurophysiology* 66 (1987): 467–82.

20. For a brief look at the hippocampus, see J. Winson and C. Abzug, "Gating of Neuronal Transmission in the Hippocampus," *Science* 196 (1977): 1223; "Neuronal Transmission Through Hippocampal Pathways Dependent on Behavior," *Journal of Neurophysiology* 41 (1978): 716–22.

21. See the immediately preceding note 15.

22. Sir John Carew Eccles, *Brain and Conscious Experience* (New York: Springer Verlag, 1966); *The Human Psyche* (New York: Springer International, 1980); *The Understanding of the Brain* (New York: McGraw Hill, 1973); and with Karl Raimund Popper, *The Self and Its Brain* (Berlin: Springer Verlag, 1977). Cf. Sir John Eccles, *Evolution of the Brain, Creation of the Self* (New York: Routledge, 1989) 241:

> I maintain that the human mystery is incredibly demeaned by scientific reductionism, with its claim in promissory materialism to account eventually for all of the spiritual world in terms of patterns of neuronal activity. This belief must be classed as a superstition. . . . we have to recognize that we are spiritual beings with souls existing in a spiritual world as well as material beings with bodies and brains existing in a material world.

Eccles, (AC, FRS, FRACP, FRSNZ, FAAS [27 January 1903 – 2 May 1997]), was an Australian neurophysiologist. He won the 1963 Nobel Prize in Physiology or Medicine (with Andrew Fielding Huxley and Alan Lloyd Hodgkin) for his work on the synapse.

23. Jacques Barbizet, *Human Memory and Its Pathology*, D. Jardine, tr., (San Francisco: W. H. Freeman, 1970).

24. Michael Marsh, *A Matter of Personal Survival: Life After Death* (Wheaton, IL: Quest, 1985), 39–40.

25. Ibid., 43–44.

26. Ibid., 48–53.

27. Alexander R. Luria, *The Working Brain: An Introduction to Neuropsychlogy*, Basil Haigh, tr., (New York: Basic Books, 1973) 281–282.

28. Christopher Upham Murray Smith, *The Brain: Towards an Understanding* (New York: Putnam, 1970), 321–322.

29. In lower primates (as in macaque monkeys) bilateral removal of the hippocampus and amygdale has prevented remembering events that occurred immediately prior (as

briefly as two minutes) to their removal. Their neuronal circuitry to the basal forebrain and its acetylcholine fiber network to the cortex has prompted the hypothesis that acetylcholine, along with other transmitters, may cause cellular changes in the brain's synapses that harden sensory impressions formed and/or mediated in the brain's neural network into physical deposits called memories. (See Tim Appenzeller and Mortimer Mishkin, "The Anatomy of Memory," *Scientific American* (separate monograph) 1987.

We have already seen the difficulty with this "trace" or "groove" theory of memory, while it is not clear whether a failure of recognition of an object after an amygdalectomy might not show simply that and not that an object cannot be remembered. Failure to recognize and failure to remember are not the same. Granting, as the neurological data in this case seem to indicate, that this failure to recognize is a failure of memory, that does not show that memory is physically stored. An electric switch, which mediates electric current, does not contain the music its mediation powers. The information for the song, in fact, is on a tape or a disc (or silicon chip), neither of which is part of the electric switch. The amygdaloid may function in the same way as the switch: remove it and you remove the memory in the same way that, in removing the electric switch you remove the sound of music.

30. See Steven Rose, *The Conscious Brain* (New York: Alfred Knopf, 1973), 197–198.

31. The killing of animals in laboratories is, to me, personally repugnant, especially those that are harmless and trusting. I do not like to report such events of laboratory killings, but am doing so here for the sake of historical accuracy and precision.

32. Colin Blakemore, *Mechanics of the Mind* (New York: Cambridge University Press, 1977). 110–111.

33. Steven Rose, *The Conscious Brain*, 203. See also Michael Talbot, *Beyond the Quantum* (New York: Bantam, 1986), 51–52.

34. Doue Draissma, *Metaphors of Memory: A History of Ideas About the Mind* (Cambridge: Cambridge University Press 2001) 178–179.

35. This tendency may or may nor derive from the spatiality of our representations. These, however, are not the only encounters of the mind, as I discuss in my *On the Existence of God* ("Fallacies and Approaches to God") the gratuitousness of Kant's doctrine that space conditions all our representations.

36. Aristotle, *Physics*, 212a 20.

37. I am thinking of the work of Father Bolzano, *Paradoxes of the Infinite*, tr., D. A. Steele (London: Routledge and Kegan Paul, 1950) and that of Baron Augustin-Louis Cauchy. In Cauchy, on handling movements of infinity and convergence see *Sur un nouveau genre de calcul analogue au calcul infinitésimal* [On a new type of calculus analogous to the infinitesimal calculus], Exercices de Mathématique, vol. 1, p. 11 (1826), and *Mémoire sur les rapports qui existent entre le calcul des Résidus et le calcul des Limites, et sur les avantages qu'offrent ces deux calculs dans la résolution des équations algébriques ou transcendantes* [Memorandum on the connections that exist between the residue calculus and the limit calculus, and on the advantages that these two calculi offer in solving algebraic and transcendental equations], presented to the Academy of Sciences of Turin, 27 November 1831, in *Oeuvres complètes d'Augustin Cauchy publiées sous la direction scientifique de l'Académie des sciences et sous les auspices de M. le ministre de l'Instruction publique* (Paris: Gauthier-Villars et fils, 1882–1974), Twenty-seven volumes. A readable and manageable presentation of his work and life is Bruno Belhoste, *Augustin-Louis Cauchy: A Biography* (New York: SpringerVerlag, 1991).

38. Poincaré, as Carl R. Boyer, *A History of Mathematics* (Princeton: Princeton University Press, 1985), 653, explains, effected a mathematical composition wherein inhabi-

tants of a certain universe would prehend their universe as infinite. Such a universe with these inhabitants is thinkable to us (for no inherent contradiction is entailed), even if not "picturable."

Whether such a universe actually exists, i.e., bespeaks an actual "infinity," is a metaphysical question. On whether space itself is actually "infinite," I would argue no, since that would be to substantialize it, make it a substance, a thing. Space is not an actually existent individual, one "thing" among, next to, others. Its "having parts" appears to us only through bodies that occupy it. What we see is different bodies in a relation of separateness to one another. That indicates space may be differently occupied, depending on the body occupying it. This differentiability of occupation gives us the basis for speaking of parts of space: if space had no parts, then whatever occupied it, it would appear, would have to occupy all of it, and thus be one. In this way, we can note, space then has a corruptibility about it inasmuch as it is into parts that corruption occurs. Space's determinability by bodies suggests a partness about it that incorruptible existents do not have.

This notwithstanding, my point here is that mathematics has not found the notion of unboundedness an inherent constraint to its abstractions. Potential unboundedness, where one is not speaking of an infinity existing altogether, but as that which is always free of any boundaries one chooses, would serve just as well in the Poincaré citation, a citation chosen only to indicate that the notion of existing without boundaries or containment is not exclusive to the profile of memory here being developed.

39. The method (first, apparently, in Plato's *Sophist*, 221c – 235a [see F. M Cornford, tr., *Plato's Theory of Knowledge: Theatetus and Sophist of Plato* {New York: Bobbs-Merril, 1957}]) of the *abscissio infiniti* (also known as division, [διαίρεσις, *diaireisis*]), continuously successive exclusions to which the inquiry points till only one object (here, *eidos*, form) remains and which, by its finality, ends the inquiry. That the procedure has epistemological probity and validity is without question. Much has been written on this as a process of eristic and definition in Plato. See. e.g., in just our day, J. L. Ackrill, "In Defence of Platonic Division" in O. P. Wood and G. Pitcher, (eds.), *Ryle* (London: MacMillan, 1970), 373–392; D. De Ciara-Quenzer, "The Purpose of the Philosophical Method in Plato's *Statesman*," *Apeiron* 31 (1998): 91–126; A. Gómez-Lobo, 1977, "Plato's Description of Dialectic in the Sophist 253d1–e2," *Phronesis* 22 (1977): 29–47; Y. Lafrance, "Métrétique, mathématiques et dialectique en *Politique* 283c–285c" in C. J. Rowe, ed., *Reading the Statesman*. Proceedings of the Third Symposium Platonicum (Sankt Augustin: Academia Verlag, 1995) 89–101); M. Miller, "The God-Given Way: Reflections on Method and the Good in Later Plato," *Proceedings of the Boston Area Colloquium in Ancient Philosophy* 6 (1990): 323–359; J. M. E. Moravcsik, "The Anatomy of Plato's Divisions" in E. N. Lee, A. P. D. Mourelatos, R. M. Rorty (eds.), *Exegesis and Argument* (= *Phronesis* Supplement 1): Festschrift for Gregory Vlastos (New York: Humanities Press, 1973) 324–348; C. D. C. Reeve, "Motion, Rest, and Dialectic in the *Sophist*," *Archiv für Geschichte der Philosophie* 67 (1985): 47–64; K. M. Sayre, *Plato's Analytic Method* (Chicago: University of Chicago Press, 1969); *Method and Metaphysics in Plato's Statesman* (Cambridge: Cambridge University Press, 2006); H. R. Scodel, *Diairesis and Myth in Plato's Statesman* (Göttingen: Vandenhoeck & Ruprecht, 1987); A. Silverman, *The Dialectic of Essence: A Study of Plato's Metaphysics* (Princeton: Princeton University Press, 2002), Chapters Five and Six; J. Stenzel, *Plato's Method of Dialectic*, D. J. Allan, tr. and ed., (Oxford: Clarendon Press. 1940); J. R. Trevaskis, "Division and its Relation to Dialectic and Ontology in Plato," *Phronesis* 12 (1967): 118–129; M V. Wedin, "Collection and Division in the *Phaedrus* and *Statesman*," *Revue de Philosophie Ancienne* 5 (1987): 207–233.

Aristotle's *De Partibus Animalium* 642b 5ff rejects the method to *infirma species* that Plato takes. For him the form comes through another process (see *Posterior Analytics* II, 19 and *Metaphysics* 1,1. which discuss the grasp of the universal [which is not the form per se, but the form as known in many things, cf. Thomas Aquinas, *Commentary on the Metaphysics of Aristotle*, John Rowan, tr.{Regnery: Chicago, 1961}, Sections 158, 251, 404–405, 1683, 2426, 2259–2264]); *Metaphysics* Z 8 seems to suggest that the form as universal exists potentially till the mind sees it as occurring in things different in every other way except one. The passive intellect (the mind that potentially knows, that is in the state of such potency [*De Anima*, 429a 22]), is what becomes the form through the activity of the intellect that is always in actuality (*De Anima*, 430a 18), and that brings that potential state into actuality (*De Anima*, 430 a12 and a15) and by which activity the mind becomes the form known. (See also *De Anima* III, 4-5 [especially 430a 10-25]). This is clearly in sharp contrast to Plato.

Plato's method, one may argue, was a process of elimination that reaches the truth of what one is trying to ascertain. Aristotle misreads the Platonic procedure, accordingly, for while Aristotelian intellective agency is the way the mind reaches form, one pronounced manner of Aristotle's eristic is to proceed through possibilities till only the plausible is reached, and the impossible excluded.

Anecdotal or Evidential?

1. We have earlier postulated that existence is the principle energizing the components of each material being into the actuality they become by way of the form that gives them intelligibility and content, and the matter that accounts for their changeability.

2. Gallup first approached this subject from a polling standpoing, as he reports in George Gallup and W. Proctor, *Adventures in Immortality: A Look Beyond the Threshold of Death.* (New York, McGraw Hill, 1982).

3. Extremely worthwhile reading of this issue one finds in J. Kerby Anderson, *Life, Death and Beyond* (Grand Rapids: Zondervan, 1980); L. Appleby, "Near-Death Experience: Analogous to Other Stress-Induced Psychological Phenomena," *British Journal of Medicine* 298 (1989): 976–977; J. R. Audette, "Historical Perspectives on Near-Death Experiences" in C. R. Lundahl ed., *A Collection of Near-Death Readings* (Chicago: Nelson Hall, 1982); Dorothy Counts Ayers, "Near-Death Experiences and Out-of-Body Experiences in a Melanesian Society," *Anabiosis: The Journal of Near-Death Studies* 3 (1983): 115–136; L. Bailey and J. Yates, *The Near-Death Experience: A Reader* (New York: Routledge, 1996); W. Barret, *Deathbed Visions: The Psychical Experiences of the Dying* (Northamptonshire: The Aquarian Press, 1986); B. C. Bates and A. Stanley, "The Epidemiology and Differential Diagnosis of Near-Death Experience," *American Journal of Orhtopsychiatry* 55 (1985): 542–549; C. B. Becker, "Views From Tibet: NDEs and The Book of the Dead," *Anabiosis: The Journal of Near–Death Studies* 5 (1985): 3–20; S. Blackmore, *Dying to Live: Near-Death Experiences* (New York: Prometheus Books, 1993); "Out of Body Experiences in Schizophrenia," *Journal of Nervous and Mental Disease* 174 (1986): 615–619; "Visions from the Dying Brain," *New Scientist* (5 May 1988):43–46; G. E. Burch, N. O. Pasquale, and J. H. Phillips, "What Death Is Like," *American Heart Journal* 76 (1968: 1438–1439; C. Carr, "Death and Near-Death: A Comparison of Tibetan and Euro-American Experiences," *Journal of Transpersonal Psychology* 25 (199): 59–110; D. Carr, Pathophysiology of Stress-Induced Limbic Dysfunction: A Hypothesis for NDE," *Anabiosis: The Journal of Near-Death Studies* 2 (1982): 75–90; N. L. Comer, L. Madow, and J. J. Dixon, "Observation of Sensory Deprivation in a Life-Threatening Situation," *American Journal of Psychiatry* 124 (1967): 164–170; J.

Cressy, *The Near Death Experience: Mysticism or Madness?* (Hanover: The Christopher Publishing House,1994); P. Fenwick and E. Fenwick, *The Truth in the Light: An Investigation of Over 300 Near-Death Experiences* (London: Headline Book Publishing, 1995); Glenn O. Gabbard, and Stuart W. Twemlow, *With the Eyes of the Mind: An Empirical Analysis of Out-of-Body States* (New York: Praeger, 1984); and F. C. Jones, "Do Near-Death Experiences Occur Only at Death?" *Journal of Nervous and Mental Disease* 169 (1981): 374–377; T. J. Green and P. Friedman, "Near Death Experiences in a Southern California Population," *Anabiosis: The Journal of Near-Death Studies* 3 (1983): 77–96; Bruce Greyson, "The Near-Death Experience Scale: Construction, Reliability and Validity," *Journal of Nervous and Mental Disease* 171 (1983): 369–375; and N. E. Bush, "Distressing Near-Death Experiences," *Psychiatry* 55 (1992): 95–110; and I. Stevenson, "Near-Death Experiences," *Journal of the American Medical Association* 242 (1979): 265–267; "The Phenomenology of Near-Death Experience," *American Journal of Psychiatry* 137 (1980): 1193–1195; Michael Grosso, "Towards and Explanation of Near-Death Phenomena," *Anabiosis: The Journal of Near-Death Studies* 1 1 (1981): 12–23; E. Haraldsson, "Survey of Claimed Encounters With the Dead," *Omega* 19 (1988–89): 103–113; D. B. Hertzog and J. T. Herrin, "Near-Death Experiences in the Very Young," *Critical Care Medicine* 13 (1985):1074–1075; R. C. Hunter, "On the Experience of Nearly Dying," *American Journal of Psychiatry* 124 (1967): 122–123; I. R. Judson and E Wiltshaw, "A Near-Death Experience," *Lancet* 2 (193): 561–562; R. A. Kalish, and D. K. Reynolds, "Phenomenological Reality and Post-death Contact," *Journal of Science and Study of Religion* (1973): 20921; V. Kirshman, "Near-Death Experiences: Evidence for Survival?" *Anabiosis: The Near-Death Studies Journal* 5 (Spring 196): 21–38; D. M. Komp, *A Window to Heaven: When Children See Life in Death* (Grand Rapids: Zondervan, 1992); C. Levin and M. Curley, "Near-Death Experiences in Children." Paper given at Perspective on Change: Forces Shaping Practice for the Clinical Nurse Specialist, Boston Children's Hospital, 11 October 1990; John Meyers, ed., *Voices From the Edge of Eternity* (Old Tappan, NJ: Revell/Spire, 1968); Raymond Moody, *The Light Beyond* (New York: Bantam, 1988); and Elizabeth Kubler Ross, *Life After Life: The Investigation of a Phenomenon. Survival of Bodily Death* (New York: HarperOne, 2001); R. Monroe, *Journeys Out of the Body* (New York: Doubleday, 1977); Melvin Morse, "A Near-Death Experience in a 7-year-old Child," *American Journal of Diseases of Children* 137 (1983) 110–114; P. L. Castillo, and D. Venecia, "Childhood Near-Death Experiences," *American Journal of Diseases of Children* 140 (1986): 110–114; and Paul Perry, *Closer to the Light: Learning from the Near-Death Experiences of Children* (New York: Villard, 1990); "Near-Death Experiences," Letters to *Lancet* 337 (1991): 386; R. Monroe, *Journeys Out of the Body* (New York: Doubleday, 1977); V. A. Negovsky, "Reanimatology Today," *Critical Care Medicine* 10 (1982): 130–133; *Resuscitation and Artificial Hypothermia* (New York: New York Consultants Bureau, 1962); R. Noyes, "Near-Death Experiences: Their Interpretation and Significance" in R. Kastenbaum, *In Between Life and Death* (New York: Springer Publishing, 1979); and R. Kletti, "Depersonalization in the Face of Life-threatening Danger: A Description," *Psychiatry* 39 (1976): 19–27; C. R. Lundahl, and H. A. Widdison, "The Mormon Explanation of Near-Death Experiences," *Anabiosis: The Journal of Near Death Studies* 3 (1983): 97–106; M. Olson, "The Out-of-Body Experience and Other States of Consciousness," *Archives of Psychiatric Nursing* 1 (1987): 201–207; K. Osis and E. Harraldsson, *At the Hour of Death* (New York: Avon, 1977); J. E. Owens, W. Cook, and I. Stevenson, "Features of Near-Death Experience in Relation to Whether or Not Patients Were Near Death," *Lancet* 336 (1990): 1175–1177; Satwant Pasricha and Ian Stevenson, "Near Death Experiences in India: a Preliminary Report," *Journal of Nervous and Mental Disease* 175 (March 1986): 65–170 Michael

Rawlings, *Before Death Comes* (Nashville: Thomas Nelson, 1980); *Beyond Death's Door* (Nashville: Thomas Nelson, 1978); Kenneth Ring, *Heading Towards Omega* (New York: William Morrow, 1984); *Life At Death: A Scientific Investigation of the Near-Death Experience* (New York: Coward McCann, and Geoghegan, 1980); and S. Cooper, *Mindsight: Near-Death and Out-of-Body Experiences in the Blind* (Palo Alto: William James Center for Consciousness Studies. Institute of Transpersonal Psychology, 1999); and E. Valarino, *Lessons From the Light: What We Can Learn from the Near-Death Experience* (New York: Plenum, 1998); Tillman Rodabough, "Near-Death Experiences: An Examination of the Supporting Data and Alternative Explanations," *Death Studies* 9 (1985): 95–113; Michael Sabom, *Light and Death* (Grand Rapids: Zondervan, 1998); and S. A. Kruetiger, "Physicians Evaluate the Near-Death Experience," *Journal of the Florida Medical Association* 6 (1978) 1–6; Michael Sabom, *Recollections of Death: A Medical Investigation* (New York: Harper and Row, 1982); F. Schoonmaker, "Near-Death Experiences," *Anabiosis: The Journal of Near-Death Studies* 1 (1979) 1–35; M. Schroeter-Kunhardt, "A Review of Near-Death Experiences," *Journal of Scientific Exploration* 7 (1993): 219–39; E. Valarino, *On the Other Side of Life* (New York: Plenum, 1997); S. Vicchio, "Near-Death Experiences: A Critical Review of the Literature and Some Questions for Further Study," *Essence* 5 (1981): 79; F. O.Walker, "A Nowhere Near Death Experience: Heavenly Choirs Interrupt Myelography." Letter in *Journal of the American Medical Association* 261 (1989): 1282–1289; Ian Wilson, *The After Death Experience* (New York: Quill, 1987); K. Woods, *Visions of the Bereaved: Hallucination or Reality?* (Pittsburg: Sterling House, 1998); Carol Zaleski, *Otherworld Journeys: Accounts of Near-Death Experiences in Medieval an Modern Times* (New York: Oxford University Press, 1987).

A skeptical view of the near-death experience as evidence for survivability by an advocate of survival as a reality is Robert Kastenbaum, *Is there Life After Death?* (New York: Prentice-Hall, 1984).

4. The reported feelings of transport and, upon return to human bodily awareness, of being pulled into the body indicate this passivity.

5. Kenneth Ring, *Life at Death*, 102–03.

6. Kenneth Ring, *Heading Towards Omega*, 83.

7. See B. Collier, "Ketamine and the Conscious Mind," *Anesthesiology* 2 (1972) 120–134; "Ketamine and the Near-Death Experience," *Anabiosis: The Journal of Near-Death Studies* 1 (1984): 87–96; Melvin Morse, *Closer to the Light*, 48; D. Scott Rogo, "Ketamine and the Near-Death Experience," *Anabiosis: The Journal of Near-Death Studies* 1 (1984): 87–96; S. M. Rothman, J. H. Thurston, G. D. Clark, et al., Ketamine Protects Hippocampal Neurons from Anoxia in Vitro," *Neuroscience* 21 (1987): 673–678. Cf. F. Strahlendorf, G. Goldstein, G. Rossi, et al., Differential Effects of LSD, Serotonin, and L-Tryptophan on Visually Evoked Responses," *Pharmacological Biochemical Behavior* 16 (1982): 51–55; F. White and T. Appel, "Lysergic Acid Diethylamide and Lisuride: Differentiation of Their Neuropharmacological Actions," *Science* 216 (1982): 535–536.

8. (Listed in chronological order): E. F. Domino, P. Chodoff, and G. Corssen, G. "Pharmacologic effects of CL–581, a new dissociative anaesthetic, in man," *Clinical Pharmacology Therapeutics*, 6 (1965) 279– 291; K. Rumpf, J. Pedick, H, Teuteberg, W. Munchhoff, and H. Nolte, "Dream-like experiences during brief anaesthesia with ketamine, thiopental and propiadid" in H. Deuscher, ed., *Ketamine* (Berlin: Springer-Verlag, 1969), 161–180; B. B. Collier, "Ketamine and the conscious mind," *Anaesthesia* 27 (1972): 120–134; R. K. Siegel, "Phencyclidine and ketamine intoxication: a study of recreational users" in: R. C. Peterson and R. C. Stillman, ed. , *Phencyclidine Abuse: An*

Appraisal (National Institute on Drug Abuse Research Monograph 21. NIDA, Rockville, Maryland, 1978), 119–140; "The Psychology of life after death," *American Psychologist* 35 (1980): 911–950; "Accounting for after-life experiences," *Psychology Today* 15 (1981), 67; Karl L. R. Jansen, "The near-death experience," *British Journal of Psychiatry* 154 (1989): 882–883; "Near-death experience and the NMDA receptor." *British Medical Journal*, 298 (1989): 1708–1709; R. L. M. Faull, and M. Dragunow, "Excitatory amino acid receptors in the human cerebral cortex: a quantitative autoradiographic study comparing the distribution of [3H]TCP, [3H]glycine, l–[3H]glutamate, [3H]AMPA and [3H]kainic acid binding sites," *Neuroscience* 32 (1989): 587–607; and B. Synek, "Alzheimer's disease: changes in hippocampal N-methyl-D-aspartate, quisqualate, neurotensin, adenosine, benzodiazepine, serotonin and opioid receptors—an autoradiographic study," *Neuroscience* 39 (1990): 613–617; Karl L. R. Jansen, "Neuroscience and the near-death experience: roles for the NMDA-PCP receptor, the sigma receptor and the endopsychosins," *Medical Hypotheses* 31 (1990): 25–29; "Ketamine: can chronic use impair memory?" *International Journal of Addictions* 25 (1990) 133–139; and R. L. M. Faull, "Excitatory amino acids, NMDA and sigma receptors: a role in schizophrenia?" *Behavioral and Brain Sciences* 14 (1991): 34–35; M. Dragunow, and R. Leslie, "Autoradiographic distribution of sigma receptors in human neocortex, hippocampus, basal ganglia, cerebellum, pineal and pituitary glands," *Brain Research* 559 (1991): 172–177; Karl L. R. Jansen, "Transcendental explanations and the near-death experience," *Lancet* 337 (1991), 207–243; "Non-medical use of ketamine," *British Medical Journal* 298 (1993) 4708–4709; "The ketamine model of the near-death experience: A central role for the N-methyl-D-aspartate receptor," *Journal of Near-Death Studies* 16 (1997): 5–26.

9. A. M. Thomson, D. C. West, and D. Lodge, "An N-methylaspartate receptor-mediated synapse in rat cerebral cortex: a site of action of ketamine?" *Nature* 313 (1985): 479–481.

10. N. A. Anis, S. C. Berry, N. R. Burton, and D. Lodge, "The dissociative anaesthetics ketamine and phencyclidine, selectively reduce excitation of central mammalian neurons by N methyl-aspartate," *British Journal of Pharmacology* 79 (1983) 565–575; D. M. Barnes, "NMDA receptors trigger excitement," *Science* 239 (1988) 254–256; Y. E. Ben-Ari, "Limbic seizure and brain damage produced by kainic acid: mechanisms and relevance to human temporal lobe epilepsy," *Neuroscience* 14 (1985) 375–403; H. Benveniste, J. Drejer, A. Schouseboe, and H. H. Diemer, "Elevation of the extracellular concentrations of glutamate and aspartate in rat hippocampus during cerebral ischaemia monitored by microdialysis," *Journal of Neurochemistry* 43 (1984): 1369–1374; D. W. Choi, "Glutamate neurotoxicity and diseases of the nervous system," *Neuron* 1 (1988): 623–634; E. J. Coan and G. L. Collingridge, "Effects of phencyclidine, SKF10,047 and related psychotomimetic agents on N-methyl-D-aspartate receptor mediated synaptic responses in rat hippocampal slices," *British Journal of Pharmacology* 91 (1987): 547–556; G. L. Collingridge, "The role of NMDA receptors in learning and memory," *Nature* 330 (1987): 604 – 605; I. Mody, and U. Heinemann, "NMDA receptors of dentate gyrus cells participate in synpatic transmission following kindling" *Nature* 326 (1987): 701–703; D. T. Monoghan, R. J. Bridges, and C. W. Cotman, "The excitatory amino acid receptors. Their classes, pharmacology and distinct properties in the function of the nervous system," *Annual Review of Pharmacology and Toxicology* 29 (1989): 365–402; R. Quirion, R. Chicheportiche, P. C. Contreras, K. Johnston, D. Lodge, S. W. Tam, J. H. Woods, and S. R. Zukin, "Classification and nomenclature of phencyclidine and sigma receptor sites," *Trends in Neurosciences* 10 (1987): 444–446; D. A. Dimaggio, E. D. French, P. C. Contreras, J. Shiloach, C. B. Pert, H. Everist, A Pert, and T. L. O'Donohue, "Evidence for an endogenous peptide ligand for the phencyclidine receptor," *Peptides* 5

(1984) 967–977; I. Mody, and U. Heinemann, "NMDA receptors of dentate gyrus cells participate in synaptic transmission following kindling" *Nature* 326 (1987): 701–703; D. T. Monoghan, R. J. Bridges, and C. W. Cotman, "The excitatory amino acid receptors. Their classes, pharmacology and distinct properties in the function of the nervous system," *Annual Review of Pharmacology and Toxicology* 29 (1989): 365–402. S. M. Rothman, J. H. Thurston, R. E. Hauhart, G. P. Clark, and J. S. Solomon, "Ketamine protects hippocampal neurons from anoxia in vitro," *Neuroscience* 21(1987): 673–683; R. P. Simon, S. H. Swan, T. Griffiths, and B. S. Meldrum, "Blockade of NMDA receptors may protect against ischaemic damage in the brain," *Science* 226 (1984): 850–852; A. M. Thomson, "A magnesium-sensitive post-synaptic potential in art cerebral cortex resembles neuronal responses to N-methyl-D-aspartate," *Journal of Physiology* (London), 370 (1986): 531–549; G. L. Westbrook, M. K. Mayer, "Micromolecular concentrations of Zn2+ antagonise NMDA and GABA responses of hippocampal neurons," *Nature* 328 (1987): 640–643.

11. L. Grinspoon and S. Bakalar, *Psychedelic Drugs Reconsidered* (New York: Basic Books 1981).

12. Ibid., 34.

13. Wilder Penfield and Theodore B. Rasmussen, *The Cerebral Cortex of Man* (New York: Macmillan, 1950); Cf. Wilder Penfield and André Pasquet, "Combined regional and general anesthesia for craniotomy and cortical exploration. Part 1. Neurosurgical considerations," *International Anesthesiology Clinics* 24 (1986): 1–20; and L. Roberts, *Speech and Brain Mechanisms* (Princeton: Princeton University Press, 1959); T. Rasmussen, "Surgical treatment of complex partial seizures: results, lessons, and problems," *Epilepsia* 24 Supplement 1 (1983): S 65–S76.

14. See Jack Hitt, "This is Your Brain on God," *Wired* 7.11 (November 1999): 1-5. Cf. Michael A. Persinger, *Neuropsychological Bases of God Beliefs* (New York: Praeger, 1987). Cf. In chronological order, "Religious and mystical experiences as artifacts of temporal lobe function: a general hypothesis," *Perceptual and Motor Skills* 57 (1983): 1255–1262; "People who report religious experiences may also display enhanced temporal-lobe signs. *Perceptual and Motor Skills* 58 (1984): 963–975; "Propensity to report paranormal experiences is correlated with temporal lobe signs," *Perceptual and Motor Skills* 59 (1984): 583–586; "Death anxiety as a semantic conditioned suppression paradigm," *Perceptual and Motor Skills* 60 (1985): 827–830.and C. F DeSano, "Temporal lobe signs: positive correlations with imaginings and hypnosis induction profiles. Psychological Reports" 58 (1986): 347–350; and K Makarec, "Temporal lobe signs and correlative behaviors displayed by normal populations," *Journal of General Psychology* 114, 2 (1986): 179–195; "Modern neuroscience and near-death experiences: expectancies and implications," *Journal of Near-Death Studies* 7, 4 (1989): 233–239; and S. D. Fisher, "Elevated, specific temporal lobe signs in a population engaged in psychic studies," *Perceptual and Motor Skills* 71 (1990): 817–818; "Preadolescent religious experience enhances temporal lobe signs in normal young adults," *Perceptual and Motor Skills* 72 (1991): 453–454; S. A. Koren, K. Makarec, P. Richards, and S. Youlton, "Differential effects on wave form and the subject's possible temporal lobe signs upon experiences during cerebral exposure to weak intensity magnetic fields," *Journal of Bioelectricity* 10, 1 & 2 (1991): 141–184; "Near death experiences: determining the neuroanatomical pathways by experiential patterns and simulation in experimental settings" in L. Bessette, ed., *Healing: Beyond Suffering or Death* (Quebec: MHH 1993), 227–286; "Transcendental meditation and general meditation are associated with enhanced complex partial epileptic-like signs: Evidence for 'cognitive' kindling? *Perceptual and Motor Skills*,76 (1993): 80–82; "Paranormal and religious beliefs may be mediated differentially by subcortical

and cortical phenomenological processes of the temporal (limbic) lobes," *Perceptual and Motor Skills* 76 (1993): 247–251; Vectorial cerebral hemisphericity as differential sources for the sensed presence, mystical experiences and religious conversions," *Perceptual and Motor Skills* 76 (1993): 915–930; Out-of-body-like experiences are more probable in people with elevated complex partial epileptic-like signs during periods of enhanced geomagnetic activity: a nonlinear effect," *Perceptual and Motor Skills* 80 (1995): 563–569; "Feelings of past lives as expected perturbations within the neurocognitive processes that generate the sense of self: contributions from limbic lability and vectorial hemisphericity," *Perceptual and Motor Skills* 83 (1996): 1107–1121; "Near-death experiences and ecstasy: An artifact of the organization of the human brain?" in S. Della Salla, ed., *Mind Myths* (John Wiley, New York: 1999) 85–99; "Experimental simulation of the god experience: implications for religious beliefs and the future of the human species" in Rhawn Joseph, ed., *Neurotheology: Brain, Science, Spirituality, Religious Experience* (San Jose CA: University Press, 2002) 267–284.

15. W. J. Serdahely, "A Pediatric Near-Death: Tunnel Variants," *Omega* 20 (1989–90): 55–62.

16. See Carl B. Becker, "Why Birth Models Cannnot Explain Near-Death Phenomena" in Bruce Greyson and Charles P. Flynn, *The Near-Death Experience* (Springfield: Thomas, 1984), 104-162.

17. See P. M. H. Atwater, "Is There a Hell: Surprising Observations About the Near-Death Experience," *Journal of Near-Death Studies* 10 (Spring 1993) 3; Robert Matthews, "Patients Near Death See Visions of Hell" @http://www.telegraph.co.uk/nhell25.html

18. Kenneth Ring, *Heading Towards Omega*, 34–35. Also George Gallup, with William Proctor, *Adventures in Immortality* (New York: McGraw Hill, 1982).

19. Zaleski does not hold that therefore the NDE evinces immortality—simply, that invoking drugs to explain the NDE does not advance our knowledge of what causes an NDE. Ring has not claimed for the NDE the status of evidence for immortality. He has suggested that the NDE phenomenon certainly does not help the denial of immortality.

20. The NDE cases of George Rodonaia and Emanuel Tuwagirairmana, two individuals closest to rigor mortis if any in the NDE were close, defy explanation in the current scientific environment. P. M. H. Atwater's *Beyond the Light* (New York: Avon, 1995) and Phillip Berman's *The Journey Home* (New York: Pocket Books, 1998) have discussed Rodonaia, while Tuwargiraimana receives coverage at http://www.near-death.com/forum/nde/000/45.htmlEmanuel Tuwagirairmana. If a scientific explanation is never found for what they have undergone it may only show that science is incapable of accounting for every experience imaginable, not that these two individuals actually underwent what they believe they did.

On the other hand, one has to be equally open to the possibility that these two individuals actually underwent the experiences they said they did. This would seem to suggest something more to earthly existence than just a body metabolizing and interacting with other bodies and the elements of nature.

A report in *Pravda* (14 September 2004) of a man "dead" for twenty-two days and then "revived" after being buried is of equal astonishment, if factual. See http://english.pravda.ru/science/19/94/378/14212_time.html.

21. See Robert Kastenbaum, *Is There Life After Death?*, 39–40. Kastenbaum, in contrast to Zaleski, is far too quick with his assertion that the NDE is "an adaptive psychobiological function"—a defense mechanism in the face of death. The evidence is far from certain, as Carol Zaleski, *Otherworld Journeys: Accounts of Near-Death Experiences in Medieval and Modern Times*, 168–83, amply points out.

22. The near-death OBE is quite specific of evidence, not to be associated with autoscopic hallucinations. The important difference between the two appears in Raymond Moody, *The Light Beyond*, 97–98.

23. Kenneth Ring, *Life At Death*, 45–46.

24. Ibid., 46.

25. Ibid., 49.

26. Rabbi Elie Kaplan Spitz, *Does the Soul Survive. A Jewish Journey to Belief in Afterlife* (Woodstock: Jewish :Lights Publishing, 2000), 16

27. Only faulty memory or recall of the OBE-reported medical/clinical details could be the other cause of the inaccuracy. Sabom's clinical records cross-check furnishes a useful buffer in this regard. The records in question were drawn up quite shortly after the OBE event(s) occurred, minimizing the possible effects of the passage of time.

28. Penny Sartori, "A Retrospective Study of NDEs in an Intensive Therapy Unit," *Christian Parapsychologist* 16. No. 2 (2004): 34-40. Dr. Sartori found several NDErs provided remarkably accurate accounts in their OBE observations. This was further reinforced in her *The Near-Death Experience of Hospitalized Intensive Care Patients: A Five Year Clinical Study* (Lewiston, NY: Edwin Mellen Press, 2008).

29. Janice Holden, "Veridical Perception in Near-Death Experiences" in J. Holden, B. Greyson, and D. James, *The Handbook of Near-Death Experiences* (Westport: Prager, 2009).

30. Cf. Janice Holden and Leroy Joesten, "Near-Death Veridicality Research in a Hospital Setting," *Journal of Near-Death Studies* 9 No. 1 (September 1990): 45–54; Kenneth Ring and Madelaine Lawrence, "Further Evidence For Veridical Perception in Near-Death Experiences," *Journal of Near-Death Studies* 11 No. 4 (June 1993): 223–229.And,http://www.esalenctr.org/display/confpage.cfm?confid=3&pageid=22&pgtype= 1. The site contains Bruce Greyson's "Near Death Experiences," paper given at the Esalen Invitational Conference, 6–11 December, 1998.

31. In addition to their *Mindsight* (note three above for this chapter) see also their co-authored "Near-Death Out-of-Body Experiences in the Blind: A Study of Apparently Eyeless Vision," *Journal of Near-Death Studies* 16 (1998): 101-147.

32. Elizabeth Kübler-Ross, *On Children and Death* (New York: Collier, 1963), 206-207.

Sentient Immortality

1. Protagoras, as Plato's *Theatetus* 152a reports held πάντων χρημάτων μέτρον ἐστὶν ἄνθρωπος τῶν μὲν ὄντων ὡς ἔστιν, τῶν δὲ οὐκ ὄντων ὡς οὐκ ἔστιν ("man is the measure of al things, of what is and what is not."

2. Prof. Dr. Adriaan Kortlandt born in Rotterdam, lived from 1918 to 2009 in Amsterdam. A Dutch ethologist. he was famous for his work on displacement activities (*overspronggedraging*) and the hierarchy of instincts and behaviors. He argued for the common characteristics between instincts in humans and other animals. In one of his experiments in Western Africa he showed a stuffed panther with an electronic moving head to chimpanzees. They attacked it with sticks. This illustrated the extent to which early man could have (instinctually) kept wild animals at bay even before spears and other weapons were invented. He also was the author of the "Rift Valley theory" (see A. Kortlandt, *New Perspectives on Ape and Human Evolution* [Amsterdam, Stichting voor Psychobiologie, 1972]).

3. See George B Schaller, *The Year of the Gorilla* (Chicago: University of Chicago Press, 1997) [e.g.] 41, 42, 43, 59, 139, 173, 194, 204, 236, 237, 239, 241, 253; cf. *The*

Mountain Gorilla: Ecology and Behavior (Chicago: University of Chicago Press, 1976). Schaller is world recognized as a preeminent field biologist, studying wildlife throughout Africa, Asia and South America.

4. Lyal Watson, *The Romeo Error: A Matter of Life and Death* (Garden City: Doubleday, 1974).

5. See Cleve Backster, *Primary Perception: Biocommunication with Plants, Living Foods, and Human Cells* (Anza, California: White Rose Millennium Press, 2003).

6. Paging through their *International Wildlife Encyclopedia* (New York: Marshall Caendish, various dates) makes this plain.

7. See, e.g., J. B. Rhine and L. E. Rhine, "An investigation of a mind-reading horse," *Journal of Abnormal and Social Psychology*, 23, 449–466. The work of the Rhines in the field of ESP and the like one can never discount or discard given the voluminous findings and details they harness in the presentation of their discussions ad conclusions. The Rhine Research Institute at Duke University is where one begins the study of their works.

8. See Robert Lestrange, *Les Animaux dans la littérature et dans r'histoire* (Gap: Ophrys, 1937), 140.

9. See Eleanor Atkinson, *Greyfriar's Bobby* (London: Puffin Books, 1962) Reprint edition. For other important accounts like, from which this chapter has especially benefitted, this see Bill D. Schul, *Animal Immortality: Pets and Their After-Life* (New York: Carrol & Graf, 1990), E. D. Buckner, *The Immortality of Animals: and the Relation of Man as Guardian, From a Biblical and Philosophical Hypothesis* (Philadelphia: George W. Jacobs, 1903), and Arch Stanton, *Animals in Heaven: Fantasy or Reality?* (Victoria, B.C.: Trafford, 2004).

10. Thomas Aquinas, *Summa Theologiae*, I^a q. 85 a. 6 co., "intellectus non est virtus utens organo."

11. Cf. Thomas Aquinas, *De ente et essentia*, 4; *In De Anima*, II, 1c, 12; *In Post.*, II, 1c, 20; *In Quattuor Libros Sententiarim Petri Lombardi*, 2 d. 17, q.1, a1.

12. Thomas Aquinas, *Summa Theologiae* I^a Q. 75 a2; 6; cf Q. 76, article 1:

(As) Dionysius says (*Div. Nom.* iv) that human souls owe to Divine goodness that they are 'intellectual,' and that they have 'an incorruptible substantial life.'

It was shown above (Articles [2],3) that the souls of brutes are not self-subsistent; the human soul, though, is. Accordingly, the souls of brutes are corrupted, when their bodies are corrupted. However, the human soul could not be corrupted unless it were corrupted "per se." This, indeed, is impossible, not only as regards the human soul, but also as regards anything subsistent that is a form alone. It is clear that what belongs to a thing by virtue of itself is inseparable from it; but existence belongs to a form, which is an act, by virtue of itself. Wherefore matter acquires actual existence as it acquires the form; while it is corrupted so far as the form is separated from it. It is impossible, however, for a form to be separated from itself. Therefore it is impossible for a subsistent form to cease to exist.

13. בְּרֵאשִׁית בָּרָא אֱלֹהִים אֵת הַשָּׁמַיִם וְאֵת הָאָרֶץ. *Gen.* 1:1 contains the same notion in its use of the word בָּרָא (*bará*), found also in 2:3, 2:4; *Ps.* 148:5, *Is.* 40:26, 42:5, and 45:18. *Bará* is a specific verb in Hebrew to indicate actively working into existence, bringing into existence, that which in no wise existed before its now being brought into existence. (See

R. Laird Harris, Gleason L. Archer, and Bruce K. Waltke, *Theological Wordbook of the Old Testament*, 1 [Chicago: Moody, 1980], 127).

14. Plato, Republic, 609b (see Loeb Classical Library edition for the works of Plato)

15. See Louis A. Berman, *The Akedah: The Binding of Isaac* (Lanham: Rowman & Littlefield. 19970; Lippmann Bodoff, *The Binding of Isaac, Religious Murders & Kabbalah: Seeds of Jewish Extremism and Alienation?* (Devora Publishing, 2005); "The Real Test of the Akedah: Blind Obedience versus Moral Choice," *Judaism* 42 1 (1993): 71-92; "God Tests Abraham—Abraham Tests God," *Bible Review* IX 3 (1993): 52; Carol Delaney, *Abraham on Trial* (Princeton: Princeton University Press, 1998); Robin M. Jensen, "The Binding or Sacrifice of Isaac: How Jews and Christians See Differently," *Bible Review* 9 (1993) 5: 42–51; Jon D. Levenson, *The Death and Resurrection of the Beloved Son: The Transformation of Child Sacrifice in Judaism and Christianity* (New Haven: Yale University Press, 1995).

16. חֶסֶד חָפַצְתִּי, וְלֹא-זָבַח; וְדַעַת אֱלֹהִים, מֵעֹלוֹת.

17. Kant's doctrine of "eschatological justice" appears throughout his thinking as a "postulate" for the soul's immortality, for we cannot actually have knowledge of either the soul or the afterlife.

18. For the translation of this word ζῷον as "animal," see H. H. Liddell and R. Scott, *Greek-English Lexicon*, with a Revised Supplement (Oxford: at the Clarendon Press, 1996) 760 under the entry ζῷον, τό.

Another World

1. The literature on reincarnation is vast, and interpretations/commentaries on it differing. One thread seems to run throughout it, however: birth without any ultimate birth explaining the subsequent, or any. See Hans Ten Dam, *Exploring Reincarnation* (New York: Arkana/Viking Penguin, 1990); Patrician Blakiston, *The Pre-Existence and Transmigration of Souls* (London: Regency, 1970); C. W. Ducasse, *A Critical Examination of Belief in Life After Death* (Springfield: Thomas, 1960); Joe Fisher, *The Case For Reincarnation* (London: Grafton Books, 1986); Joseph Read and S. L. Cranston, *Reincarnation: the Phoenix Fire Mystery* (New York: Crown Publishers, 1977); Hans Holzer, *Life Beyond Life: the Evidence for Reincarnation* (West Nyack: Parker, 1985); J. M. E. McTaggart, *Human Immortality and Pre-Existence* (New York: Kraus, 1970); Wendy D. O'Flaherty (ed.), *Karma and Rebirth in Classical Indian Tradition* (Berkeley: University of California Press, 1980); Ian Stevenson: *Twenty Cases Suggestive of Reincarnation* (New York: SPR, 1966). Stevenson's work, like those of clairvoyant claims of speech with the dead (of which books abound), is not conclusive to his claim. There are explanations other than claims of contact with the dead that equally account for how various things presumably only contact with the dead (and thus a post mortem world) or a prior existence could reveal were known.

2. For a look at the evidence of and epistemological arguments regarding the reality of miracles one can begin with my, *The Christ From Death Arisen* (Lanham: Rowman and Littlefield, 2008), 19–30.

3. See Aristotle, *De Anima*, 431a 16: διὸ οὐδέποτε νοεῖ ἄνευ φαντάσματος ἡ ψυχή. Cf. 432a 3–6; 403a 8–10; 429a 1–2; 433a 9–10; *De Memoria*, 449b 30–450a 25. Phantasm is "image," or "sensuous content." It is a tenet that tersely states the Aristotelian view of the necessity of sense content as the basis for all cognition. Aquinas explains it in *De Veritate*, q. 3, art. 3, arg. 19) "nothing is in the intellect that was not first in the senses (nihil est in intellectu quod non sit prius in sensu)."

4. The argument is from C. D. Broad, *The Mind and Its Place in Nature* (New York: Harcourt, Brace, 1929), 623.

5. Descartes' original statement in this insight (perhaps anticipated in Augustine's *De Civitate Dei*, {XI, 26}, "Si [...] fallor, sum" ("If I am mistaken, I am," and even rudimentarily in Aristotle, "whenever we perceive, we are conscious that we perceive, and whenever we think, we are conscious that we think, and to be conscious that we are perceiving or thinking is to be conscious that we exist," {*Nicomachean Ethics*, 1170a 25 ff"}) was "Je pense donc je suis," from his 1637 *Discours de la méthode pour bien conduire sa raison, et chercher la vérité dans les sciences*. (Descartes wrote the *Discourse* in French, not in Latin, thus reaching a wider audience in his country. The Latin expression "Cogito ergo sum" appears in the later *Principles of Philosophy* [1644], Part 1, article 7: "Ac proinde hæc cognitio, ego cogito, ergo sum, est omnium prima & certissima, quæ cuilibet ordine philosophanti occurrat." In the *Second Meditation*, he does not use this phrase, but writes instead, "the proposition, I am, I exist, is necessarily true whenever it is put forward by me or conceived in my mind." Arguably many library shelves would be needed to contain the books written on this subject. It is quite clear, though, that Descartes held his existence to be indubitable whenever he would think of it. This could not be said of matter or the thought of it.

6. The principle first appears in Aristotle's *Metaphysics*, 1006a 1–11. Its impenetrability is defended by Aristotle pointing out the impossibility of language, or thought, without the principle being true.

7. Continuity is not the cause or basis of selfhood, but rather selfhood is the precondition for continuity. Selfhood itself is not continuity, for a human being could exist for an instant only but so long as it was human it possessed selfhood, however brief its span of existence was.

Without personal identity (identity of the self through time) memory is impossible. Memory is of something that occurred at a time different than that at which memory occurs. Two different times are implicit in its structure. Two different referent points for the event eliminate the time factor that memory requires. One self then must perdure, that is be the same at "time 1" and "time 2."

INDEX

Abel, 159
Abib, 131
aboutness, 18, 79, 151, 154, 166
Abraham, 159
accretion, 72
acquaintance, 55, 56, 59
Adam, 157, 158
adenine, 124
Adonai-jireh, 159
adverbial seeing, 50
afferent output, 99
afterlife, 156, 160, 161, 164, 165
akedah, 159
algorithm, 47, 102, 104
algorithmic, viii, 18, 103
amino acid, 128
analogically, 152
analogizing, 30–31
analogue, 130
analogy, 120, 123, 130
anecdotal, 135, 137, 146
animal, 6, 9, 30, 31, 33, 49, 50, 73,
152–162
animal awareness, 30–33
animal consciousness, 31, 32. 33, 34
animal species, 11
animal experiments, 117
animal world, 31, 33
annihilation, 11, 159, 163, 164, 170
ant, 153
antipolar, 47
Apostle, 161

appearance, 17
apperceptive agnosia, 84
Aquinas, Thomas, 11, 49, 73, 155, 162
Aristotle, ix, 28, 50, 53, 54, 61, 104,
112, 115, 165
Aristotelian, 52
artificial intelligence, 103, 104
asterognosia, 84
atom(s), 48, 50, 53, 67
atomistic, 52, 77
atomistic theory of light propagation,
50
automata, 32, 152
automaticity, 154
autopagnosia, 81
awareness, 3, 5, 22–27, 29–32, 58, 113,
115, 116, 117, 118, 123, 128, 132, 136,
137, 142, 143, 144, 145, 146, 147, 150,
165, 167
axon, 126
Ayer, A. J., 55, 56

Backster, Cleve, 153
Bakalar, S. 142
bará, 156
Barbizet, Jacques, 122
bears, 154
Beauregard, Mario, 109, 141
Begley, Sharon, 106
behavior modification, 125
behaviorists, 153
being of light, 141

Berkeley, Bishop, 60, 71, 114
Bezymyanny, 154
bicameral splitting, 108
binary, 18, 101, 102, 167
biochemical identity, 132
bird, 154
birth tunnel, 142
bitless, 7
bits, 66, 67,68, 69, 70, 72, 73, 76, 129, 130
blind, 44, 45
bodily, 144
bodily embedded, 145
body, 3, 4, 23, 6, 27, 28, 29, 31, 136–142, 144–149
Botvinick-Cohen, 4, 5, 36, 93, 94, 95, 97, 100, 113
Braille, 128
brain, vii, 4, 18, 27, 44, 48, 5, 79, 80, 83, 84, 85, 89, 91–102, 104–110, 113, 120–124, 127133, 141, 142, 143, 145, 164–168.
brain dish experiment, 101
Brass, M., 109
breath, 156, 159
Burton, Robert and Maurice, 150

Cain, 159
Cartesian, 152
Cartesian dualism, 88
cat, 152, 153
causal efficacy, 30
causal theory of perception, 55
causality, 82, 125, 126, 129, 132, 164
causation, 8, 151
cell damage, 141
cerebral commisneurotomy, 107
cerebral cortex, 141
chayahim nepheshim, 159
chemically based, 164
chimpanzees, 153
chip, 167
Chisolm, Roderick, 87
Christ, Jesus, 158, 159, 161, 163
Christian, 155, 162, 163
Christianity, 154, 155
Churchland, Patricia, 89, 92
Churchland, Paul, 85, 89, 92, 99
circular argumentation, 7, 63
coherence, 50, 83, 84, 96, 105

color, 25, 27, 45–53, 58, 60, 79, 167
    as ratio, 50
color blindness, 46
color spectrum, 58
comatose, 145, 146, 147, 148
Comman, James, 50
common sense, 18
composition, 66
conatus, 170
conceivability, 28, 29
concept, 40, 41, 42, 45, 57, 58, 59, 63, 109, 128
concept formation, 115, 133, 151
conceptualization, 27, 109
cones, 49
conscious, 152
consciousness, vii, viii, ix, x, 3, 4, 5, 6, 7, 10, 11, 17, 18, 19, 23–33, 35–45, 47, 48, 51, 53, 55, 56, 57, 58, 59, 61, 65, 66, 67, 70, 73, 78, 79, 83–97, 99, 100, 104, 105, 106, 107, 108, 113, 114, 117, 118, 120, 121,131, 135, 136, 139, 140, 142, 144, 145, 148, 149, 151, 152, 154, 160, 163–171
    and body, 27
    and its object, 24
    indivisibility of, 26,
    is without parts, 34
    not positionable, 27
content, 26, 29, 30, 31, 32, 35,38, 76
continuity, 87, 116
contradiction, 27
control group, 124
Cooper, S., 147
Corinth, 163
Corinthians, First Epistle to the, 155, 158, 163
corpus callosum, 107, 108
correlate(s), 5, 24, 29, 30, 31, 94, 96, 98, 104, 105, 138
    of consciousness, 6
correlation, 106, 151
correlative being, 24
corruption, 145
cortex, 47, 48, 53, 83, 94, 95, 98, 99, 101, 106. 109, 121, 126, 141, 166, 167
cortical, viii, 4, 47, 53, 97, 98, 129, 164, 165, 167
cortical neuronal cells, 167
cortical substrate, 4

Coutts, Baroness Burdett, 154
covalence, 49
creatio ex nihilo, 29
Creator, 157
cutaneous rabbit, 97

DNA, 124, 127, 128, 129, 130, 131, 132, 134
DNA gates, 101
dark matter, 45
Davidson, Richard, 109
day (yom), 157
death, vii, ix, 3, 6, 7, 15, 16, 17, 19, 34, 36, 38, 64, 69, 75, 76, 88, 89, 93, 122, 133, 136–148, 152, 153, 154, 157, 158, 159, 165
Deceiver, 22
decomposing, 24, 73
decomposition, 8, 11, 66, 67, 68, 69, 70, 95, 136, 152, 170, 171
defense mechanism, 141, 143
DeMarse, Thomas, 101
Deiters cells, 117
Deity, 159, 164
Democritean, 53, 59
Democritus, 50, 67
Demon, Evil, 28
demonic, 170
dendrites, 166
Dennet, Daniel, 88, 91, 97, 99, 100
  Kinds of Minds, 91
density, 71, 72
depth psychiatry, 123
Descartes, Rene, 22, 32, 57, 86, 93, 108, 116, 166
destruction, 10, 68, 69, 70, 72, 73
diminution, 66, 71
direct acquaintance, 58
directedness, 154
directed towards, 59
direction, 23
direction-towards, 26, 35
directionality, 23, 24, 26, 28, 32, 35, 36, 42, 59, 154
disbonding, 68
disembodied, 142
disintegration, 61
disjunctive agnosia, 84
dissolution, 4, 25, 66

Divine, The, 155, 157, 159, 160, 161, 170
divisible, 78, 79, 80
divisibility, 66, 86, 156, 158, 164, 166
dog, 152, 153, 154, 160
dopamine, 109
Draisma, Jan, 130
dual awareness, 138

Eccles, Sir John, 122
Ecclesiastes, 156, 162
Eden, 157
efficient causality, 35
electrical, 152
electrical polarity, 47
electro, 97, 114
electro bits, 117
electro charge, 119
electro content 96
electro data, 92
electro-encephalography, 120
electro exploration, 120
electro integration, 92
electro modelings, 114
electro process, 117
electro representation. 92
electro stimulation, 102
electrochemical, viii, 96
electrochemistry, viii
electrocorticograpy, 120
electrode(s), 94, 101. 98, 101, 120, 121, 130, 143
electromagnetic, 45, 47, 90
electromagnetic, 167
electromagnetic radation, 46, 140, 142
electromagnetic reverberation, 51
electromagnetic wavelength, 49
electromagnetism, 48
electron(s), 48, 52, 152, 166
electron microscopy, 15, 72
elephants, 153
eliminative materialism, 19, 88, 89, 90, 91, 92
embodied, 11, 26, 139, 165
embodied consciousness, 23
empirical, 166
endopsychosins, 141
endorphin(s), 141, 147
Endy, Drew, 102
energy, 68, 164

enfoldment, 130
entropy, 75
epileptic, 107, 120, 129, 141
epilepsy, 120, 121, 122, 141
error, 22, 146
essence, 17, 78, 136
essences, 31
Esther, Book of, 156
eternal being, 155
eternity, 140, 169
Euclidean, 133
Evangelist, 161
Evil Demon, 29, 37
Evil Genius (*genium malignum*), 22
excitatory, 120, 122
excitatory wires, 102
excitotoxicity, 141
excluded middle, 133
existential synthesis, 30
expanse theory, 53
extension, 71, 89, 140, 166
external world, 5, 6
extinction, 3, 5, 6
extralinguistic, 51, 57
eye-brain, 50

fMRI (functional magnetic resonance imaging), 110
Fall, The, 158, 159
fradic coil, 120
firings, 8
First Kings, 156
first person, 86, 88, 92
First Samuel, 156
fish, 153
flatline, 165
Flood, The, 159
folk psychology, 94, 100, 101, 151
folkwise, 18
form, 52, 78, 136
form (εἶδος), 115
Fortran, 126
foveal, 42
frequencies, 45, 67, 140
frequency, 8, 11, 12, 15, 45, 127, 128
frontal lobes, 141
Frontiers in Neurobiotics, 101

GNCC, 100, 104
Galatians, Epistle to the, 155

Gallup, 137, 138, 143
galvanic current, 120
gamma band. 84
ganglion, 45
Genesis, 11, 155, 157, 158, 159
ghost in the machine, 100
Gihon, the river, 149
givenness (*Gegebenheit*), 29
Glassman, Edward, 126
glial, 124, 168
glomeruli, 94
glutamate, 141
goldfish, 153
gorillas, 153
God, 142, 157
Gödel (Incompleteness Theorem), 103, 104
Godhead, 158
Greischar, Lawrence, 109
Greyfriar's Bobby, 154
Grinspoon, L., 142
groove, 124
growth principle, 153

habit(s), 120, 127, 132
Haggard, P., 109
hallucination, 51, 130, 133
hallucinatory, 149
Harth, Eric, 88
    Creative Loop, The, 88
heaven, 5, 163
Hebrews, Epistle to the, 155, 159
hell, 5, 158
hippocampal region, 131
hippocampus, 122, 128, 129
histological, 160
histological structure, 132
histology, 47, 154, 167
Holden, Janice, 147
hologram, 129, 130, 131
holographic, 123, 124
holography, 131
holonomic, 130
homecoming, 140
homunculus fallacy, 131
Hosea, 159
Hume, David, 4, 28, 36, 56, 60, 78, 104, 118
    "shade of blue," 104
    Treatise, 5

Humean, 56
Husserl, Edmund, 23, 30, 32
Hyden, Holger, 124, 126
hydrocephalic, 167
hydrocephalus, 107, 108, 167
hypoxic/ischaemic, 141

immanently objective, 23
immaterial, 11, 47, 66, 79, 83, 88, 107,
   126, 127, 152
immaterialism, 127
immateriality, 7, 102, 113, 133, 134
immaterially, 30
immortal, viii, ix, 5, 6, 8, 1, 13, 17, 19,
   35, 54, 56, 114, 137, 151, 155, 160,
   163, 164
immortalist, 134
immortality, vii, viii, ix,x, 4, 5, 6, 7, 8,
   13, 14, 16, 18, 19, 32, 33, 36, 37, 38,
   52, 56, 58, 59, 61, 65 66, 83, 95, 113,
   133, 151, 152, 154, 158, 160, 161, 163,
   170, 171
impartible, 74
incommunicable, 27, 46
incorporeal, 144
indemonstrable premise, 104
independence, 73
indestructibility, 11
individual, 36
indivisible, 66, 67, 77
indivisibles, 67
indivisibility, 26
inextension, 89
inference, 151
infinite regress, 40, 51, 103
infinitesimal, 72
info bits, 100
infrared, 45
inhibitory wires, 102
insensate, 149
instinct, 153, 154, 155, 160
intention, 155
intentional, 23, 25, 29, 79, 89, 92
intentional object, 51
intentionality, 23, 24, 26, 32, 33, 37,
   56, 57, 79
introspection, 166
intuition, 103
involuntary, 93
ionization, 71, 103

ions, 46, 48, 142
irreducible, 7, 67, 70, 116
irreducible bits, 135, 136
Isaac, 159
Isaiah, 155, 156

Jackson, Frank, 46
James, William, 119
Jeremiah, 156
John, E. Roy, 122, 123
John, Gospel of Saint, 158, 161

Kant, Immanuel, 87, 152, 160
Kastenbaum, Robert, 144
ketamine, 141, 142
Kisoro, 153
knowledge as immaterial synthesis, 22
knowledge by acquaintance, 41
Kortlandt, Adrian, 153
Kübler-Ross, Elizabeth, 147

LSD, 142
language, 22, 30, 32, 37, 38, 39, 40, 41,
   42. 45, 50, 51 59, 60, 61, 147
laser light, 129, 130
lateral geniculate, 126
lateral inhibition, 49
Latin language, 22
Lazarus, 144
Levinas, Emmanuel, 3
Leviticus, 156
Lewin, Robert, 107
Libet, Benjamin, 97, 98, 100, 141
life, 73
life principle, 15
limbic time, 99
linquistic, 5, 38, 39, 45, 58
linguistic turn, 59
light, 37, 45, 46, 49, 50, 53, 140, 141,
   142
light waves, 56
Liu, Guosong, 101, 102, 103
living animal (ζώων), 161
Lobaschevskian, 133
locatability, 86
Long, Dr. Jeffrey, viii
   Evidence of the Afterlife. The Science
      of Near-Death Experiences, viii
long-term memory, 117, 120, 122–127,
   131, 133, 167

Longuet-Higgins, Christopher, 129
loopback theory, 84
Luke, Gospel of Saint, 158
luminous matter, 45
Luria, A. R., 124
    The Working Brain, 124
Lutz, Antoine, 109

macromolecular, 120
macula, 45
magnesium, 142
magnetic field, 152
magnification, 9, 10, 65
Malebranche, Père Nicolas, 32, 152
malevolent, 170
malin génie (mauvais *génie*), 22, 93
Marsh, Michael, 122, 123
    *A Matter of Personal Survival: Life
    After Death*, 122
mass, 89, 90, 91 108
material, 19, 26, 27, 33, 58, 60, 61, 66,
67, 79, 113–117, 119, 120, 124, 126,
127, 129, 132, 133, 151
material being, 26, 76
material reality, 75
materialism, x, 77, 79, 83, 86, 88, 89,
90, 91, 92, 108, 127, 141, 159
materialist, 18, 26, 48. 53, 89, 114, 117,
119, 120, 126 127, 131, 133, 148, 149,
168
materiality, 7, 99, 106, 126 133
materially derived, 100
Mathieu. Ricard, 104
matrix, 18, 91
matter, 6, 7, 8, 11, 14, 15, 26, 33. 44.
45, 46, 47, 48, 66, 67, 68, 69, 72, 73,
75, 78, 79, 85, 88, 92, 93, 95, 100, 106,
108, 114, 115, 124, 144, 14, 151, 154,
155, 159, 160, 163, 164, 166, 16, 169,
170, 171
Matthew, Gospel of Saint, 158
meaning, 23, 30, 31, 32, 35, 40, 41, 74
medulla, 124
megahertz, 86
memory, 107, 114, 116–134, 160
Merleau-Ponty, Maurice, 33
mesial thalamus, 122, 128, 129
metabolism, 164
method, 89, 138
methodic doubt, 57

methodology, 13–19, 33, 146
mind, viii, ix, 8, 9, 11, 22, 23, 27, 28,
29, 32, 40, 41, 65, 66, 71, 72, 75, 78,
88, 89, 90, 91, 94, 98, 101, 10, 108,
109, 114–118, 121, 122, 123, 129, 138,
139, 142, 144, 148, 155, 16, 165, 168
*Mind and the Brain, The: Neural Plas-
ticity*, 100
mind-body, 89, 90
minimalist, 67,68, 69, 72
miracles, 155, 163
modal argument, 79
model(s), vii, ix, 7, 53
modeling, viii
molecular, 120, 125, 127
molecular thesis, 128
molecule(s), 117, 119, 121, 122, 124,
125
mortality, 137
Moody, Raymond, 138
Moriah, 159
motherboard, 167
multiple personality, 26

NCC, 104, 105
NDE, 136–149, 157, 165, 168
NMDA receptor, 141
Nagel, Thomas, 85
nanometer 45
nanotechnology, 102
nature, 9, 22, 28, 30, 144, 150
Nature, 30, 31, 75, 76, 141, 143, 160
Nature Neuroscience, 101
near-death, viii, 136, 138, 139, 140
143–148
necromancy, 163
nephesh(im), 155,
nephesh chayah, 156, 158
nerve cells, 124, 126
nerve pathway, 50
neural, 44, 45, 46, 48, 90, 91, 92, 93,
94, 95, 96, 100, 101, 156
neural circuitry, 104
neural correlates, 94, 95, 98, 104, 105
neural fibers, 103
neural mapping, 102
neural network, 101
neural pathway, 52,106, 164
neural plasticity, 104
neural receptor, 49

neural reverberations, 154
neural signal, 45
neural topography, 105
neuro-reductionist(s),vii, 18
neurochemical, 4, 91, 117, 127, 131
neuroelectric, 47, 53, 79, 83, 84, 85, 93,
100, 107, 114, 119, 132, 165, 166
neuroepistemology, 19, 151
neurological sites, 129
Neurology, 107
neuromaterialist, 47
neurons(s), 84, 91, 122, 123, 124, 125,
130, 132, 156, 164
neuronal, 83, 113, 120, 122, 125, 126,
127, 128, 129, 130, 132, 133, 135, 141,
154, 160
neuronal cell, 125, 126, 127, 128, 129
neuronal correlate, 104
neuronal DNA, 91, 131, 132
neuronal firings, 49, 80
neurnal fluid, 167
neuronal histology, 18
neuronal matrix, 90
neuronal matter, 160
neuronal moments, 18
neuronal trace, 120
neurophilosophy, ix, x, 4, 5, 18, 89, 93,
94, 95, 96, 99, 105, 106, 107
neurophilosophic, 5, 34, 79
neurophysiologic, 94, 95, 102
neurophysiology, 124
neuroprocessing, 80
neuroreductionism, viii
neuroscience, viii, 18
neurosignal, 46
neurotransmitter, 141
neutrons, 14
New Scientist, 90
New Testament, 156
nigostratial dopamine, 109
Noah, 159
nominalism, 60
nominalists, 114
non-bodily, 148, 149
non-bodily awareness, 147
non-control group, 124
non-corporeal, 149
non-hallucinatory, 143
non-material, 114, 148
non-materiality, 126

non-partibility, 9, 10
non-*qualia*, 91
non-quantitative, 49
nucleic (acid[s]), 124, 127, 128
Numbers, 156

OBE, 136, 137, 138, 141–149, 151, 164
O'Leary, Denyse, 109
O'Reilly, Randal, 101
object(s), 4, 9, 17, 21, 22, 23, 26, 27,
29, 30, 31, 33, 42, 57, 54–59
object-directed, 24
object-related, 24
objectification, 31, 41
obsessive-compulsive, 164
Occam, 22
ocular neurology, 154
of-ness, 79
Old Testament, 155, 156
olfactory, 154
olfactory lobe, 94
ontological simultaneity, 38
optic pathway, 50
optical receptors, 49
ornithologists, 153
ostensive, 46
other, 6, 18, 23, 35, 36, 38, 40, 45, 52,
73
other-directed, 34, 35
other directionality, 42
otherness, ix, 6, 29, 35, 36, 43, 111
out-of-body, 136, 142, 144, 145, 147,
148, 149
outside percept, 100
outside world, viii, 89, 93, 94, 95
oxygen, 156

PCP, 141
pain, 79, 166
Paradise,158, 159
paramormal, 163
Parkinsons, 10
Parot, Phaner, 122
partibility, 8, 10, 63, 78, 86, 95, 116,
135, 158, 160, 164, 166
partible, 33, , 79, 13, 136
partless, 33
parts, 66, 67, 78, 80, 81, 87
Paul the Apostle, 155, 158, 163
peace, 139, 143, 157

Penfield, Wilder, 120, 142
The Mystery of the Mind, 122
percept(s), 4, 44–53, 56, 58, 78, 79, 80,
81, 83, 84, 85, 86, 88, 89, 90 91, 95, 96,
97, 100, 105, 106, 113, 114, 119, 123,
149, 165, 167
perception, 21, 22, 24, 28, 47, 48, 49,
50, 51, 53, 55, 63, 88, 133
perception at a distance, 55
perceptuality, 116
perishing, 10
Persinger, Michael, 142
Personal Existence After Death, ix, 7
personhood, 11, 19, 136, 139, 151, 169
Peter, Epistle of, 155
petitio principii, 71
phantasm, 165
pharmacological, 142, 143
phencyclidine, 141
phenomenology, 17, 19
phenomenological, 35
pheneomenological method, 17
phota, 50
photographic plate, 129, 130
photon wavelength, 49
photons, 44
photoreceptor(s), 46, 142
physical, 79, 115, 117, 124, 130, 131,
132, 133
physical body, 144
physical matter, 7, 15
physical properties, 128
physically constricted, 165
Picower Center For Learning and
Memory, 101
pictorial memory, 120
place, 8, 24, 66,71, 88, 120, 129, 131,
132, 133
placebo, 109
planaria, 125
planarian, 126
Planck's constant, 68
plants, 153
Plato, 156, 157
Poggio, Tomasso, 101
points, 68
possible world, ix, 28
pre-nominalist, 115
Preacher, 156, 162
prefrontal cortex, 101

prejudice, 16, 17
presuppositions, 17
Pribam, Karl, 129, 130, 131
principle, 71
principle of non-contradiction, 166
privacy, 166
private, 27, 86, 88, 92, 120, 137, 138,
166, 168
property dualist, 88
proportion, 10, 78, 110, 111
proportionality, 110, 111
proportions, 74
Protagoras, 152
protons, 14
Proverbs, 156
Psalmist, 156, 159
Psalms, 156
psychedelic, 142
psychosis, 144
publicly accessible, 43, 137
publicly observable, 165, 166
pure, 17, 35
pure description, 17
purely appears, 33
purity, 17
purpose, 75, 76

qualia, 5, 79, 83, 88, 91
quantify, 85
quantitative, 5, 46, 47, 49, 50, 52, 58,
164
quantity, 26
quantum, 3, 7, 8, 136
quantum mechanics, 67, 135
quantum physics, 7, 8, 9, 10, 13, 14, 16,
48, 65, 67, 139
quantum science, 21, 65

REM, 105
RNA, 124–128
radiation wavelength, 50
randomness, 132
rat cells, 101
Rawlings, Nancy, 109
receptor cells, 90
Redeemer, 161
reductionism, ix, x, 19, 83, 103, 151,
167
reductionist(s), 4, 5, 7, 58, 85, 119,
120, 128, 167

redundancy, 107, 108
regress, 130
regress argument, 6
reincarnation, 163
representational content, 93
res extensa, 86
resistance, 55, 77, 80, 165
resuscitation, 138, 146
Revelation, 15, 158, 161
retina(e), 49, 50, 126, 142
retinal, 142, 147
retinal thrombosis, 142
Rhine, Joseph Banks, 153
ribonucleic acid, 125
Ricard, Mathieu, 109
right temporal lobe, 142
rigor mortis, 144
Ring, Kenneth, 138, 139, 140, 143, 145
    Heading Towards Omega, 140
    Life at Death, 143, 145
rods, 49
Roman Catholic, 155
Romans, Epistle to the, 155, 157
Rorty, Richard, 60
rote, 120
rubber ball illusion, 93
Russell, Bertrand, 41
Ruth, Babe, 28

Sabom, Martin, 138, 145, 146,
    Recollections of Death: A Medical
    Investigation, 146
sadism, 158
Sagan, Carl, 142
Saint Bernard, 160
Sartori, Penny, 147
Savior, 160
Schaller, Geeorge bal, 153
Scripture, 11, 155, 156, 157, 158, 159,
    162, 169
Schoolmen, 115
Schwarz, Jeffrey, 109
Science, 107
scientific method, 89
scripting DNA, 102
self, 3, 5, 18, 56, 86, 93, 100
self-consciousness, 166
self-contradiction, viii
self-correcting, 17
self-determination, 72, 73

self-origination, 73
self-refutational, 7, 8, 14, 17
self-subsistent, 155
self-verifying, 114
selfhood,116, 144, 152, 168
sensation, 26, 75, 77, 78, 83. 85, 86,
    140
sense(s), 11, 15, 127, 128, 132, 137,
    140
sense-apparatus, 15
sense-bound, 165
sense capacity, 19
sense content, 165
sense data, 16
sense faculties, 145
sense imagery, 133
sense organ, 49, 155
sense perception, 9
sense power(s), 9, 11, 13, 29–30, 168
sense-prehension, ix
sense receptors, 80
sense stimuli, 140
sensible form, 50
sensibly originated, 15
sentience, 35
sentient, 10, 18, 23, 26, 27, 30, 32, 33,
    86, 88, 89, 120, 151, 152, 154
sensory capacity, 145
short-term, 113, 120
sight, 9, 154
Singer, Wolf, 105, 106, 114
singular, 115
skepticism, 56, 137, 146
Skye Terrier, 154
software applications, viii
solid, 78, 139, 141
solidity, 165
solipsism, 29
solipsistic, 36
Solomon, 154, 162
somaethetic cortex, 97
sound, 79
space, 8, 9, 10, 14, 21, 31, 68, 77, 89,
    138, 139, 140, 144, 167, 169
space-time, 133, 168, 169
spatial, 8, 9, 10, 27, 59, 167, 169
spatiality, 66
spatio-temporally, 167
speedwell, 155
spine, 167

Spinoza, Benedictus de, 116
spirit, 169
split brain, 107
split-personalities, 26
Spiritual Brain, The, 109
spontaneity, 132
sporadic, 132
squirrel, 153
standby context loop, 84
Storm, Michael, 110
   The Anatomy of Evil, 110
sub-atomic, 7, 8, 72, 152
subject, 5, 22, 24, 25, 27, 30, 32, 33
subjective, 5, 84, 85
subjectivism, 5, 56, 58
subjectivist(s), 5, 104
subjectivity, 31, 85, 86, 87, 94, 114
suicide, 144
syllogism, 18, 155
syllogistic method, 18
syllogistic process, 104
Sylvan fissure, 142, 167
synaptic, 126, 127, 141, 166
synchrony, 84, 85, 91, 106, 117
synchrony of firings, 80
synthetic biology, 102

telescoping, 154
temporal lobe, 129, 141
third person, 88, 91
thyratron, 120
Tempter, 158
time, 30, 98, 116, 118, 119, 138, 169
time delay in sensation, 55
Timothy, Second Epistle to, 155
trace, 120, 123,
trace hypothesis of memory, 123
trans-bodily, 146
trans-material, 27
transparency, 31, 35, 97
transparent, 30
trinary, 18, 101
Turing machine, 4

unitive, 47
universal(s), 7, 55, 56, 60, 73, 113, 114,
115, 116, 133, 140, 155
unquantifiable, 86

valence, 47

veridical, 151
veridicality, 147, 149, 151
vibration(s), 15, 25, 67
vibrational, 7, 15, 67
vibrational band, 14, 15
vibrational frequency(ies), 14, 15, 136
vibrational frequency field, 15
vibrational matrix, 91, 95
vibrationality, 15
vicious circle, 6
vision, 140, 154, 161
visual apparatus, 140
visual cortex, 141
voluntary, 91, 140

Watson, Lyall, 153
   The Romeo Error, 153
Watson, Peter, 90
wave frequencies, 68
wavelength(s), 25, 45, 46, 49, 50, 52,
58
waves, 68
wicked demon, 23
Williams, Bernard, 87
Wilson, Donald, 107
world, viii, ix, 3, 4, 5, 21, 22, 24–30,
32, 36, 38, 39, 168
world independent of perceiver, 18, 51,
56
world of light, 139

Zaleski, Carol, 143
zinc, 142
Zola, Emile, 154
zombie, 18, 77, 80, 81

ABOUT THE AUTHOR

Robert Geis has authored book length philosophical and theological studies on sexual ethics, papal infallibility, and the philosophy of God. *In My Ever After* is his third philosophical study on immortality, following on his scriptural exegetical study of the Resurrection, *The Christ From Death Arisen*. He is a Prelate Protosyncellus in the Eastern Orthodox Catholic rite.